ספר

מלחמות השם

להפלוסוף האלהי הרב הגדול רבי
לוי בן גרשון זצ״ל

הוגה יהדרים סולת מתוך כפרי
ארטטו ושאר פלוסופי
אש׳ כיעולם אנשי
שם

נדפס פה רלוח רעק״זא
פ״ת שך לסוך

LEVI BEN GERSHOM
(GERSONIDES)

THE WARS
OF THE LORD
· BOOK ONE ·
IMMORTALITY OF THE SOUL

VOLUME ONE
Translated with an introduction and notes by
SEYMOUR FELDMAN

THE JEWISH PUBLICATION SOCIETY OF AMERICA
Philadelphia · 5745/1984

109968

Library of Congress Cataloging in Publication Data
Levi ben Gershom, 1288-1344.
The wars of the Lord.
Includes bibliographical references.
Contents: v. 1. Immortality of the soul
1. Philosophy, Jewish. 2. Philosophy, Medieval.
I. Feldman, Seymour. II. Title.
B759.L43M5413   1983   181'.06   83-4348
ISBN 0–8276–0220–0 (v. 1)

Designed by ADRIANNE ONDERDONK DUDDEN

This volume is being published with the assistance of a grant from
THE ABRAHAM M. WOLFMAN FUND

In Memory of My Beloved Mother
Anna Feldman

גולדא בת לייבוש ז"ל

· CONTENTS ·

· ACKNOWLEDGMENTS ·

Levi ben Gershom's *Milḥamot ha-Shem* has not fared as well as some of the other classics of medieval Jewish philosophical literature. Saadia's *Emunot ve-deot* became *The Book of Beliefs and Opinions,* and Maimonides' *Moreh nevuḥim* the *Guide of the Perplexed.* And before the English translations were made of these works, there existed German or French versions. Until now, no complete translation in any language of the *Milḥamot ha-Shem* has ever appeared. Lacking a translation into a modern European language, Gersonides' magnum opus has been an unknown and closed treasure except to those capable of unlocking its somewhat heavy and formidable doors. This has been most unfortunate. Those scholars who have been able to penetrate the work's outer walls have recognized the philosophical brilliance, originality, and boldness of its inner sancta. Some have recoiled from these virtues, but few have denied them. It has been my goal to make these erstwhile hidden treasures known to a wider audience.

The stimulus for this undertaking came from Professor Salo Wittmayer Baron. While chairman of the Publication Committee of The Jewish Publication Society of America, he suggested to me (too many years ago to mention) that I consider doing a translation of the *Milḥamot ha-Shem.* After some study of Gersonides' cosmology, which resulted in an essay devoted to his theory of creation, I decided to undertake the translation despite the lack of a critical text, any previous complete translation in any language, and a relatively small scholarly literature on Gersonides' philosophy. Needless to say, translating the *Milḥamot* was no easy task.

Yet I was both encouraged and assisted by a number of individuals and institutions throughout the project, whose support I would now like to acknowledge. First I want to thank Professor Baron for suggesting the project. Whatever its ultimate fate—*habent sua fata libelli*—the *Milḥamot* has been for me more than just a piece of scholarly research. It opened up to me the vast world of medieval science and philosophy, whose richness I had previously only glimpsed. But more than just mere learning did the book give me: I became acquainted with someone who, although dead for over six hundred years, became for me a living person, a man whose personality, profundity, and universality I have come to love and admire.

Venturing on virtually virgin territory I needed some guides, people who if they had not yet completed the journey before me, still had acquired some knowledge of the terrain, its hazards and rough spots. Professor Charles Touati of the Sorbonne was most helpful in this respect, giving me invaluable information about the various manuscripts of the *Milḥamot* as well as useful suggestions about difficult passages. He has been most generous in sharing his knowledge. Others too have contributed both moral and scholarly support, among whom were Professors Gerson Cohen, Chancellor of The Jewish Theological Seminary of America, Alfred Ivry, Norman Bronznick, Arthur Hyman, Bernard Goldstein, Yosef Hayim Yerushalmi, Isadore Twersky, David Silverman, and Herbert Davidson.

Not only were individuals helpful. I have had to make use of several libraries in acquiring the needed manuscript material as well as in having ready service in their use. In this regard the library and staff of the Jewish Theological Seminary of America have been outstanding. Without their assistance I doubt whether the translation would have been accomplished. I also wish to acknowledge the cooperation of the Bibliothèque Nationale, Oxford, and Vatican libraries for supplying me with several of the much needed manuscripts of the *Milḥamot*. In addition thanks are also due to Rutgers University and the Memorial Foundation for Jewish Culture for providing me with both financial support and free time to do some of the research and writing needed for the project.

During the preparation of the many drafts that preceded this final version I have had to call upon the indulgent and steady services of three people who did not flag in their attempt to decipher my penmanship and continual corrections. Julie Schumann, Celia Wallace, and Sylvia Falk provided constant and priceless help with their ever-ready hands. In its later stages the editorial staff of The Jewish Publication Society of America contributed much to the final text of the translation. Maier Deshell, the editor of the Society, and Thomas Waldman were most helpful in stylistic matters.

Most languages, I suspect, have some kind of equivalent for the English proverb "Last, but not least . . ." The Hebrew analogue adds a nuance that is most appropriate for the people whom I now want to thank. "*Aḥaron, aḥaron, ḥaviv*—last, but beloved." Translating the *Milḥamot* was a most arduous task, and there were many times when it seemed insuperable. Throughout it all, my family remained confident that I would bring it to light. Without their patience and encouragement this book—*The Wars of the Lord* by Levi ben Gerson (Gersonides)—would probably still be on my desk. For its existence I owe my father, wife, and sons a great deal, more than I can ever express.

PART ONE

INTRODUCTION

· 1 ·

LIFE AND WORK OF GERSONIDES

Life

LEVI BEN GERSHOM (Gersonides), the author of *The Wars of the Lord* (*Milḥamot ha-Shem*), stands out as one of the more creative and philosophically daring figures within the medieval Jewish world. Mathematician, astronomer, biblical exegete, and philosopher—he assumed all these roles and excelled in each. Yet, almost one hundred years after Adolf Neubauer's biographical sketch, we can still repeat his cautious remark, "We have very few details on the life of Levi."[1] Unlike Maimonides, Levi did not leave a large number of letters to contemporaries from which facts about his personal life and social environment can be gleaned. Nor did he, like Maimonides, occupy an established social position in the Jewish community, such that he would have been frequently mentioned in the letters of others. Actually, we possess not even a handful of letters written by or to him. Nor does he tell us much about himself in his writings. Hence, whereas biographies of Saadia and Maimonides have been written, only a biographical sketch of Levi ben Gershom can be written. Nevertheless, by virtue of the pioneering work of Moritz Steinschneider and Adolf Neubauer and the recent work of Joseph Shatzmiller and Charles Touati, we are now able to fill in this sketch with additional information, so that a fairly recognizable picture of Levi the man emerges.[2]

It is certain that Levi was born in 1288. This date is provided by Levi

---

1. E. Renan and A. Neubauer, *Les écrivains juifs français* (Paris, 1893), p. 246 (592).

2. Moritz Steinschneider, "Levi ben Gerson," *Gesammelte Schriften* 1 (Berlin, 1925): 233–70; Renan and Neubauer, *Écrivains juifs français*, pp. 240–98 (586–644); J. Shatzmiller, "Gersonides and the Jewish Community of Orange in his Day" (in Hebrew), *University of Haifa Studies in the History of the Jewish People and the Land of Israel* 2 (Haifa, 1972): 111–26, and "Some Further Information about Gersonides and the Orange Jewish Community in His Day," *University of Haifa Studies in the History of the Jewish People and the Land of Israel* 3 (Haifa, 1974): 139–43; Charles Touati, *La pensée philosophique et théologique de Gersonide* (Paris, 1973), pp. 33–48.

himself in several of his writings in which he gives both the date of completion of the book in question and his own age when he completed it.[3] It is also evident that he was born in Provence, although the exact town of his birth is uncertain. Both Latin, Provençal, and Hebrew sources refer to him by titles indicating that the village of Bagneols (Bagnols) was either his birthplace or his town of residence for a considerable period of time. Bagneols was a small village in the county, or district, of Orange, the administrative center of that part of Provence. Levi did not spend all his life here, since we find him residing in Avignon during his latter years. It is important to note that during his lifetime Provence was under the rule of either Robert of Anjou or the pope, both of whom were hospitable to intellectual pursuits and tolerant of Jews. Unlike Abraham ibn Ezra or Maimonides, who both traveled extensively, Levi spent all his life in Provence.

Ever since the chronicles of several Renaissance Jewish historians, there has been some controversy concerning Levi's family, especially his genealogy. Who is the Gershom, his father? One tradition claims that his father was Gershom ben Solomon of Arles, the author of the Hebrew encyclopedia *The Gates of Heaven*.[4] Another possibility is that his father was the noted talmudic scholar Gershom ben Solomon of Béziers. On the basis of the information provided by the 1372 work of Isaac Lattes, Touati has persuasively argued that Gershom of Béziers was Levi's father.[5] Levi himself mentions his father several times in his biblical commentaries as the source of information about the meaning of biblical phrases, indicating that his father was well versed in biblical exegesis, a field in which Gershom of Arles is not known to have excelled.[6] Moreover, both Levi and Isaac Lattes refer to his father as "Rav," a title that was used to refer to talmudic scholars, among which Gershom of Béziers can be included, but not Gershom of Arles. Accordingly, I think we can dispense with the tradition that ascribes the paternity of Levi to Gershom of Arles.[7] In several places in his writings Levi refers to a brother, but not by name. External sources show that he had a brother Solomon, about whom we shall say more later.[8] Levi himself never mentions anything that would indicate that he married or had children, but one tradition reports

---

3. In his *Ma'aseh Hosheb* and *The Wars of the Lord*, bk. 5, pt. 1.

4. Abraham Zakuto, *Sefer Yuḥasin*, ed. H. Filipowsky (London, 1857), p. 224a; Gedalya ben Yahya, *Shalshelet ha-Qabbalah* (Venice, 1587), p. 61a.

5. Touati, *Gersonide*, pp. 34–35.

6. Gersonides, *Commentary on the Pentateuch*, 71a.

7. Levi also mentions his maternal grandfather Levi Ha-Kohen in his biblical commentaries (*Commentary on the Pentateuch*, 114a), but his identity is not clear.

8. Touati believes that Levi had more than one brother (*Gersonide*, p. 36).

that he married his first cousin.[9] There is no solid evidence that he had any offspring.

A similar reticence is evident about his education. Although Levi occasionally mentions his father and grandfather as sources of certain exegetical information, he does not tell us anything about his Jewish schooling or acquisition of secular learning. If his father was the Talmudist Gershom of Béziers, it is highly probable that he acquired his initial biblical and talmudic education from his father and perhaps his grandfather. As his literary output clearly shows, Levi was a master of all the secular learning of his age, but we do not know how he acquired this immense knowledge.

A closely related question concerns Levi's knowledge of languages and his literary sources. All his books were written in Hebrew. Occasionally he gives a Provençal rendition of a difficult or rare Hebrew word. His citations from Aristotle, Averroes, and Maimonides, the only philosophers of whom he had firsthand knowledge, were all from Hebrew texts; indeed his knowledge of Aristotle was most probably based on the Hebrew translations of Averroes's commentaries on Aristotle in which the Aristotelian text was included in translation. With these facts in mind we can now address ourselves to a question that has vexed scholars ever since the nineteenth century: did Levi know Arabic or Latin, the other two languages of medieval philosophy? I believe that he knew neither, at least to the extent of having a workable reading knowledge of Arabic or Latin philosophical texts. Most scholars now agree that his knowledge of Arabic was at best rudimentary. Now and then he makes a comparative grammatical point involving some knowledge of Arabic, but these discussions are always elementary and could have been derived from Abraham ben Ezra, whom he often cites. The question of Levi's Latinity is, however, more complicated. In recent years two scholars have defended Neubauer's original claim that Levi did know Latin and have claimed that Levi was indebted to Latin sources for his knowledge of certain Aristotelian ideas and current medieval philosophical doctrines. Since this point is of some importance for a general understanding of Levi's philosophy, I shall briefly discuss here this latter claim.

About fifty years ago Jacob Teicher argued on the basis of a phrase in Book 1, chapter 6 of *The Wars of the Lord* that Levi employed a Latin translation of Aristotle's *On Generation of Animals*.[10] Nevertheless, Charles Touati has

---

9. Ibid.

10. Jacob Teicher, "Studi preliminari sulla dottrina della conoscenza di Gersonide," *Rendiconti della Reale Academia Nazionale dei Lincei*, 6th ser. 8 (1932): 500–510. This has been recently reprinted in *Medieval Jewish Philosophy*, ed. Steven Katz (New York, 1980).

convincingly demonstrated that Teicher's argument rests on a faulty reading of Gersonides' text.[11] Nor is Shlomo Pines's attempt to prove Levi's debt to the Latins any more successful; on the basis of similar-sounding passages in some Latin philosophical author (e.g., Aquinas) and in Gersonides, Pines suggests that the latter was indebted to the former.[12] This kind of argument is doubtful in general and fails in particular in the case of Levi. In almost every instance of an alleged similarity cited by Pines, parallel passages in Aristotle or Averroes can be found. And where no such passage can be found in the latter authors, there is no reason why a brilliant and original mind, such as Levi's, could not have reached the same conclusion independently. Moreover, since, as we shall see, Levi had numerous contacts with Christian clerics, there is the possibility that he learned of some contemporary Latin philosophical ideas orally. Finally, there is the important fact that Levi *never* cites any Latin text or mentions by name any Christian author.[13] The Latinity of Levi still remains to be proved.

What about Gersonides' occupation? The dominant view has been that Levi was a physician, like his philosophical predecessors in medieval Jewish thought, Judah Halevi and Maimonides.[14] The chief pieces of evidence for this opinion are the unpublished essay on the gout attributed to Levi, some scattered references in his other works to medical writers such as Galen and ibn-Zohr, and Isaac de Lattes's report that Levi wrote on medicine.[15] But none of these pieces of evidence is decisive. At best they show that Levi was well read in the scientific corpus of his day and that he had a *theoretical* interest in certain areas of medicine. Of great importance is the recent work of Joseph Shatzmiller, who has explored in detail the archives of the Provence to discover the realia of Gersonides' life and times. He has shown that, first, in none of the archives investigated so far is Levi ever referred to by the Latin title *physicus* ("physician"), whereas his brother Solomon is so referred to. On the other hand, Levi is referred to in Latin as *magister*, a general title indicating proficiency in some branch of learning, e.g., philosophy or Ha-

---

11. Touati, *Gersonide*, p. 38; see also the present translation, Bk. 1, chap. 6, n. 18.

12. Shlomo Pines, "Scholasticism after Thomas Aquinas and the Teachings of Hasdai Crescas and His Predecessors," *The Israel Academy of Sciences and Humanities, Proceedings* 1 no. 10 (1967).

13. Touati, *Gersonide*, pp. 38, 148–49, n. 93.

14. M. Joël, *Levi ben Gerson als Religionsphilosoph* (Breslau, 1862), p. 45; Renan and Neubauer, *Écrivains juifs français*, p. 251 (597); Steinschneider, "Levi ben Gerson," pp. 235–36; Touati, *Gersonide*, p. 43; D. Bloch, *Providence in the Philosophy of Gersonides* (New York, 1973), p. 11.

15. Isaac de Lattes, in A. Neubauer, *Medieval Jewish Chronicles*, 2 vols. (Oxford, 1895), 2:240.

lakhah. Second, the archives do record that Levi was active in moneylending, an occupation that was becoming increasingly widespread among French Jewry.[16] Although this latter phenomenon was brought about primarily by external economic and political factors, it is important to note that money-lending had its positive side too: it afforded scholars ample time to pursue their scholarly work.[17]

Shatzmiller and Touati have raised the question whether Levi was a professional astronomer. Levi himself mentions his contacts and work with Christian clerics who had astronomical interests, and some of Levi's writings in this area seem to have been prompted or commissioned by these church-men. The astronomical tables included in Book 5, part 1, chapter 99 were written at the behest of several Christian notables. The treatise *De Numeris Harmonicis* he wrote at the request of Philippe de Vitry, the bishop of Meaux. Indeed, the last work written by Levi was an essay in astrology that may have been commissioned by the Avignonese pope, Clement VI. It is thus likely that at various times Levi provided professional information on astro-nomical and astrological topics for highly placed Provençal clerics.[18]

In trying to answer the question of Levi's occupation, we should not retrodict our own occupational requirements and situation. Today a physi-cian must complete at least six years of university training as well as several years of clinical apprenticeship, and must pass certain standard examinations before he may practice medicine on his own. Obviously this is a full-time profession. But such requirements did not obtain in the Middle Ages. Thus a learned man could be engaged, at least at different stages of his life, in several pursuits, and perhaps in some at the same time. Maimonides, for example, was occupied in business before he concentrated on medicine. Hence it is possible that Levi was a moneylender and astronomer, and even perhaps a physician, at different times during his life.[19] Finally, Shatzmiller suggests that Levi was related to a family of moneylenders of considerable importance. It is possible that Levi was independently wealthy, at least to the extent that he was able to carry out his scholarly pursuits without eco-nomic pressure.

---

16. Shatzmiller, "Gersonides and the Jewish Community," pp. 113–15, 120.

17. Salo W. Baron, *Social and Religious History of the Jews*, 17 vols. (New York, 1957), 4:224.

18. Shatzmiller, "Gersonides and the Jewish Community," pp. 120–23; Touati, *Gersonide*, pp. 43, 53.

19. In his important monograph on Jewish economic activity in the southern French town of Perpignan in the thirteenth century, Richard W. Emery (*The Jews of Perpignan in the Thirteenth Century* [New York, 1959]) cites a case of a physician who was also a moneylender (p. 27) and a case of a Talmudist who was also a moneylender, the noted R. Menahem Meiri (p. 28).

Our biographical sketch is virtually complete. Although we do not know how Levi died, the date of his death is given as the twentieth day of April in the year 1344. This information is supplied by the Latin translator of the previously cited prognostication that may have been provided by Levi for the illumination of the pope.[20] Although the reader of a philosophical book is often and naturally interested in the life and personality of its author, it is not always possible to supply him with such information or with much of it. This has been the case with Levi ben Gershom. We shall have to be content, therefore, with his writings, which, as we shall see, were plentiful and varied. These, more than any biographical fact, are what are significant for our understanding of Gersonides the philosopher.

Literary Work

Without any doubt Levi was the most prolific and versatile Jewish author in the Middle Ages. In his fifty-six years he produced an enormous corpus of scientific, philosophical, and Judaic writings that encompass the whole domain of medieval learning. Levi appears to have written on everything, ranging from astronomy to zoology. Naturally, even such a "renaissance man" as Levi would concentrate on one or several areas rather than others, and we find a decided preference on his part for philosophical and mathematical-astronomical sciences among secular studies, rather than purely literary or historical work. Again, in his strictly Judaic pursuits, Levi seems to have been more interested in biblical exegesis than in either halakhic or grammatical research, although we shall see that his talmudic scholarship was considerable. In the catalog that follows, Gersonides' writings are classified according to four categories: (I) Judaica (including both Halakhah and biblical exegesis), (II) mathematics, (III) science, and (IV) philosophy. Within each classification his writings will be listed chronologically.[21]

JUDAICA

Although Gersonides' halakhic writings add up to less than a handful of works, he had a considerable reputation as a Talmudist, as attested to not

---

20. Touati, *Gersonide*, pp. 47–48, 58.

21. In this section I am deeply indebted to the work of Renan and Neubauer, Steinschneider, and Touati.

only by his overall admirer Isaac de Lattes,[22] but also by a man who was quite unsympathetic to his philosophical commitments and ideas, Rabbi Isaac bar Sheshet (1326–1408). In a responsum dealing with the study of Greek philosophy, R. Isaac bar Sheshet (the Ribash) singles out Gersonides for special discussion, along with Maimonides, and criticizes several specific Gersonidean theories. But he says quite explicitly that Rabbi Levi was "a great Talmudist who wrote a fine commentary on the Torah and Prophets. . . ."[23] This evaluation is borne out not so much by the extant halakhic corpus of Gersonides, which is minuscule, but by his Commentary on the Pentateuch, in which he shows his halakhic acuity and erudition throughout all the legal portions of the Pentateuch. Since this commentary has been published and recently reissued, it can serve as an excellent testimony to Gersonides' talmudic mastery. His Judaica will now be discussed under three rubrics: Halakhah, biblical exegesis, and miscellaneous Judaica.

· *Halakhah* ·

Commentary on the Treatise Berakhot of the Babylonian Talmud. This commentary is referred to by Levi himself in his Commentary on Deuteronomy (p. 207b). Unfortunately, this work has not survived, and we do not know the exact date of its composition or its specific content, but since the commentary on Deuteronomy was completed in January 1338, this work antedates that year. It would appear from the Commentary on Deuteronomy that the commentary on Berakhot was concerned with the explication of certain aggadic passages and the nature of biblical and rabbinic language.

Responsa. A responsum is included in Isaac de Lattes's collection of responsa (published in Vienna, 1860, pp. 87, 93) that deals with the question of the 'agunah, a woman whose husband has disappeared without testimony of his death by two Jewish witnesses. In this particular case there was one Christian witness who reported that he had heard from a Jew, who had testified in another town, that the husband had been killed by a Christian. Basing his decision solely on the Talmud, Levi ruled that the report of this Christian

---

22. Isaac de Lattes writes: "He [Gersonides] wrote commentaries on the whole Torah, both written and oral." This is, however, an exaggeration. See Neubauer, *Medieval Jewish Chronicles*, 2:240.

23. Menahem M. Kellner, "Rabbi Isaac bar Sheshet's Responsum Concerning the Study of Greek Philosophy," *Tradition* 15, no. 3 (1975): 116.

should be admitted as testimony. Although Renan and Neubauer had doubts about the authenticity of this responsum, Touati has no reservations in accepting its provenance from Levi.[24]

There is a responsum that deals with the *Qol Nidrey* prayer. This responsum evidently had been a subject of controversy in fourteenth-century Provence.

There exists a letter written by the Talmudist and poet Rabbi Isaac Kimchi that gives further evidence of Gersonides' halakhic reputation. Evidently, Gersonides had been consulted on a question of divorce and had asked Isaac Kimchi for his opinion of the matter. The latter was disinclined to intervene, but makes an exception because of Gersonides' reputation, wisdom, and piety. The closing lines of this letter are also revealing: Isaac writes to Levi, "May He who dwells on High give you strength and success with the highest of the kings so that it will be well with all of us!" Apparently, Levi's contacts with the Christian aristocracy or clergy were well known among his coreligionists in Provence and he was, at least once, asked by them to intercede in their behalf.[25]

There are two works that have been traditionally attributed to Gersonides but whose authenticity has been recently questioned by Touati on stylistic and substantive grounds.[26] Without entering into a discussion of this topic, I merely list these works below.

Sha'arey Zedeq (The gates of righteousness). This is a short commentary on the traditional thirteen hermeneutic rules of Rabbi Ishmael that are used by the rabbis in legal derivations. It has been published twice: in 1800 (Jacob Fitussi: Livorno) and in 1884 (Isaac J. Wolfinsohn: Jerusalem).

Meḥoqeq Safun (A [portion of a] ruler reserved [Deut. 33:21]). This work is attributed to Levi by Rabbi Solomon ben Simeon Duran, his grandnephew. According to Duran, this work was a commentary on certain aggadic passages in the talmudic tractate of Baba Batra (chapter 5). This work was not available until Steinschneider discovered it and attributed it to Gersonides. Both Renan, Neubauer, and Touati, however, question its authenticity, especially since some of the ideas contained in it are incompatible with Gersonides' views in *The Wars of the Lord* and the biblical commentaries.[27]

---

24. Touati, *Gersonide*, p. 61.

25. This letter has been published by Israel Lévi in *Revue des Études Juives* (henceforth abbreviated as *REJ*) 44 (1902): 82–86 (cf. Touati, *Gersonide*, pp. 46–47); Shatzmiller, "Some Further Information about Gersonides," pp. 141–42.

26. Touati, *Gersonide*, pp. 61–62.

27. Renan and Neubauer, *Écrivains juifs français*, pp. 252–53; Touati, *Gersonide*, pp. 62–63.

· *Biblical exegesis* ·

Unlike his contributions to Halakhah, Levi's biblical commentaries were many, important, and influential. Besides being significant and interesting in their own right, they are valuable guides and aids in understanding *The Wars of the Lord*. As we shall see, some of these commentaries were written concurrently with the latter work, and Levi frequently cites the one in the other. Some of the commentaries can be regarded as companion pieces to several of the books of *The Wars*. For example, the *Commentary on Song of Songs* is concerned with the Agent Intellect, and hence nicely supplements Book 1 of *The Wars;* and the Commentary on Job fits in neatly with Book 4 of *The Wars*, which is concerned with the problem of providence. Because of these cross-references and actual quotations from *The Wars*, the commentaries sometimes contain readings that are helpful in ascertaining the text of the latter work.

Some of Levi's commentaries exemplify a definite and specific literary structure having three parts. The first consists of a fairly literal explication of words or short phrases of the biblical text. The second considers the meaning of the biblical narrative of a given portion as a whole. Finally, Levi concludes the latter section with a list of "useful lessons" (*to'aliyot*) that summarize the main points in his overall explanation of the biblical text in a clear-cut, didactic manner. The latter provides then a valuable, popular analogue to the more technical and philosophical *Wars*.[28] Although Levi's biblical commentaries do attempt to provide a literal understanding of the text, it is clear from even a cursory glance that they are chock-full of his philosophical ideas and theories. For example, following the rabbinic tradition of regarding Song of Songs as an allegory and not as an erotic poem, Levi interprets this book as an allegorical drama whose main protagonists are the human intellect and the Agent Intellect (not as the rabbis claimed, God and the community of Israel). Similarly, in his explanation of the creation scene in chapter 1 of Genesis, he injects the philosophical theories of Book 6 of *The Wars*. This is not to suggest that all his commentaries are *wholly* philosophical. As mentioned earlier, Levi does try to explain words and phrases literally. In his commentaries on the historical books of the Bible he is less philosophical than elsewhere and he does not digress or depart too much from the historical narrative. Whatever the merits of Levi's commentaries as biblical exegesis, they are interesting specimens of a certain genre of medieval Jewish biblical interpretation, represented

---

28. This third part was published separately in 1865 in Warsaw by Yehiel ben Solomon under the title *Sefer ha-de 'ot ve-ha-middot*.

by such figures as Saadia, Maimonides, and Joseph Caspi, all of whom see the biblical text as having a layer of philosophical meaning. Most importantly, however, they are valuable supplements to his philosophical writings.

Levi's commentaries have been quite influential in Jewish biblical exegesis and biblical learning. They were read and cited throughout the late medieval period and thereafter; the commentaries on the Former Prophets were included in the first publication of the rabbinic Bible (*Miqra'ot Gedolot*) in the time of the Renaissance. Indeed in the very next generation the great Spanish rabbi, Nissim ben Reuben Gerondi (1315–75), quotes Gersonides frequently, often with approval, in his sermons and commentary on the Torah. After the catastrophes of 1391 and later in Spain, a reaction against philosophy developed in Spain, and Gersonides' commentaries were attacked and criticized. Isaac Abrabanel is a good example of the critical approach toward Gersonides' biblical exegesis. In modern times the last great Jewish traditional biblical exegete Malbim (Meir Loeb ben Jehiel Michael) also makes use of Gersonides' commentaries and characterizes him as a man of great erudition and his commentaries as containing "rare pearls."[29] Gersonides' biblical commentaries are listed below in chronological order.

Commentary on Job (Perush 'al Sefer Iyob), December 30, 1325. Of all of Levi's commentaries, this has been the most popular and has been frequently published. Indeed it was one of the earliest Hebrew books to have been printed (Ferrara, 1477). It was reprinted in the rabbinic Bible and has become one of the standard traditional commentaries of this biblical book. It is also the only one of his biblical commentaries that has been translated into English (A. L. Lassen, *The Commentary of Levi Ben Gersom (Gersonides) on the Book of Job* [New York 1946]). This commentary supplements Book 4 of *The Wars*, which like the Book of Job is concerned with the problem of divine providence. It is one of the more philosophical of the commentaries, with each of the protagonists of the biblical work representing a specific philosophical position on the question of providence. Job, for example, voices at first the position of Aristotle that divine providence does not extend over individuals within the human species. Elihu, on the other hand, represents the "true view" that divine providence does reach individuals but only those whose moral and intellectual attainments warrant it.[30]

---

29. Malbim, Commentary on Job, quoted in Touati, *Gersonide*, p. 554.
30. See this translation, Bk. 4, chaps. 2 and 7, and also the Commentary on Job, chap. 42.

Commentary on Song of Songs (Perush 'al Sefer Shir ha-Shirim), June or July 1326. This is perhaps the most allegorical of Levi's commentaries. Indeed he regarded this biblical book as intended for the elite, whereas the Book of Proverbs was for the masses. The philosophical allegory contained in Song of Songs is, as mentioned earlier, the story of the human intellect and its attempt to reach intellectual perfection. It is very helpful in understanding Book 1 of *The Wars*, which is concerned with the topic of human immortality. In fact, Book 1 of *The Wars* is explicitly referred to in this commentary, which was probably written concurrently with or shortly after the former work. It also contains the outlines of Levi's epistemology and a classification of the sciences. In particular, we find there a decided preference for mathematical proofs and logical demonstrations as the paradigm of cognitive certainty. Nevertheless, scientific empiricism is also advocated.

Commentary on Ecclesiastes (Perush 'al Sefer Qohelet), October 13, 1328. Unlike the rabbis of the Talmud, Levi considered the Book of Ecclesiastes to have been the first, not the last, of the three books written by King Solomon, whereas Song of Songs was the last, not the first.[31] In his view the former concerns itself with general questions of ethics, collecting (thus the title *Qohelet*, i.e., "gathering") various competing theories about the nature of the good, and finally opting for the doctrine that intellectual perfection is the *summum bonum*. It also contains occasional passing comments on epistemological topics. Instead of the "useful precepts," which do not appear yet in his commentaries, the Commentary on Ecclesiastes contains "general principles" (*Kelalim*) at the end of certain sections of the text that Gersonides himself has arranged and divided.

Commentary on Esther (Perush 'al Sefer 'Ester), March 1329 and Commentary on Ruth (*Perush 'al Sefer Rut*), May 30, 1329. These two commentaries are short, providing relatively literal explanations of certain words and passages. The "useful lessons" are appended for the first time.

All four commentaries on the Megillot were published together in 1560 in Riva di Trento, Italy, and were reprinted several times. No commentary on the Book of Lamentations survives or appears to have been written.

Commentary on the Pentateuch (Perush 'al Sefer ha-Torah), 1329 to January 14, 1338. This long commentary, begun right after the completion of *The Wars*, which is mentioned frequently throughout, was also one of the first Hebrew books to have been printed—before 1480 (Mantua)—and has been reprinted

---

31. Preface to his Commentary on Ecclesiastes; cf. Shir ha-Shirim Rabbah 1, paragraph 10, end.

several times afterward—1547 (Venice), 1724 (Amsterdam), 1958 (New York), and 1967 (Israel). It is prefaced by an important introduction in which both Levi's method and some of his leading philosophical ideas are set forth. In it Levi tells us that he wants to continue this work with a commentary on the commandments (*Sefer ha-Mizvot*) and a commentary on the Talmud in which the various talmudic tractates would be analyzed in terms of the biblical precepts contained under or presupposed by that particular division of the Oral Law. We shall see that Gersonides was quite concerned with establishing a close link between the Written and Oral Laws, and that these two latter books, which were never written, were part of this overall enterprise.

It is in the Commentary on the Pentateuch that the tripart analysis of literal explication of words, general explanation of biblical narrative, and the "useful precepts" is consistently and thoroughly applied for the first time. Although Levi is by no means reluctant to read his philosophical theories, already worked out in *The Wars*, into his commentary, he does not see this as in any way a departure from the real meaning of the Torah. Indeed he sets himself off from the homiletic method (*derash*) of the talmudic sages, which he regards as valuable for pedagogic reasons, but which has no authoritative or dogmatic status. Believing completely in the identity of the true meaning of the Torah with his own philosophy, he cannot see that his own commentary is itself but another kind of midrash. Nevertheless, in his explanation of words, Gersonides is usually nonphilosophical and frequently cites the paragon of strict philological analysis in medieval Jewish biblical exegesis, Abraham ibn Ezra; occasionally he utilizes the similar method of David Kimchi.[32] Although he does cite Rashi a few times, he is evidently not too sympathetic with the homiletic interpretation of Scripture as developed by the talmudic rabbis and so beautifully exemplified by Rashi.

In his Preface, Levi puts forth one of his more unique ideas. Contrary to the method of the rabbis in deriving the Oral Law from the Written Law by means of the standard thirteen rules of legal inference, Levi rejects this approach and claims that he will attempt to derive the Oral Law directly from the biblical precepts. That is, in his view the laws of the Mishnah, for example, are part of the *literal* meaning of the biblical commandments. To this end Levi proposes a different set of canons of interpretation (*meqomot;* τόποι) in terms of which he believes he can defend this approach.[33] When he gets to the legal portions of the Pentateuch, his commentary is most detailed and his halakhic erudition and acuity clearly evident.

---

32. See the Commentary on the Pentateuch, 77d.
33. Ibid., 2b.

   Although the Commentary on the Pentateuch is philosophical in content, it is not as difficult as *The Wars*, and hence can be utilized as a prolegomenon for the latter work. Indeed, it may have been intended as a popular introduction to or substitute for *The Wars*. Yet it does presuppose some familiarity with medieval philosophical literature and terminology. Whatever its original purpose, the commentary is an excellent exposition of Levi's philosophy and an interesting specimen of the philosophical genre of biblical Midrash that Maimonides himself undertook in the *Guide of the Perplexed* but did not carry out to the same extent as did Levi.

Commentaries on the Former Prophets: Joshua, Judges, Samuel, and Kings. Only the date of completion of the Commentary on 2 Samuel is known: January 22, 1338. The first printed edition was in 1494 (Portugal), and these commentaries were included in various editions of the rabbinic Bible. The "useful precepts" of these commentaries were translated into Yiddish by Jekuthiel Blitz and published in 1678 in Amsterdam.

   These commentaries are probably the least philosophical of Levi's biblical commentaries. From a structural point of view, he dispenses with the tripart form and uses a line-by-line commentary, which is both linguistic and semantic, and concludes with the "useful precepts." Of interest to the reader of *The Wars* are his more detailed comments on the miracles performed for Joshua (Josh. 10) and Hezekiah (2 Kings 20:8–11) that are discussed in Book 6, part 2, chapter 11 of *The Wars*.

Commentary on Daniel (Perush 'al Sefer Daniy'el), January–February 1338. Printed in Italy for the first time before 1480, this work was included in some but not all rabbinic Bibles: 1518 (Venice), 1724 (Amsterdam), 1954 (Tel Aviv). The Aramaic portions of Daniel are translated into Hebrew. This commentary is especially noteworthy for its eschatological concerns, which are not too evident in most of Levi's other writings. In it Levi, like many other medieval Jews, indulged in messianic speculations and actually suggests a date for the appearance of the Messiah: 1358. This will be a time of considerable conflict, especially between Christianity (King of the North) and Islam (King of the South), with the former invading the Near East, especially the Holy Land. As Touati notes, Gersonides' speculations reflect the contemporary tensions between Christianity and Islam, especially in Armenia.[34] This apocalyptic war will end, Gersonides continues, in 1403, at which time the resurrection of the dead will take place at the hands of the Messiah. All

---

34. Touati, *Gersonide*, pp. 531–32; Gersonides, Commentary on Daniel, 8b.

the nations of the world will then recognize the dominion of the Lord and will abandon their false faiths and accept the Torah. The Kingdom of God will then become a universal reality.

Commentaries on Ezra, Nehemiah, and Chronicles (Perushim 'al Sifrey 'Ezra, Neḥemyah, ve-Divrey ha-Yamim), February–March 1338. Unlike the other commentaries, these were not published until modern times (Krakow, 1888). This work was reprinted in Israel in 1970. As in the Commentary on Daniel, the Aramaic portions of Ezra and Nehemiah are translated into Hebrew. Gersonides makes the interesting comment at the end of these books that all three were written by the same author.

Commentary on Proverbs (Perush 'al Sefer Mishley), April 23, 1338. This too has been a popular commentary. Printed early (1492), included in almost all rabbinic Bibles, it was even translated into Latin by Christian scholars.[35] It has been maintained that this commentary had some influence on the great English poet John Milton.[36] This is a highly philosophical commentary. Levi sees Proverbs as a genuine "Wisdom Book" and finds in the various Solomonic sayings proof-texts for his philosophical ideas. It is a valuable auxiliary for the study of *The Wars*.

Commentary on Isaiah (Perush 'al Sefer Yesh'ayahu). Unfortunately this work is lost. We know of its composition since Levi refers to it in his Commentary on the Pentateuch (197b, 227b) and in the Commentary on Kings (2 Kings 19:25). Evidently it was written before 1337.

· *Miscellaneous Judaica* ·

Although Levi had little talent in poetry, he did try his hand at writing several liturgical hymns and a poetic parody for the Purim festival. These pieces are useful in revealing to us other dimensions of Levi's personality.

Three poems for the Feast of Shabuot. One interesting feature of these poems is the identification of the Torah, which is the dominant theme of this holiday, with wisdom, a notion that goes back to the Book of Proverbs and is central in both Hellenistic Jewish thought and in some rabbinic aggadot.

---

35. Steinschneider, "Levi ben Gerson," p. 240.
36. H. Fletcher, "Milton and Ben Gerson," *The Journal of English and Germanic Philology*, 29 (1930): 41–52.

A confessional poem (viduy) for the Day of Atonement. This and the three poems above have been published and translated into French by Touati.[37] All four poems have been incorporated into the liturgy of the French Jews of the Comtat Venaissin. The confessional poem is quite moving and reflects Levi's deep religiosity and piety, which he here expresses poetically rather than intellectually. He is quick to point out his religious and moral shortcomings, especially his self-assertiveness and independence. The prayer reveals to us an aspect of Levi's personality that is not apparent in his other writings.

The Scroll of Secrets (Megillat Setarim). Purim is for the Jew a holiday of joy and merriment, on which certain activities not normally typical of Jews or Judaism (e.g., drunkenness) are permitted, indeed encouraged. It was customary for Hebrew poets to write Purim parodies for the day, and Levi composed such a parody.[38]

MATHEMATICS

Although Levi's contributions to mathematics have been studied in modern times, a new comprehensive study of this area of his intellectual activity based on all the known sources and complete translations of them is still needed. The textual information was provided by Steinschneider.[39] Joseph Carlebach wrote a doctoral dissertation on Levi's mathematics, but it is not easily accessible and needs supplementation and correction.[40] In English, George Sarton gave a brief general description of some of Levi's results, and this is still useful.[41] Two recent scholars, G. Sarfatti and N. Rabinovitch, have made important contributions to our understanding of Levi's mathematical ideas.[42] Nevertheless, more needs to be done. As a mathematician

---

37. C. Touati, "Quatre compositions liturgiques de Gersonide," *REJ* 17 (1958): 97–105.

38. I. Davidson, *Parody in Jewish Literature* (New York, 1907), p. 23.

39. Steinschneider, "Levi ben Gerson," pp. 224–52; idem, "Die Mathematik bei den Juden," *Bibliotheca Mathematica*, 11 (1897): 103–7. A. Marx, "The Scientific Work of Some Outstanding Medieval Jewish Scholars," in *Essays and Studies in Memory of Linda Miller*, ed. I. Davidson (New York, 1938), pp. 154–60.

40. Joseph Carlebach, *Levi ben Gerson als Mathematiker* (Berlin, 1910).

41. George Sarton, *Introduction to the History of Science*, 5 vols. (New York, 1975), vol. 3, pt. 1: 594–607.

42. Gad Sarfatti, "Mathematical Terminology in Hebrew Scientific Literature of the Middle Ages" (in Hebrew) (Jerusalem, 1968), pp. 220–27; Nahum Rabinovitch, "R. Levi Ben Gershon and the Origins of Mathematical Induction," *Archive for History of Exact Sciences* 6 (1970): 237–48.

Gersonides wrote on three distinct areas in mathematics: arithmetic, geometry, and trigonometry. Some of these works were written fairly early in his professional career.

The Work of a Counter (*Ma'aseh Hoshev* [Exod. 26:1]), April 1321. This is probably the first work that Levi completed. This book has been published twice in modern times with a German translation: by Gerson Lange, *Sefer Maasei Choscheb—Die Praxis des Rechners, Ein hebraisch–arithmetisches Werk des Levi ben Gerschom aus dem Jahre 1321* (Frankfurt am Main, 1909) (this edition contains the complete Hebrew text); and by Joseph Carlebach, *Levi ben Gerson als Mathematiker* (Berlin, 1910) (this edition contains only selections of the original in German translation, and according to Rabinovitch these excerpts are not trustworthy).[43]

This book is concerned with various fundamental arithmetical operations and comprises two parts: a theoretical introduction, based on books 7–9 of Euclid's *Elements*, and a part dealing with their practical applications. Of special interest are his use of a symbolic notation for number variables, his discussions of fractions and permutations, and his utilization and justification of mathematical induction, which Rabinovitch claims was original and pioneering.[44]

Commentary on Books 1–5 of Euclid's Elements. This work was published by Carlebach in 1910. It is in the tradition of the medieval philosophical-scientific commentaries, especially those of Averroes. Euclid's *Elements* had been translated into Hebrew from the Arabic at the end of the thirteenth century by Jacob ben Machir ibn Tibbon and again by Moses ibn Tibbon, whose translation was used by Gersonides. Levi's commentary may have been the first Hebrew commentary on Euclid. One quite peculiar feature of this book is Levi's general aim of proving all of Euclid's axioms and of dispensing with all axioms whatsoever. As Sarfatti observes, it is difficult to see what Levi had in mind in undertaking this self-defeating enterprise.[45]

Treatise on Geometry (*Hibbur Hokhmat ha-Tishboret*), 1324–25. Only a fragment of this work is extant and was published by Carlebach.[46] In the fragment that survives Levi attempts to prove the notorious Fifth Postulate of Euclid

---

43. Rabinovitch, "R. Levi ben Gershon," p. 239, n. 10.
44. Ibid., p. 238.
45. Sarfatti, *Mathematical Terminology*, p. 226.
46. In Joseph Carlebach, *Liqqutim me-kitvey ha-Ralbag*, in *Levi ben Gerson als Mathemetiker*, pp. 174–78, Hebrew section.

dealing with parallel lines that had vexed ancient, medieval, and modern mathematicians until 1837, when non-Euclidean geometry was invented independently by Bolyai and Lobachevski.

Book 5, part 1, of *The Wars of the Lord* includes a number of chapters that constitute a self-contained treatise on trigonometry. This section, along with the chapters dealing with an astronomical instrument invented by Levi (to be discussed below), was translated into Latin under the title *De sinibus, chordis et arcubus* in 1342 at the behest of Pope Clement VI and has been published in modern times by Maximilian Curtze.

Although Sarton characterized this work as "very important" and "original," more recent work in both medieval Arabic and Hebrew mathematics has revealed that Levi's treatise was neither as original nor as advanced as some medieval Arabic trigonometric texts.[47] Nevertheless, it was the most original and advanced trigonometric treatise in Western Europe and had some influence on the development of trigonometry in the Christian Latin cultural orbit. Regiomontanus (or Johann Müller, 1436–76), for example, knew of Levi's treatise. One of its more significant features was its use of sines instead of chords in developing the foundations of trigonometry.[48]

De numeris harmonicis, 1343. This work, extant only in Latin, was the last of Levi's completed works, written at the behest of the bishop of Meaux, Philippe de Vitry. The Latin text was published by Carlebach in his *Levi ben Gerson als Mathematiker* (pp. 129–38). Philippe de Vitry was a musician who appears to have been interested in the arithmetical aspects of harmony, an ancient Greek preoccupation. He requested Levi to write a treatise dealing with certain mathematical presuppositions of musical theory. The fact that Levi was asked to provide such information testifies to his reputation as a mathematician, especially in Christian circles.[49]

---

47. B. R. Goldstein, "Preliminary Remarks on Levi ben Gerson's Contributions to Astronomy," *Proceedings of the Israel Academy of Sciences and Humanities* 3, no. 9 (Jerusalem, 1969):244. Maximilien Curtze, "Die Abhandlung des Levi ben Gerson über Trigonometrie und den Jacobstab," *Bibliotheca Mathematica*, n.s. 12, no. 4 (1898): 97–112.

48. Sarton, *History of Science*, pp. 598–99. A. C. Crombie, *Medieval and Early Modern Science*, 2 vols. (New York, 1959), 1:96–97.

49. Eric Werner and Isaiah Sonne, "The Philosophy and Theory of Music in Judaeo-Arabic Literature," *Hebrew Union College Annual* 17 (1942–43): 564–72; Eric Werner, "The Mathematical Foundation of Phillippe de Vitri's *Ars Nova*," *Journal of the American Musicological Society* 9 (1956): 128–32. I owe this last reference to Professor Martin Picker of the Department of Music, Rutgers University.

SCIENCE

In the Middle Ages the various intellectual disciplines were not considered to be as distinct and mutually exclusive as we believe them to be today. Much of the scientific material of the medieval world was developed out of or in close conjunction with the philosophical corpus of Aristotle, whose writings encompassed virtually every field of intellectual inquiry. Many medieval thinkers considered science to be a part of philosophy, and in some instances the same individual was active in both science proper as well as in philosophy. Such a man was Gersonides, whose mathematical talent and interests naturally led him into scientific pursuits, especially astronomy, which was usually considered to be a branch or application of mathematics and was classified together with mathematics and logic as the "propaedeutic sciences" (*ha-ḥokhmot he-limudiyot*). Scientific interest was also an outgrowth of the commentaries written on Aristotle's writings. Some of the major Aristotelian texts are scientific in nature, and the commentaries on them often read like scientific textbooks. This is especially true in the case of the most illustrious of the medieval Aristotelian commentators, Averroes (ibn-Rushd, 1126–98, born Cordoba, Spain). Once Averroes's commentaries became the standard expositions of Aristotle's writings, commentaries were in turn written on them, giving rise to a whole literature of supercommentaries on Averroes's commentaries on Aristotle, among which those of Gersonides are of capital importance. Many of these commentaries are quite important for an understanding of the history of medieval science; for the basic texts of medieval science were often Aristotle's *Physics, On the Soul, On the Heavens,* and his biological writings. On and around this corpus the Arabs and Jews of the medieval world developed an enormous literature, in the form of both commentaries and independent treatises.

In the following list of Levi's scientific corpus I include both some of his supercommentaries on Averroes's commentaries on Aristotle and parts of his philosophical magnum opus *The Wars of the Lord,* and hence I depart from the practice of Steinschneider and Touati, who place these writings in the philosophical part of their catalog. Levi wrote no scientific treatise as such; all his scientific writings were included in "philosophical" books. Most classification schemes of this sort are to some extent arbitrary, and arguments can be made for and against subsuming these commentaries under the heading of either philosophy or science. I have adopted the procedure of considering some of the Aristotelian texts and commentaries as being more scientific than philosophical in our sense of these terms. To be sure, the dividing lines are not sharp or fixed; but I believe that in some instances it is more justified to place a work under the category of science than that of philosophy. In other cases the distinction is, I admit, not so clear, and individual preferences enter the judgment. Levi's scientific writings can be grouped into three categories: astronomy, natural sciences other than astronomy, and medicine.

· *Astronomy* ·

It is in astronomy that Levi made his most important and original scientific contributions. In his own lifetime he was recognized by his Jewish and Christian contemporaries to have been an important astronomer, and he was awarded the posthumous distinction of having one of the craters on the moon named after him—"Rabbi Levi." (Abraham ibn Ezra is similarly recognized.) In recent years Levi's astronomical contributions have elicited the attention of contemporary scholars, one of whom, Bernard Goldstein, has made some important studies in this field. A general description of some features of Levi's astronomy is given in the synopsis of book 5. Here I shall only cite the important literary facts pertinent to the astronomical works Levi composed and mention some of their specific astronomical features.

Book 5, part 1 of The Wars of the Lord. Like the rest of *The Wars*, this part was composed over an extended period, being completed in 1340 after having been begun in 1328. Levi originally conceived of this work as an integral part of *The Wars*, but its length (136 chapters) and technical, mathematical character led to its separation from the rest of the treatise.[50] In the first printed edition of *The Wars* this part was omitted. In fact, it survives separately in four manuscripts. Only one manuscript contained it together with the rest of *The Wars* and that manuscript was destroyed in the fire that decimated the Turin library. This work was translated into Latin during Levi's own lifetime under the sponsorship of high figures in the Provençal clergy, including the Avignonese pope. Actually, this work consists of several different parts, which can and will be considered separately.[51]

Megaleh 'amuqot. A description of the *megaleh 'amuqot* (revealer of profundities)—an astronomical instrument invented and used by Levi for measuring the angular distances of the heavenly bodies—is given in chapters 4–11 of Book 5, part 1. Along with the chapters dealing with trigonometry, which were discussed in part II above, this material was separately translated

---

50. A complete list of all the chapter titles, in both Hebrew and Latin, can be found in Renan and Neubauer, *Écrivains juifs français*, pp. 278–95; 624–41.

51. B. R. Goldstein's essay "Preliminary Remarks on Levi ben Gerson's Contributions to Astronomy" is most important; cf. Sarton, *History of Science*, pp. 599–602.

into Latin at the behest of Pope Clement VI in 1342 and survives in several manuscripts. In these Latin translations the instrument is called *Baculus Jacobi*, the title probably referring to the term *maqel*, "staff," in Gen. 32:10, which Levi himself uses to refer to this instrument in the poems he composed on it.[52] He usually refers to this implement by the general term *keli*, "instrument." Both Sarton and Goldstein have convincingly argued that this instrument was indeed invented by Levi, despite the traditional ascription to Regiomontanus, who was indebted to Levi's work, as we indicated earlier.[53] Both Sarton and Goldstein have discussed the structure and mechanics of this instrument and have provided a diagram of it. It consisted of a long rod along which a plate slides. To determine the angular distance between two stars, for example, one places the staff in front of the eye with the other end directed toward the sky. With the cross-plate the observer lines up the two stars such that each one is seen at either side of the plate. The distance is then calculated on the basis of the ratio of the size of the plate to its distance from the eye as measured on the staff. In both the theory and the application of the instrument, Levi introduces his trigonometric ideas.

Astronomical tables (luḥot). These tables are included in chapter 99 of Book 5, part 1. They were commissioned by several Christian clerics and exist separately in several manuscripts. Chapter 99 is comprised of five parts: a general explanation of the tables; instructions on how to compute the mean, or average, conjunction and opposition of the moon and sun; a method for deriving the true conjunction or opposition of the moon and sun; a computation of true solar time; and a discussion of eclipses, containing tables for position of the moon for each day.[54]

Critique and exposition of astronomical theories. In these chapters (chapters 39–44) Levi discusses a variety of astronomical topics, dealing with the motions of the various heavenly bodies, their sizes and distances, the order of the planets, and in particular the motions of the moon. In the course of these discussions, he is quite independent, criticizing both Ptolemy and the new astronomical theories of al-Bitruji. Nevertheless, he still works within the geocentric model of the universe in presenting his own theory, although he does briefly mention the heliocentric hypothesis, only to reject it quickly

---

52. See Bk. 5, pt. 1, chap. 9. The poems have been published by Carlebach in *Liqqutim, S. Carlebach Festschrift*, pp. 152–53.

53. Sarton, *History of Science*, p. 601; Goldstein, "Preliminary Remarks," pp. 244–45.

54. An edition of these tables has been prepared by Bernard R. Goldstein, *The Astronomical Tables of Levi ben Gerson* (New Haven, Conn.: The Connecticut Academy of Arts and Sciences, 1974).

and unsympathetically.[55] In this respect Levi was more conservative than his younger French Christian contemporaries Nicholas of Oresme (1325–82) and Jean Buridan (1300–58), both of whom entertained the Copernican hypothesis and discussed it in detail before rejecting it.[56]

Book 5, part 2. This part of *The Wars* is included in most of the manuscripts of the whole treatise as well as in the printed editions, although it is devoted almost entirely to astronomical matters. It was probably included because, except for chapter 9, it is nonmathematical. Yet it is highly technical, comprising chapters whose philosophical import is not readily apparent. For example, in Book 5, part 2, chapter 2 Levi discusses the nature of the interspherical matter, whose existence he proved in part 1 of Book 5. It is, however, only in Book 6, part 1, chapter 18 that the philosophical significance of this kind of celestial matter is made evident. Among the specific astronomical topics considered in part 2 are the following: the interspherical matter (chapter 2), certain topics in astronomy concerning the diurnal sphere, the sphere of the fixed stars, the Milky Way, and the movements of the planets (chapters 4–5, 7–9). In chapter 6 Levi takes up the question of how the sun heats the air. Here he refers to experiments made with "burning mirrors"— a topic of some interest to medieval scientists.[57]

Book 5, part 3. Although most of the topics in this part of Book 5 are not concerned with astronomy, two chapters do consider issues of some importance to medieval astronomers. In chapter 6 Levi discusses the Aristotelian question of how many celestial spheres are needed to explain the movements of the heavenly bodies. He also criticizes several features of Aristotle's theory of celestial mechanics and anticipates in part the Cartesian-Newtonian theory of inertia. Chapter 10 deals with a topic that was of considerable interest to medieval and early modern astronomers: are the velocities of the heavenly bodies mathematically related by a commensurate, i.e., rational, number? Some thinkers believed that a negative answer was dictated by the beliefs in divine omnipotence and in human freewill. On the one hand, if God is all powerful, He is not bound to create these velocities according to a commensurate number, which to a human mind may appear to be more logical;

---

55. See chap. 51. Gersonides also alludes to the heliocentric theory in his Commentary on Deuteronomy, 213c.

56. Edward Grant, *A Source Book in Medieval Science* (Cambridge, Mass., 1974), pp. 500–510.

57. Crombie, *Medieval and Early Modern Science*, 1:102.

on the other hand, if these velocities were commensurate, they would be fixed and man would be subject to their dominion.[58] Gersonides, however, believed that if these velocities were mathematically related by an irrational number, they would be disorderly and unknowable. Characteristically, he preferred order and knowability.

Prognosticon de conjunctione Saturni et Jovis et Martis (A prediction of the conjunction the planets of Saturn, Jupiter and Mars), 1345. This work was not completed by Levi himself, but by its Latin translator, Peter of Alexander, and Levi's brother, Solomon. It survives in the Latin translation and in a partial Hebrew copy discovered by Touati.[59] It is possible that the work was originally commissioned by Pope Clement VI. This work stands on the borderline between astronomy and astrology, two disciplines Levi generally kept distinct, although he was a fervid believer in astrology. This particular piece seems to have been one of several such prognostications made by contemporary astronomer-astrologers that were considered a few years later as omens predicting the Black Death. In it Levi records a number of astronomical observations taken over a period of time, including those of an eclipse. Interestingly, Levi points out that despite the influence of the heavenly bodies over the affairs of men, this influence can be avoided or annulled either by human freedom or by divine intervention—a theme that is to be important in *The Wars*.[60]

· *Natural sciences other than astronomy* ·

As indicated earlier, in this section we will discuss the supercommentaries of Levi on Averroes's commentaries on the more scientific texts of the Aristotelian corpus. Certain portions of *The Wars* will also be listed because of their technical and scientific character. Despite their connections with philosophy—sometimes close, at other times remote—these scientific chapters can be considered apart. Although a few modern investigators have described some of Levi's scientific ideas, no comprehensive study of this part of his literary output exists.[61]

---

58. N. Oresme, *Tractatus de commensurabilitate vel incommensurabilitate motuum caeli*, ed. and trans. Edward Grant (Madison, Wis., 1971).

59. Touati, *Gersonide*, p. 58.

60. Lynn Thorndike, *A History of Magic and Experimental Science*, 6 vols. (New York, 1934), 3:303–11; Marx, "Scientific Work," p. 160

61. Sarton, *History of Science*, p. 602; Touati, *Gersonide*, pp. 249–58, 311–15; Nahum Rabinovitch, *Probability and Statistical Inference in Ancient and Medieval Jewish Literature* (Toronto, 1973), pp. 125–27.

Supercommentaries on Averroes. Averroes's commentaries on Aristotle's writings were of three types: the long commentary containing complete translations of the original Aristotelian text with the commentaries being distinguished from the text; the intermediate commentary containing partial translations or paraphrases of the original with the commentaries interspersed in the text; and the epitome, or résumé, comprising a summary of the text written in the form of an independent monograph rather than a commentary. These commentaries were so widely utilized that Averroes became known as "The Commentator." Moreover, the translations contained in the long and intermediate commentaries eventually replaced independent translations of the original text. This was especially true in the Hebrew orbit, where Hebrew translations of Aristotle were rare. Gersonides knew his Aristotle almost entirely from Hebrew translations of the long and intermediate commentaries of Averroes. In his own supercommentaries on Averroes, Levi did not compose a single commentary on any of Averroes's long commentaries. Levi's own comments are both expository and critical; he is not reluctant to depart from either Aristotle or Averroes, although less so from the former than from the latter. For example, in his supercommentary on Aristotle's *On the Heavens*, he finds Aristotle's proofs for the unicity of the world to be wanting. Frequently, Averroes's explanations or ideas are sharply criticized.[62]

Levi's supercommentaries were written fairly early in his literary career. They antedate the final version of *The Wars*, although they were probably written shortly after or during the original drafts of parts 5 and 6 of this work. It is most likely that these commentaries were written as part of Levi's own "preparation" for writing *The Wars*, which is, as we shall see, quite scientific in nature.[63]

The first five supercommentaries, *Epitome of the* Physics (June 1321), *Intermediate Commentary on the* Physics (July 1321), *Epitome of* On Generation and Corruption (August–September 1321), *Epitome of* On the Heavens (September 1321), *Epitome of the* Meteorology (December–January 1322), were written as a continuous series during a period of six months. Taken together, they constitute a critical exposition of the basic themes and ideas of Aristotle's

---

62. In Bk. 5, pts. 2 and 3, Averroes's commentaries are frequently cited and almost always criticized in detail.

63. For the details concerning the manuscripts of these commentaries, consult Moritz Steinschneider's *Hebräische Übersetzungen* (Berlin, 1893), paragraphs 47, 51, 57, 60, 63, and 66; Harry A. Wolfson, "Plan for the Publication of a Corpus Commentariorum Averrois in Aristotelem," reprinted in *Studies in the History of Philosophy and Religion*, ed. I. Twersky and G. Williams, 2 vols. (Cambridge, Mass., 1973), 1:430–47.

physics and cosmology. They are quite important in understanding certain portions of books 5 and 6 of *The Wars*, to which the commentaries on the *Meteorology*, *On the Heavens*, and *On Generation and Corruption* refer.

Under the title of *Epitome of* The Book of Animals (January 1323) several of Aristotle's biological treatises were collected by the Arabic translators, who grouped together Aristotle's *Parts of Animals* and *Generation of Animals* under the heading "The Book of Animals" (*Kitāb al-ḥayawāh, Sefer ba'aley ḥayyim*). This work consists of nine books corresponding to the four books of *Parts of Animals* and the five books of *Generation of Animals*. At the end of his own commentary Levi notes that he found this particular commentary of Averroes to be especially difficult, since he lacked a copy of Averroes's intermediate commentary. The Commentary on the pseudo-Aristotelian text *On Plants* is mentioned in the supercommentary in *The Book of Animals*. Unfortunately, it has not come down to us.

The Wars of the Lord. Various portions of *The Wars of the Lord*, besides the astronomical portions of Book 5, which we have grouped under Levi's astronomical writings, are quite clearly scientific in nature. Indeed, the whole treatise is full of technical scientific discussions, some of which are set off in distinct chapters. Three sections in particular of *The Wars* can be singled out as especially scientific in content (with the understanding that these sections may have some philosophical import and that other sections of *The Wars* also contain some scientific matter).

Chapter 4 of Book 3. In this book, Levi discusses the general problem of divine cognition, but in this particular chapter he considers a theory of divine cognition that links the thesis of divine omniscience with the scientific theory of atomism. Gersonides proceeds to give an extensive and deep analysis of certain topics in the concept of matter, including a critique of Averroes's answer to the atomists.

Part 3 of Book 5. Although the main concerns of this section are philosophical, several of the chapters do have lengthy discussions on scientific matters. In particular, chapters 2–4 contain discussions of embryology and reproduction, with particular emphasis on the role of the Agent Intellect in these processes. The basis for these discussions is Aristotle's treatise in embryology, *On Generation of Animals*.

Part 1 of Book 6. Chapters 8–9 contain criticisms of Aristotle's cosmology; chapters 10–12 and 20–24 take up the concepts of time and motion; chapter 13 considers the problem of the emergence of dry land out of the primordial waters; chapter 24 is a critique of Aristotle's theory of natural change; and chapter 27 contains a very interesting discussion of the infinite.

· *Medicine* ·

In our biographical sketch we pointed out that for centuries Levi was thought to have been a physician. One argument in favor of this hypothesis was the report of Isaac de Lattes that Levi wrote books on medicine. Perhaps one such book is an item that has been traditionally ascribed to him: a prescription for the gout, a work that exists in two manuscripts.[64]

PHILOSOPHY

Levi's philosophical writings comprise two types: supercommentaries on Averroes's commentaries on Aristotle's philosophical texts and independent treatises. Fairly early in his career (1317) Levi decided to take up the vexing question of the creation of the universe, a problem that Maimonides had, at least in Levi's view, left unsolved. After writing a "first draft" of a monograph devoted to this topic entitled *The Wars of the Lord*, Levi realized that this problem was not philosophically isolated from other philosophical problems, nor was it divorced from some fundamental concepts in the natural sciences. He therefore set aside *The Wars* for a while and proceeded to make a thorough study of the Aristotelian-Averroist literature. This study in turn gave rise to Gersonides' own contributions to the literature: his supercommentaries on Averroes. His study of and writing on these basic philosophical texts eventually led him back to *The Wars*, but with a new conception of its structure. Meanwhile, he had produced a number of new works, of which the scientific supercommentaries were described above. Here we shall examine the philosophical portion of this literature.

· *Supercommentaries on Averroes* ·

Commentaries on the Intermediate Commentaries of Aristotle's logical treatises. All of Levi's commentaries on the Aristotelian logical corpus are based on Averroes's intermediate commentaries. Aristotle's logical writings comprise eight distinct books, to which a ninth, Porphyry's *Isagogue* (Introduction), was added in the early Middle Ages. The whole set was often referred to under the title *Organon*, on the basis of Aristotle's own characterization of logic as a preparatory study that provides the *tools* (ὄργανα) for further inquiry. These books were an essential part of the philosophical curriculum of the

---

64. Touati, *Gersonide*, p. 57; Renan and Neubauer, *Écrivains juifs français*, p. 262 (608).

Middle Ages, although the Latins did not have the whole collection until the twelfth century. In the Arabic-Hebrew world the following writings had been translated and commented on quite early:[65]

· Porphyry's *Isagogue* (*Mavo*)
· Categories (*Ma'amarot*)
· On Interpretation (*Melizah*)

Although Levi supplied no dates for these three supercommentaries they appear to have been written relatively early. They were translated into Latin and included in the complete Latin Averroes edition of Aristotle in 1550 (Venice). A recent edition of Averroes's intermediate commentary on the first two has appeared which includes citations from Levi's supercommentary.[66]

· Prior Analytics (*Heqesh*), February 1323
· Posterior Analytics (*Mofet*), July 1323

In these two supercommentaries Levi expresses his dissatisfaction with Averroes's exposition of Aristotle and provides an alternative commentary on these treatises of Aristotle.[67]

· Topics (*Nizuah*), August 12, 1323
· Sophistical Refutations (*Hat'a'ah*), August 24, 1323

Levi did not comment upon the last two books in Aristotle's *Organon*— the *Poetics* and the *Rhetoric*. Since neither subject was of great interest to him, this lacuna may be attributed to his philosophical and scientific bents of mind. However, these two works were not translated into Hebrew until 1337, more than ten years after Levi had commented on the "core" of Aristotle's logic.

---

65. Steinschneider, *Hebräische Übersetzungen*, paragraphs 14–44; F. E. Peters, *Aristoteles Arabus* (Leiden, 1968), pp. 7–29.
66. Herbert Davidson, *Commentarium Medium in Porphyrii Isagogen et Aristotelii Categorias* (Cambridge, Mass., 1969).
67. Steinschneider, "Levi ben Gerson," p. 70.

Commentary on Averroes's Fifth and Ninth Questions on Aristotle's Prior Analytics, after 1320. Averroes had written a set of "questions" (*Quaesita*) on various difficulties in Aristotle's theory of the syllogism as presented in the *Prior Analytics*. Some of Averroes's solutions did not appeal to Levi, who attributes some of the difficulties to the faulty condition of Aristotle's text.[68]

Commentary on Averroes's Epitome of On the Soul, December 1323. Here too Levi remarks that his text is not in good condition, and indeed that he was forced to make several emendations. He warns his reader that his comments must be understood under these conditions.

Commentary on Averroes's Epitome of the Parva Naturalia, (February 27, 1324). The title *Parva Naturalia* was given by the Latin commentators to the short treatises Aristotle composed on such topics as sensation, memory, and dreams (Περὶ αισθήσεως καὶ αισθήτον). These books were collected in their Arabic-Hebrew version under the heading *Book of Sensation and Sensible Objects,* which is the title of the first of these monographs (*Sefer ha-ḥush ve-ha-muḥash; Kitāb al-ḥiss w'al-maḥsūs*). However, the Arabic-Hebrew version is not complete, lacking the essays on youth and old age, life and death, and breathing.

One interesting feature of Levi's commentary is that he provides two particular instances from his own experience of the phenomenon of precognition, which he discusses theoretically in Book 2 of *The Wars.*[69] One such example was the vision he had of his being struck with a sword without serious injury; soon thereafter the event occurred.

Commentary on the Intermediate Commentary of the Metaphysics. Despite the efforts of Steinschneider and Touati, this work remains lost. This is most unfortunate, since it would have provided elucidation of some important ideas and passages of *The Wars,* which contains several references to this lost commentary. This is especially the case with two very difficult discussions of the *Metaphysics,* 4.2 and 12.10, that appear in Book 5, part 3 of *The Wars,* chapters 12 and 3, respectively. This commentary is also mentioned in Levi's Commentary on Ecclesiastes (25b). Since the latter as well as Book 5, part 3 were written by the end of 1328, the supercommentary on the *Metaphysics* was written earlier.

---

68. Touati, *Gersonide,* pp. 73–74; Steinschneider, "Levi ben Gerson," pp. 101, 103.

69. These have been described by Harry Blumberg in his edition of *Averroes. Epitome of Parva Naturalia* (Cambridge, Mass., 1961), p. 109, n. 49a. A part of Gersonides' commentary to this work has been edited by Alexander Altmann in the *Jubilee Volume of the Procedings of the American Academy for Jewish Research* 46, pt. 1 (1978–79): 1–31.

Commentary on Averroes's Essays on the Conjunction of the Separate Intellect with Man. (The exact Hebrew title is *Be'ur qezat 'iggrot nimz'au le-qezat ha-aharonim*.) Averroes had written several "epistles," or essays, on one of his favorite themes: the union of the Agent Intellect with the human intellect. Since this idea grows out of Aristotle's *On the Soul*, Averroes's *Epistles* were usually grouped together with his commentaries on Aristotle's *On the Soul*. Gersonides himself, for example, refers to these essays in connection with Averroes's commentaries on *On the Soul* and included his own supercommentary on them in his supercommentary on *On the Soul* (1323). Averroes's *Epistles* consist of three essays, two of which Levi considers to have been written by Averroes, whereas the third he falsely attributes to Averroes's son. The original text of Averroes was published in the Hebrew translation of Samuel ibn Tibbon with a German translation by J. Hercz as *Drei Abhandlungen über die Conjunction* (Berlin, 1869). Since Levi discusses this important topic in Averroes's philosophy in Book 1 of *The Wars*, this commentary upon Averroes's *Epistles* is a valuable supplement.

· *Independent Treatises* ·

On Valid Syllogisms (Sefer Ha-heqesh Ha-yashar), August-September 1319. This work may have been the first complete treatise composed by Levi. It was translated into Latin under the title *Liber Syllogismi recti*. Both the Hebrew and Latin versions are extant in manuscript. In this essay Gersonides considers several problems connected with Aristotle's modal syllogism as developed in the *Posterior Analytics*. Since modal logic is of great interest today, a translation of Levi's monograph is a desideratum.[70]

The Wars of the Lord. A discussion of the text and problems of *The Wars* will be given in chapter 3 of this Introduction.

---

70. A translation of this treatise is currently being prepared by Charles Maniken as a doctoral dissertation at Columbia University.

· 2 ·

GERSONIDES' PLACE IN THE HISTORY OF
PHILOSOPHY

Gersonides' Cultural Milieu

DURING the Middle Ages, Provence was one of the more intellectually alive and culturally creative areas in western Europe. It was one of the first regions to create a vital vernacular literary language, Provençal, which found its expression both in poetry and in song. From the twelfth through the fourteenth centuries it was the center of religious ferment, which ultimately broke out into various heretical groups such as the Cathars, Albigensians, and the Waldensians. The papacy itself went into exile in Avignon in the fourteenth century, a period known as the "Babylonian captivity of the papacy." Until the late fifteenth century, Provence was politically independent of the rest of France, being ruled by either the counts of Toulouse, the Angevin princes, or in some regions the popes. This political independence accounts in part for its cultural and religious diversity and heterogeneity.

For the cultural history of Jews as well Provence was of great importance. Under the rule of the counts of Toulouse and the house of Anjou, Provençal Jewry was for the most part protected, even favored; and the popes in Avignon too had a benign policy toward the Jews.[1] Although this region of France contained a relatively small Jewish population, compared, for example, with Spain, in the Middle Ages it produced a long series of distinguished Jewish scholars in a wide range of intellectual pursuits. Indeed, in two areas of Jewish learning—talmudic and biblical exegesis—it was most distinguished, and it became the center of certain fields of secular study, e.g., philosophy and mathematics, during the thirteenth and fourteenth centuries. With the decline of Jewish philosophical creativity in Spain from 1200–1380 and in the Muslim East, Provençal Jewry, along

---

1. Thomas Okey, *The Story of Avignon* (London, 1911), p. 247, describes medieval Avignon as "the promised land of the children of Abraham."

with Italy, was the main center of philosophical-scientific activity.[2]

Until the middle of the twelfth century Jewish Provence was primarily the locale for Talmudists, with the town of Lunel being one of the chief centers for the study of Halakhah. However, during the second half of this century Jewish families steadily migrated from Spain to Provence because of the Almohade invasions. Among these émigrés were two important families, the Kimhis and the Tibbonids, the former settling in Narbonne, the latter in Lunel. These two families were outstanding representatives of the Spanish Judeo-Arabic cultural synthesis, and in coming to Provence they brought to this region their interest in Hebrew grammar, Jewish-Christian polemics, and philosophy. The Kimhis were most important in the study of Hebrew grammar and in biblical exegesis; but David Kimhi, the great commentator on the Bible, was also a disciple of Maimonides the philosopher. Yehudah Tibbon, on the other hand, was primarily interested in philosophy, and he began the great family tradition of translating the chief classics of Judeo-Arabic philosophy into Hebrew for the benefit of Provençal Jewry, where Arabic was by and large not known. Yehudah and his son Samuel produced Hebrew translations of Saadia, Bahya, Halevi, and Maimonides, and by the middle of the thirteenth century Provençal Jewry was probably the most philosophically sophisticated Jewish community.

One new feature contributed to this attainment. Although he was either ignored or condemned by his Muslim coreligionists, the great Spanish-Muslim philosopher Averroes had a great influence on Spanish and Provençal Jewry. His philosophical writings, especially the commentaries on Aristotle, virtually revolutionized the history of philosophy, particularly with respect to the understanding of Aristotle. Whereas Maimonides became familiar with some of these materials only at the end of his life, after the *Guide of the Perplexed* had been written, the subsequent generation of Jewish philosophers deeply felt the impact of the Cordoban commentator, so much so that the history of Jewish philosophy until Spinoza reflects the Averroist reading of Aristotle.[3] The Tibbonid tradition in translation continued with Moses ibn

---

2. Although no comprehensive history of medieval Provençal Jewry has yet appeared, there are several important monographs dealing with various aspects of Jewish life in medieval Provence: Richard W. Emery, *The Jews of Perpignan in the Thirteenth Century;* Isadore Twersky, *Rabad of Posquières: A Twelfth-Century Talmudist*, rev. ed. (Philadelphia, 1980); Frank Talmage, *David Kimhi, the Man and the Commentaries* (Cambridge, Mass., 1975); Salo W. Baron, *Social and Religious History of the Jews*, 10:82–91.

3. For the role and destiny of Averroes among the Jews, see Harry A. Wolfson, "The Twice-Revealed Averroes" and "Plan for the Publication of a Corpus Commentariorum Averrois in Aristotelem," both reprinted in Twersky and Williams, eds., *Studies in the History of Philosophy and Religion*, 2: 371–401 and 430–47.

Tibbon, among others, translating into Hebrew many of the Averroes commentaries, as well as the Arabic translations of the Greek mathematicians and astronomers. Once the basic Aristotelian corpus as interpreted by Averroes and the scientific legacy of the Greeks were made available to Provençal Jewry, it was not long before Jewish philosophers and scientists emerged and began to contribute to this literature. The period from 1220 to 1390 is filled with the names of many Jewish commentators on Averroes, philosophers, philosophical biblical exegetes, and scientists.[4]

The combined impact of Maimonides and Averroes not only revolutionized Jewish religious and philosophical thought but also gave rise to several open struggles between various segments of the Jewish community. Samuel ibn Tibbon completed his Hebrew translation of Maimonides' *Guide* in 1204. Twenty-five years later the opponents of philosophy began their opening attack against the followers of Maimonides, including David Kimhi and the Tibbonids. For the next generation Provençal and Spanish Jewry were rife with religious controversy over the legitimacy of philosophy and in particular over the position of Maimonides in the Jewish curriculum of studies. To those who saw "Greek wisdom" as leading to religious heresy, Maimonides was indeed a great Halakhist, but his philosophical side was aberrant and had to be suppressed. On the other hand, those who tried to accommodate Greek thought into Judaism saw Maimonides as the one who had successfully achieved the desired synthesis between Aristotle and Moses. The conflict was bitter, and edicts of excommunication were issued by both parties. Even the Church was brought into the fray, with the opponents of Maimonides appealing to the clergy for support against the philosophical party. In 1232 or 1233 some of Maimonides' writings were actually burned at the command of the Church in Provence. This last act, however, had a sobering effect. Some of the most bitter opponents of Maimonides had second thoughts and began to relent. For a while the struggle abated and all was quiet for another two generations.[5]

But the fire continued to smolder, and in 1303 the conflagration broke out again. Charges were made against certain Jews that they were allegorizing the Torah to such an extent that they no longer subscribed to its plain meaning and were therefore lax in their observance of the commandments—an old complaint, as Philo in the first century testifies. Both the extreme allegorizing

---

4. Israel Zinberg, *History of Jewish Literature*, trans. Bernard Martin, 12 vols. (Cincinnati, 1972, 1973), 1 and 3.

5. The best work on this subject is still Joseph Sarachek's *Faith and Reason: The Conflict over the Rationalism of Maimonides* (Williamsport, Pa., 1935). Zinberg's *History of Jewish Literature*, 3, is also useful.

and the religious laxity were attributed to the influence of Greek philosophy, especially as it was interpreted by Averroes, on Jewish intellectuals, who began to interpret Scripture "not according to its proper meaning."[6] The attack again elicited defenders of philosophy, most notably Yedayah Bedersi and Menaḥem ben Shlomo Meiri, the former writing a special essay defending the practice of philosophy.[7] This time too an external force intervened, which had as its consequence the cessation of the conflict: the expulsion of the Jews from northern France by Philip the Fair in July 1306. The Jews were now faced with a more serious threat, and they could no longer afford internal religious and philosophical quarrels. The conflict diminished and eventually died down (although it hasn't disappeared entirely even in our own century). By the middle of the fourteenth century Jewish philosophy was relatively secure in Provence, although its practitioners were declining in number. The conflict, however, took its toll.

This was the general cultural and philosophical environment in which Gersonides lived and wrote. Although he makes several general references to the expulsion of the Jews from northern France (in his Commentary on Leviticus, chapter 26:38, and The Wars, Preface), he does not refer explicitly to any of the internal intellectual conflicts that we have just described, even though he lived through the second struggle between the philosophers and their opponents. Perhaps he alludes opaquely to the opponents of philosophy in his Preface, where he mentions a group of people who resent any novelty in theological thought. Since Levi's literary career began roughly thirteen years after the second conflict had begun to diminish, there was probably little need for him to refer to it. It was only after his death that he began to be singled out as a representative of the philosphical party by those who wanted to suppress the pursuit of philosophy.[8]

The Character of Gersonides' Philosophy

The roles of Maimonides and Averroes in the intellectual history of Provençal Jewry are important not only for understanding that particular period of Jewish history; these two philosophers were the dominant intellectual influences on the philosophy of Gersonides. To be sure, Aristotle's influence is

---

6. Mishnah, Sanhedrin 10.
7. Abraham Halkin, "Yedaiah Bedershi's Apology," in *Jewish Medieval and Renaissance Studies,* ed. Alexander Altmann (Cambridge, Mass., 1967), pp. 165–84.
8. Menahem M. Kellner, "Rabbi Isaac bar Sheshet's Responsum," pp. 110–18.

virtually on every page of *The Wars*, explicitly or implicitly. But in the later Middle Ages the understanding of Aristotle was mediated by Averroes's commentaries, and in the Jewish tradition Aristotle's philosophy was also perceived in the light of Maimonides' qualified assimilation of it into the Jewish philosphical-theological tradition. When we speak, then, of Aristotle's influence on Gersonides, or for that matter on any Jewish philosopher from the thirteenth through the sixteenth centuries, we are referring to Aristotle as interpreted by Maimonides and Averroes. Indeed, Gersonides' knowledge of Greek philosophy is almost entirely taken from Averroes's commentaries, and he cites no Jewish philosophical text other than those of Maimonides. Thus Averroes and Maimonides were for Gersonides more than just general philosophical influences; they were his chief philosophical teachers.

It is possible to present Levi's general philosophical outlook in terms of his positions vis-à-vis Maimonides' conservative and qualified acceptance of Aristotle and Averroes's radical and unconditioned adherence to the philosophical teachings of the great Greek philosopher. Maimonides considered Aristotle to be the greatest philosopher that ever lived. But this unqualified admiration of Aristotle did not lead him to an unqualified acceptance of all of Aristotle's ideas. On some of the more fundamental issues that were vexing medieval thinkers, Maimonides adopted the "conservative," or traditional religious view *against* Aristotle. This is most evident when we consider the questions of creation, divine omniscience, and divine providence. In each of these three cases Maimonides adopted a position that was either explicitly or implicitly at variance with the views of Aristotle.[9] Moreover, he was not afraid to criticize Aristotle on matters pertaining to astronomy and cosmology. Although Maimonides did utilize Aristotle's physics and metaphysics for the formulation and demonstration of several important theological principles, such as the existence, unity, and incorporeality of God, he broke with Aristotle whenever the latter clearly departed from a view that Maimonides believed to be central to classical Judaism, e.g., creation.[10]

Averroes, on the other hand, rarely, if ever, strayed from Aristotle's path.

---

9. Maimonides, *Guide of the Perplexed* 2.13; 3.16–17, 20–21.

10. Although Maimonides explicitly rejects Aristotle's theory of the eternity of the universe in chap. 13–25 of pt. 2 of the *Guide*, there has been a persistent tradition of Maimonidean commentators who have claimed that he really believed in some version of the eternity theory. Moses Narboni in the fourteenth century and Leo Strauss in our own day were suspicious of Maimonides' explicit teaching on this topic, and they have been supported by several recent Israeli scholars. I incline toward the traditional view of reading Maimonides as rejecting Aristotle's theory of eternity. This was the interpretation of Gersonides, and we shall follow it. See Colette Sirat, *Hagut filosofit bi-mey ha-beynayim* (Jerusalem, 1975), p. 253.

Even on the issue of creation, he interpreted the passages in the Koran pertaining to this topic in such a way as to reconcile them with Aristotle's theory on eternity.[11] Rather than give up Aristotle, Averroes preferred to twist the Koran to fit Aristotle's theories, which he regarded as true. It is no wonder that he was accused of heresy and his books were burned, some of them lost forever or extant only in Hebrew or Latin. But whatever his true beliefs or real intentions, Averroes saw himself primarily as an interpreter of Aristotle, and he was regarded by his contemporaries and successors as "the Commentator." Averroes's adherence to Aristotle may appear to be slavish and uncritical, but a study of his commentaries shows how deep his understanding of Aristotle was and where occasionally he was prepared to strike out on his own. Ultimately Averroes's attachment to Aristotle was construed by others as so strict that he was charged with teaching the doctrine of the "double-truth." This view was especially current among certain thirteenth-century Latin philosophers, such as Siger of Brabant. According to this reading of Averroes there are two truths: philosophical, as found in Aristotle, and religious, as expressed in a divinely revealed book. The two do not always coincide, and indeed they may be in conflict. How they are to be reconciled constitutes the "riddle of Averroism."[12] Whether such an idea was really the view of Averroes may be questioned, but what is important for us is the fact that Averroes was perceived as *the* disciple of Aristotle in the Middle Ages, and not merely as his commentator.

Gersonides' philosophy represents, if only unconsciously, a more sympathetic reception of Aristotle into Judaism than is found in Maimonides, but at the same time a more critical appreciation of Aristotle than is seen in Averroes. Words like "compromise" and "synthesis" do not adequately express Gersonides' intentions or achievement. Convinced of the logical *identity* of philosophical truth and revealed truth, Gersonides attempted to construct a system of thought that was philosophically demonstrable yet compatible with Scripture. Every major issue of theological or philosophical significance in the Middle Ages was for him capable of philosophical analysis and resolution. There were for him no dangling threads in the fabric of Judaism that could be tied up only by resorting to revelation, as Maimonides had counseled. But, unlike Averroes, Gersonides realized that Aristotle was human, and that not every proposition in the Aristotelian corpus was true. On several

---

11. Averroes, *On the Harmony of Religion and Philosophy*, trans. George Hourani (London, 1961).

12. Frederick Copleston, *A History of Medieval Philosophy*, 8 vols. (Westminster, Md., 1962), 2, chap. 42; Ernest Renan, *Averroés et l'Averroisme: essai historique* (Paris, 1866).

important issues Aristotle was in fact totally wrong. Gersonides' attitude toward Aristotle was, then, more independent than that of Averroes, yet more appreciative than that of Maimonides. But this is only a rough characterization. To grasp the true significance of Gersonides' philosophical position, one has to examine specific crucial issues in which the differences between Aristotle, Maimonides, and Averroes are especially pronounced. Such an examination will reveal how and why Gersonides was labeled by Salomon Munk over one hundred years ago as "the most daring of all Jewish philosophers."[13] Although Munk's characterization may have been excessive, it is nevertheless not too far from the truth.

Perhaps the best illustration of Gersonides' philosophical autonomy from both Aristotle and Averroes is his discussion of creation, the topic that was the sole theme of the original version of *The Wars*. As Maimonides formulated the issue, there were three main rival hypotheses to be considered: the Aristotelian theory of eternity; the Platonic theory of creation from some primordial matter; and the biblical doctrine of creation ex nihilo. For Maimonides, to accept the eternity of the universe is to give up the belief in the miraculous, especially the belief in divine revelation. Hence, for the believer in Scripture, a theory of creation, whether Platonic or ex nihilo, is dogmatically necessary. Maimonides' procedure in resolving this issue was, first, to invalidate the philosophical arguments against creation, some of which were Aristotelian in origin, whereas others were advanced by Al-Farabi and Avicenna. Having shown the logical possibility of creation, Maimonides then argued for its greater empirical plausibility, although he explicitly said that no argument on this issue is decisive and demonstrative. Finally he opted for creation ex nihilo on traditional grounds, claiming that since Plato did not prove his theory, there is no need to accept it. Thus, on the issue of creation Maimonides vigorously rejected Aristotle by means of philosophical argument, but mildly reproved Plato on traditional theological grounds.

Gersonides found this whole treatment to be inadequate. In the first place, he didn't like the logical character of Maimonides' arguments for creation, which were inductive and nondemonstrative. If Aristotle was to be refuted, the strongest kind of argument would be needed: the deductive, demonstrative syllogism. Thus Gersonides constructed his own arguments against Aristotle, which he believed had greater probative force. Second, unlike Maimonides, Gersonides believed that the idea of creation ex nihilo, regardless of its status in the Jewish tradition, was false, indeed absurd. He proceeded to demonstrate its absurdity and to argue for a version of the Platonic

---

13. Salomon Munk, *Mélanges de philosophie juive et arabe* (Paris, 1857), p. 497.

theory. Despite the authority of Aristotle and the respect he had for Maimonides, Levi forged his own path through these philosophical thickets. Aristotle was completely wrong, and to the extent that Averroes shared Aristotle's belief in the eternity of the universe, so was he; Maimonides was, on the other hand, only partly wrong, but still in error.

Gersonides' philosophical and theological independence, and even his radicalism, can also be illustrated in his theory of divine cognition, which, along with his defense of the Platonic theory of creation, may be the most novel feature of his philosophy of Judaism. Medieval discussions of divine cognition focused on two central issues: (1) Can God know particular events? (2) If He does, is this knowledge compatible with human freedom? The first question is generated from the Aristotelian principle that God is a timeless, incorporeal entity, and thus incapable, at least prima facie, of apprehending temporal particulars in the physical universe.[14] The second question derives from an Aristotelian dilemma between the unrestricted application of certain laws of logic and the contingency of future events. For if *every* sentence is either true or false *now*, then if there *will* be, say, a battle at sea tomorrow, that battle cannot, it would seem, not take place. And thus free will appears to be an illusion.[15] In its theological formulation the dilemma becomes one in which divine omniscience appears to be incompatible with human freedom. For if God knows all events, including future events, then any future act I perform is such that it cannot not eventuate. Thus, it would appear, I am not free to refrain from performing it.

In medieval philosophy there were a variety of proposals to resolve this dilemma. Some thinkers held that God's knowing some future event does not imply His making this event occur.[16] Others maintained that since God is eternal, His knowledge is also eternal, and that in His *eternal* cognition all events, past, present, and future, are grasped and encompassed.[17] Maimonides and Averroes too believed the dilemma to be spurious. Rejecting the previously mentioned attempts to evade the dilemma, they claimed that God's knowledge cannot be described in terms of human categories, such that it is general or particular (Averroes) or that it is subject to the laws governing human cognition (Maimonides). Since God's knowledge is identical with His essence, to understand the logic of His knowledge would be to comprehend His essence, which is of course impossible for man. We simply have to admit

---

14. Aristotle, *Metaphysics* 12.9; Maimonides, *Guide* 3.16.
15. Aristotle, *On Interpretation*, chap. 9.
16. Augustine, *On Free Choice of the Will*, 3, chaps. 2–4.
17. Boethius, *The Consolation of Philosophy*, bk. 5.

here that we cannot understand both how God can know particular future events and how such events can still retain their contingency.

Not a single one of the previously cited solutions of this dilemma was accepted by Gersonides. Indeed he rejected their common point of departure: the spuriousness of the dilemma. On the contrary, he believed that the dilemma is genuine, and that one must choose one and only one of its two horns. Since Gersonides, like all of his predecessors, insisted on the centrality of human freedom, he surrendered the belief in divine foreknowledge of particular contingent events. Divine omniscience is radically redefined in terms of knowing what is knowable. For Gersonides, knowing the outcomes of particular contingent events in the future is a logical impossibility, even for God. God's knowledge consists only of general laws.[18] We can clearly see here his independence from his two teachers, Maimonides and Averroes, who were in this respect philosophical-theological "conservatives."

The two issues discussed above were chosen to illustrate Levi's philosophical autonomy. But it will not do to stop here and to generalize, making Levi into a thoroughgoing philosophical-theological "radical." Such an approach would be simplistic as well as incorrect. There was another side to Gersonides' philosophical personality that is expressed in his willingness to defend traditional theological doctrines against current philosophical dogmas if he thought that the latter were philosophically unpersuasive. We shall illustrate this dimension to his philosophy with two examples.

One idea that was common to both some Greek philosophers and the Judeo-Christian-Muslim tradition was the belief in human immortality. To be sure, this idea was variously interpreted among and within these traditions. Nevertheless, there was here a convergence of Greek philosophical thought and divine Scripture. In the Muslim philosophical tradition a special theory of immortality was developed, which was Aristotelian in origin but had assumed almost mystical overtones. This was the notorious doctrine of the conjunction of the human intellect with the Agent Intellect. Aristotle's mysterious "intellect from without," whose role in knowledge and organic generation had been cryptically hinted at by Aristotle, became in the hands of his Greek commentators a full-blown theory of human immortality. In Averroes this theory reached perhaps its most mature and thorough form. The main thesis of this theory is the claim that at the highest level of human cognition the individual knower attains some kind of unification with the Agent Intellect, the suprasensible and incorporeal cause of cognition in man.

---

18. Gersonides, *The Wars*, Bk. 3.

In the achievement of this stage of perfection the individual becomes one with the Agent Intellect and hence "loses" his individuality.[19]

This doctrine was fairly influential among the Christian philosophers to whom we have alluded earlier under the title "Latin Averroists." They were particularly attracted to Averroes's idea of the union with the Agent Intellect, even though its corollary of no individual immortality was incompatible with traditional Christianity. The vigor with which these Latin Averroists advocated their mentor's doctrine naturally elicited a counterattack, which was led by the great Dominican Thomas Aquinas, who wrote a special essay sharply criticizing the Averroist teaching. And in 1277 this doctrine, along with many other "propositions," was condemned by the Church as heretical.[20]

To the philosophically and religiously conservative mind the loss of individual immortality was too much to surrender. And on this score Gersonides was a conservative, departing from Averroes and perhaps Maimonides as well, if Shlomo Pines's interpretation of the latter thinker is correct.[21] The weight of traditional Jewish religious teaching was too heavy to throw off easily, especially if the arguments against this teaching were not valid, as Gersonides attempted to show. In his Commentary on Song of Songs, one of his earlier essays in biblical exegesis, Levi constructs an allegory between the human intellect and the Agent Intellect, replacing or supplementing the traditional rabbinic allegory between Israel and God. Nevertheless, throughout the allegory the distinction between the two intellects is preserved. In Book 1 of *The Wars* Averroes's doctrine is treated in detail and is rejected on philosophical grounds. Moreover, Levi meets Averroes face-to-face in his supercommentary on Averroes's essays on conjunction and again criticizes the doctrine from a philosophical standpoint. Gersonides' defense of individual immortality exemplifies both his independence from Averroes and his sensitivity to more traditional religious themes and demands.

Nor is this example of the conservative side to his personality unique. On another important and controversial issue in medieval philosophy Levi

---

19. Alfred Ivry, "Averroes on Intellection and Conjunction," *Journal of the American Oriental Society* 86 (1966): 76–85; Philip Merlan, *Monopsychism, Mysticism, Metaconsciousness* (The Hague, 1963).

20. *Condemnation of 219 Propositions*, trans. Ernest Fortin and Peter O'Neill, ed. Ralph Lerner and Muhsin Mahdi, *Medieval Political Philosophy: A Sourcebook* (New York, 1963), propositions 113–49; Copleston, *History of Medieval Philosophy*, 2, chap. 42.

21. Pines has argued that this was the view of Maimonides. See his introduction to his translation of the *Guide*, cii-ciii. The passage in the *Guide* is found in pt. 1, chap. 74, 7th argument.

aligned himself with the traditionalists. In Book 4 of *The Wars* he discusses the various views on the topic of divine providence. As the "philosophical view," or the theory of Aristotle, Gersonides describes the claim of those who restrict divine providence in the earthly domain to the human species, with individuals within the species not receiving divine protection as individuals. This thesis then would admit *general* providence but deny individual providence for man. On the other hand, there is the view that divine providence extends to *all* members of the human species as individuals and is exhibited in every experience, good or bad, of an individual. According to this latter theory, God's providence is continually being manifested in rewards and punishments received by all men as individuals.

Although Aristotle's views on this topic are somewhat ambiguous, it is clear that some medieval thinkers understood him to have denied one of the key doctrines of Judaism: God's concern for individual men. But what sense can we make out of the Bible if Aristotle's claim are accepted? Clearly, Aristotle had to be rejected on this matter. This was the response of Maimonides, and on this issue Gersonides followed suit.[22] But in taking the conservative position against Aristotle, Gersonides departed from his usual method. Whereas in his defense of creation, for example, he argued directly against Aristotle, attempting to prove both the truth of creation and the invalidity of Aristotle's arguments for the hypothesis of the eternity of the universe, on this topic Levi was more defensive in his tactics and more theological than philosophical in his exposition. Most of his argument in Book 4 of *The Wars* is really directed against the second view he discusses, the doctrine of the masses, who would have God distributing His providence over everyone and at all times. There is relatively little direct argument against Aristotle, or the philosophical position, except for one paragraph in which Levi merely appeals to the phenomena of prophecy, divination, and true dreams, and the chapter in which he attempts to show the compatibility of his theory of divine cognition, which is basically the philosophical view of divine cognition, with his account of individual providence.[23]

Indeed a good deal of space is devoted to showing that the Book of Job is to be read as a philosophical dialogue among Job (Aristotle) and his friends (representing various versions of the general view of the religious masses), which is resolved by the character Elihu, who represents the true view advanced by Maimonides and Gersonides that individual providence is evidenced among individual men *who deserve it*. Moreover, the longest chapter

---

22. Maimonides, *Guide* 3.17.
23. Gersonides, *The Wars*, Bk. 4, chaps. 3 and 5.

in Book 4 is concerned with interpreting various rabbinic sayings in accordance with the previous theory. Of all six books of *The Wars*, Book 4 is the least philosophical in style, content, and points of reference. Citations from the Bible and rabbinic literature abound; and there is no doubt that at least in this book of *The Wars* it is Levi ben Gershom the rabbi who is speaking. Of course, Levi does not advocate the views of the average Jew of his day, whoever he was supposed to be. But by Levi's time, there was enough diversity in theological nuance to allow Levi to express the views on divine providence that he advocates. And on this particular topic his doctrine was not much different from the theory of Maimonides. His solution to the problem of divine providence reveals him to be both independent from Aristotle and yet at the same time not completely representative of any random Jewish believer. Nevertheless, Levi was a firm believer in individual providence, a theme that is repeated continually throughout his biblical commentaries.

These various dimensions of Levi's philosophy cannot be easily characterized by a label. He was too good of a philosopher to allow himself to be captured by a philosophical slogan or catchword. It would be incorrect and anachronistic to see him as a "pure" philosopher pursuing the truth wherever it led him. A *medieval* philosopher did not live in a world in which pure philosophy was practiced. Even the most "liberated" philosophers in the Middle Ages, such as Al-Farabi and Averroes, had to pay their respects to the established religious traditions in which they lived. The presence and importance of religion was too pervasive to be ignored by medieval philosophers. In Gersonides' case fidelity to certain conventional religious beliefs was sincere, and was motivated by a deep conviction that Judaism *properly* interpreted was identical with philosophical truth—perhaps not with Aristotle or Averroes, yet with truth, and that is what matters.

Gersonides' Position in the History of Medieval Jewish Thought

When we try to locate and evaluate Levi's position within the Jewish tradition, we are immediately faced with a problem, indeed a paradox. On the one hand, his biblical commentaries were highly regarded and studied and in some cases included in printed editions of rabbinic Bibles, a fact which endows a commentary and its author with a certain status and authority. Yet his philosophical ideas were often criticized, and he was regarded by some thinkers as having strayed too far from the traditional mainstream of Judaism. Indeed his philosophical magnum opus was called "The Wars Against the Lord" by Shem Tob ibn Shem Tob (1390–1440), the Spanish Kabbalist and fierce opponent of all philosophical speculation.[24] A kind of intellectual schizophrenia in the Jewish soul, similar to the kind that occurred during the controversy over Maimonides, manifests itself with respect to Gersonides. In the case of Maimonides the opponents of philosophy made a distinction between *Rambam* the Halakhist and Maimonides the philosopher; in the case of Gersonides the distinction was drawn between *Ralbag* (acronym for Rabbi Levi ben Gershom) the biblical exegete and Gersonides the philosopher. To the opponents of philosophy Maimonides and Gersonides were unacceptable; they were, however, acceptable as commentators of holy books. This compartmentalized attitude is clearly expressed in the letter of Rabbi Isaac bar Sheshet (1326–1408), to which we have alluded earlier and a part of which we now quote:

> And the sage Rabbi Levi of blessed memory, a great Talmudist who wrote a fine commentary on the Torah and Prophets, followed in the footsteps of our teacher Rabbi Moses bar Maimon, of blessed memory. But those sciences, i.e., philosophy and physics, turned his heart from the true path. He contradicted the opinions of our teacher Rabbi Moses, of blessed memory, in a number of matters. These include the issue of God's knowledge of future contingents, the stopping of the sun for Joshua, and the turning of the shadow back ten degrees, about all of which he wrote things which are forbidden to hear. In his book called *Wars of the Lord* he wrote about the immortality of the soul and about the Providential punishment of the wicked in this world.[25]

Beginning with words of praise, Rabbi Isaac bar Sheshet testifies to Levi's talmudic learning and excellent biblical commentaries, which were well known by the late fourteenth century. But he quickly points out that Levi did not accept Maimonides' more traditional position on several philosophical-theological matters, especially the issues of divine foreknowledge and miracles.

This ambivalence is evidenced in the survey of attitudes toward Gersonides provided by Charles Touati in his extremely important and comprehensive study of Gersonides' philosophy.[26] If one were to make a chart of all the authors cited by Touati and arrange them in two columns, opponents and proponents, the column of opponents would be longer. Nevertheless, this evaluation by majority vote should be assessed in the light of the following considerations. First, many of the stronger condemners of Gersonides were

---

24. Shem Tob ibn Shem Tob, *Sefer ha'-Emunot* (Ferrara, 1556), 4th gate, chap. 19, p. 45b.
25. Kellner, "Rabbi Isaac bar Sheshet's Responsum," p. 116.
26. Touati, *Gersonide*, pp. 541–59.

people who lived through or soon after the catastrophe of Spanish Jewry in 1391, whereas the most positive reactions to Gersonides came from those who lived before 1391 or in modern times. This is not accidental or unimportant. After 1391 a fundamental change took place in European Jewry's attitude toward secular learning, especially philosophy. The severe social and religious upheavals that rocked Spanish Jewry had their impact on the place of philosophy within the European Jewish community. To some authors who lived through or close enough to the pogroms, forced conversions, and forced debates, philosophy, and more generally the "wisdom of the Greeks," was the stranger and enemy from within the gates that led to apostasy. To others the very last act of this tragedy—the expulsion from Spain in 1492—was divine punishment for the reception of the beauty of Japhet into the tents of Shem.[27] A general disapproval of philosophy again emerged, and Gersonides was one of its victims. The historian of Jewish religious and philosophical thought must admit then that Gersonides the philosopher was pretty much a peripheral and suspect figure within traditional Jewry after 1391, whereas as a biblical exegete he occupied a more secure and central place in the Jewish study of the Bible. It is not altogether clear how this schizophrenic attitude could have been adopted—no more than it is easy to understand how people could have believed, or at least tried to believe, that the author of the *Guide of the Perplexed* was not the author of the *Mishneh Torah*—for many, if not all, of Gersonides' philosophical theories are found in his biblical commentaries. But not everything in the human soul is easily explained.

Second, one must remember that after 1492, if not before, philosophy in Judaism had been virtually eclipsed by mysticism, a phenomenon that had occurred several centuries earlier in Islam. This fact, not irrelevant to the period of crisis and tragedy in Judaism from 1391–1492, explains in part why the more philosophically daring of the medieval thinkers, such as Gersonides, were sharply criticized and even condemned by such Kabbalists as Shem Tob ibn Shem Tob, Meir ibn Gabbai, and the Judah Loeb ben Bezalel of Prague. Although Kabbalah is as speculative and metaphysical as is *The Wars*, the Aristotelian conceptual framework of medieval Jewish philosophy was regarded as dangerous and foreign by the adherents of the Kabbalah, and one can detect a gradual but definite hostility

---

27. Solomon Alami, *Iggeret ha-Musar* (c. 1415), a selection of which is reprinted in *The Judaic Tradition*, ed. Nahum N. Glatzer (Boston, 1969), pp. 397–403. The contemporary historian of medieval Spanish Jewry, Yitzhak Baer, is inclined to this view; Yitzhak Baer, *A History of the Jews in Christian Spain*, trans. L. Schoffman, 2 vols. (Philadelphia, 1961, 1966), 2:253–59.

among the Kabbalists toward the more Aristotelian philosophers of Judaism.

Third, a significant change in philosophical fashion had taken place. By the end of the fourteenth century the position and status of Aristotle in the *entire* medieval philosophical world had begun to decline. Within the Christian orbit a very important group of thinkers emerged who assumed a more critical stance toward Aristotle than that taken by Thomas Aquinas in the thirteenth century or by Levi in the first half of the fourteenth century. William of Ockham, Levi's great English contemporary and sometime co-resident in Avignon, Nicholas of Oresme, Jean Buridan, Nicholas of Autrecourt, and others chipped away at the Aristotelian edifice, so that by the Renaissance it was beginning to totter. During the Renaissance there was an important Platonic revival, and by the seventeenth century no significant philosopher was working within an Aristotelian framework.

This latter development also manifested itself within the Jewish intellectual world. In the first decades of the fifteenth century the Jewish anti-Aristotelians began to make themselves heard, the first, and perhaps most decisive, step being made by Hasdai Crescas in 1410 with the publication of his *'Or 'Adonay* (The light of the Lord). Thereafter, Aristotle steadily lost status among Jewish philosophers and theologians. The Abrabanels, Isaac and Judah, were respectively anti-Aristotelian and Platonic in spirit. The most important Jewish philosopher in the seventeenth century other than Spinoza, Joseph Solomon del Medigo (1591–1655), abandoned Aristotelian physics and cosmology almost entirely. Thus, even among those who still found philosophical theorizing to be valid or important, Aristotelian philosophy was virtually obsolete. It is no wonder that Gersonides, one of the more Aristotelian philosophers within the Jewish tradition, was either criticized sharply or completely ignored.

But a philosopher's significance is not measured merely by the quantitative preponderance of detractors or defenders. Even the opponents testify to a philosopher's importance. After all, there have been, relatively speaking, very few Cartesians since the seventeenth century, yet who would gainsay Descartes's philosophical legacy? It is possible, moreover, to characterize modern philosophy as a series of alternative answers to Cartesian questions. A philosopher's significance is measured in a variety of ways, not the least of which is the reaction, positive or negative, he elicited either in his lifetime or afterward. And when we look at Gersonides from this perspective, we can see that his philosophical impact was anything but negligible. There is hardly a significant Jewish philosopher or theologian during the period 1400–1650 who does not refer to Levi, directly or indirectly, even if only to criticize him. This point may be demonstrated by citing the most important Jewish philosophical author after Gersonides, Hasdai Crescas, and one of the most important biblical exegetes after Gersonides, Isaac Abrabanel.

As mentioned above, Hasdai Crescas was a critic of Aristotle. But in his *'Or 'Adonay* he continually contends with Maimonides and Gersonides, the chief representatives of Jewish Aristotelianism in Crescas's eyes. Although he is quite critical of, indeed even hostile toward, Gersonides, Crescas pays his respect to him, if only unwittingly, by devoting considerable attention to his views, only to reject them.[28] Gersonides' more "radical" doctrines of divine omniscience, creation out of primordial matter, immortality, and miracles are discussed in detail and criticized. But throughout Crescas's debate with Gersonides, it is quite evident that he takes Gersonides' views seriously. One does not devote so many pages to an opponent whom one despises or dismisses intellectually.

The other side of Levi's legacy to Jewish religious literature—his biblical commentaries—was also attacked, most notably by Don Isaac Abrabanel (1437–1509). But again, in reading Abrabanel's criticisms one is impressed with the fact that regardless of Abrabanel's negative remarks, Gersonides is someone who Abrabanel feels needs to be criticized. Gersonides' fame as a biblical exegete was sufficiently significant to warrant a critique. Abrabanel's concern, indeed obsession, with Gersonides is especially evident in his response to Levi's interpretation of miracles, particularly the miracle that occurred during Joshua's defeat of the Canaanites at Gibeon (Josh. 10). Abrabanel devoted considerable space both in his own Commentary on Joshua and his more philosophical work *Mif'alot 'Elohim* [The works of God] (book 10, chapters 8–9) to refuting Gersonides' interpretation of this episode as well as the general theory of miracles that is evident throughout Levi's biblical commentaries. Abrabanel correctly perceived that Levi's theological work was all of one piece: one could not divorce his biblical exegesis from his philosophical speculations, preserving the former but discarding the latter. The biblical commentaries, Abrabanel recognized, were just a different literary expression of the same philosophical content that is found in *The Wars*. Just as this work had to be criticized, so too the commentaries could not pass unchallenged. It was perhaps too much to expect of Levi's philosophical posterity that he be received with open arms, but neither could he be ignored. This too is a testimonial to his importance and influence.

---

28. Some of Crescas's criticisms were blunted by Abraham Shalom, who was a more moderate and appreciative critic of Gersonides. See Herbert Davidson, *The Philosophy of Abraham Shalom* (Berkeley, 1964).

Gersonides and Christian Scholasticism

So far we have concerned ourselves with Gersonides' place within Jewish thought. What about his relationship to the Christian Latin philosophers? Medieval philosophy was far from being a hermetical pursuit; philosophical books written in one language were frequently translated into the other languages of medieval philosophical discourse. As our catalog of Gersonides' works indicates, a few of his supercommentaries on Averroes and several of his astronomical-mathematical writings were translated into Latin. The latter did have some impact upon subsequent developments in mathematics and astronomy. Analogously, Gersonides' astronomical instruments, especially his invention known as "Jacob's Staff," were employed in both astronomy and navigation.[29] Indeed, in the seventeenth century Kepler wanted to read Levi's works but could not find copies of them. However, when we turn to Gersonides' philosophical writings, it is not clear whether he influenced or was influenced by any Latin philosophers. We have discussed above the probability of Levi's latinity and have expressed our doubts as to his having a knowledge of Latin philosophical literature. Nor do we have any evidence that any Latin philosopher mentions Levi. Although Maimonides' *Guide of the Perplexed* had been translated into Latin by the middle of the thirteenth century, no corresponding rendition of Levi's *The Wars* exists. Thus, it seems unlikely that his philosophy influenced Christian medieval philosophy.

Nevertheless, there is another way whereby we can see the significance of Levi's philosophy relative to Christian medieval thought. Often a philosopher's position is better understood by means of a comparison with his near contemporaries. By comparing Levi's philosophical style with that of some Latin medieval thinkers and by recognizing the similarities and the differences between them, we can appreciate what is common or novel in Gersonides' philosophy. To this end we shall consider two of the most eminent Scholastic philosophers, Thomas Aquinas (1225–74) and William of Ockham (c.1285–c.1349). Although Aquinas preceded Levi, he is especially relevant for our purpose because of his familiarity with Maimonides' *Guide*. Ockham, however, was not only a contemporary but actually lived in Avignon for a few years while Levi resided there. Whether they ever met or heard of each other is unlikely. During this time Ockham was living in seclusion in a Franciscan monastery protected by his fellow Franciscans from the pope, whom he had offended by his political views and before whom he was summoned for an

---

29. Crombie, *Medieval and Early Modern Science*, pp. 96–97; Goldstein, "Preliminary Remarks," pp. 239–54.

inquiry. Levi, on the other hand, was probably on good terms with the pope and his court. In spite of the improbability of their personal contact, a comparison between Levi and Ockham will be instructive in so far as it will indicate how two contemporaries viewed philosophy and its relation to religion. Let us begin with Levi and Aquinas.

Unlike Maimonides, Aquinas had been able to benefit from Averroes's commentaries upon Aristotle. As we have mentioned he also knew Maimonides' *Guide*. Thus, in Aquinas we see a sophisticated synthesis of the philosophical ideas of Aristotle, Maimonides, and Averroes with the Christian theological tradition. With Maimonides, but against Averroes, Aquinas claimed that there were definite and specific limits to human reason: certain key issues are not solvable or provable by philosophical methods. One such issue was the same problem that had vexed Maimonides, namely, the temporal origin of the world. Neither Maimonides nor Aquinas accepted the standard arguments in behalf of this theological dogma and advised their readers to rely upon religious tradition.[30] Aquinas went on to draw an explicit distinction between those theological propositions that reason can prove—the preambles of faith—and those that philosophy cannot demonstrate—the articles of faith—claiming however that the latter are compatible with reason. Hence, although the preambles of faith fall within the scope of philosophy, the articles of faith transcend the reach of logic. An instance of the former would be the existence of God; an instance of the latter, besides the temporal origin of the world, is the Trinity.

This kind of philosophical peacemaking between the competing and contrary claims of revelation and reason did not appeal to Levi. He was absolutely convinced that the truths of reason and those of revelation are identical. For him philosophy is in principle competent to reach all the truths needed for man's true happiness; conversely, Judaism teaches nothing that reason cannot justify. Philosophy has no antinomies that revelation has to resolve: revelation has no mysteries that we have to leave obscure. In this respect he was closer to Averroes than to Maimonides, and reminds us more of some of the eighteenth-century Enlightenment philosophers than the standard or stereotypical medieval theologian.

When we turn to Ockham, our comparison reveals something quite different. For although he and Levi are nearly contemporary, their outlooks are quite contrary, and for reasons other than those which differentiated Levi

---

30. Maimonides did believe, however, that there were some good inductive arguments in favor of this thesis, but he explicitly stated that these arguments were not decisive (Maimonides, *Guide*, 2.16, 18–19, 22–24).

and Aquinas. In several important respects Levi was a "backward-looking" philosopher, standing firmly within the Aristotelian-Averroist philosophical framework. Not so Ockham. He was part of the rising tide of Aristotelian criticism that was to reach its high point in the Christian world during the Renaissance and in the Jewish orbit with Hasdai Crescas. In this respect Ockham can be considered "forward-looking."

First, Ockham, along with some other Scholastics, was beginning to have doubts about the adequacy of Aristotelian physics, especially as it was interpreted in the Latin tradition. Although it would be inaccurate and anachronistic to see Ockham as a fourteenth-century precursor of Galileo—unlike the Italian genius, Ockham performed no experiments to refute Aristotle—Ockham did raise serious reservations about some of the Aristotelian physical principles and concepts. True, these questions were more "internal" criticisms in that they still presupposed the general framework of Aristotle's natural philosophy, yet they went deeper than Levi's own critical comments upon Aristotle or Averroes. One example helps illustrate this development in fourteenth-century Latin natural philosophy. The standard Aristotelian definition of motion was that it was the actualization of that which was potential in a body.[31] Ockham replaced this cumbersome metaphysical definition with the simpler notion of a body successively occupying different places. No unperceived or unperceivable potentialities have to be postulated, only the perceived body in different perceived positions.[32]

In metaphysics, Ockham's "revisionism" went even further. He rejected the standard interpretation of Aristotle's theory of universals, according to which natural kinds, or species, have some real foundation in nature, a theory that was accepted by Averroes, Maimonides, and Aquinas. Instead, species, for Ockham, are mental constructs that we make up for purposes of classification. Although they may be useful, they can be harmful if they suggest to us that there exists in the world the *species* dog in addition to any particular Fido, Lassie, and Checkers. Together with his rejection of Aristotelian realism there is in Ockham a complete revision of the meanings of the Aristotelian metaphysical categories of substance, quality, relation, quantity, etc. Again, in all but substance and quality, these features turn out to be mental constructs. Finally, and perhaps most importantly, Ockham began to express doubts about causality, at least the necessity allegedly inherent in causal and inductive laws.[33]

---

31. Aristotle, *Physics*, bk. 3.

32. Crombie, *Medieval and Early Modern Science*, pp. 62–63.

33. For a very good yet concise discussion of these matters see Julius Weinberg, *Short History of Medieval Philosophy* (Princeton, 1964), chaps. 11–12.

These various departures from Aristotle were not merely expressions of dissatisfaction with Aristotle's philosophy. They manifested a growing distrust in human reason, in the possibilities of philosophy itself. Ockham narrowly restricted the scope of reason in theology; for him philosophy could prove only one proposition in theology—the existence of God. It could not even prove that God is one! At this point we begin to see the divorce between philosophy and religion on the one hand and philosophy and the sciences on the other. Ockham didn't believe that philosophy has much to contribute to religion, at least in the sense of proving or justifying religious beliefs. Moreover, his metaphysical agnosticism suggested to some of his successors that the proper domain of human reason is not metaphysics, as Aristotle had claimed, but the natural sciences. Indeed, outside logic and the sciences it doesn't seem that for Ockham rational inquiry has any positive role to play.[34]

All of this is alien to Gersonides. Scepticism was as foreign to his mentality as polytheism. Although he was unafraid to express doubts or criticisms of Aristotelian physics, he remained a believer in Aristotelian metaphysics and its relevance to theology. He accepted the Aristotelian theory of universals as *real species* and the categorical scheme of substance and accidents as *real features* of individual items. He had no doubts about causality or inductive inference; hence the latter could be used in proofs for the existence of God. If the later Middle Ages is to be characterized by growing disaffection with reason and greater reliance upon blind faith, Gersonides was "behind his time"; yet, we might say, he was "ahead of his time," looking forward to the Age of Reason.

Gersonides and Contemporary Thought

How can we view Gersonides today? Can contemporary Jewish thinkers find in Gersonides—either the philosopher or the exegete—anything that would be of more than just historical interest? In part the answer to this question is simply a specific version of the answer we give to the question of how any living community conceives of and assimilates its past. In this respect Gersonides is no different from Saadia, Halevi, Maimonides, or Crescas. Indeed, even the more "traditional" medieval figures such as Rashi, the Ramban, and the mystics have to be reinterpreted by modern traditionalists. Some modern Jewish thinkers have expressed preferences for one or another of the medieval philosophers: Hermann Cohen was an avid admirer of Maimonides; Franz

---

34. Ockham did not believe in a philosophical or rationalistic ethics either.

Rosenzweig was most sympathetic to Judah Halevi. In some cases these preferences rest on a genuine conceptual affinity between the modern thinker and his medieval mentor, as in the case of Rosenzweig and Halevi. In other instances the link is not so much intellectual but emotional, as, I believe, was the case with Cohen and Maimonides. Can the Jewish thinker of today go back to the Middle Ages and appropriate something in the Jewish philosophical literature that will clarify or solve any of the problems that he himself poses? To a large extent the answer depends on the nature of the problems defined by our contemporary thinkers.

Some of the issues hotly debated by Maimonides, Gersonides, or Crescas are no longer current philosophical problems; the creation of the universe is an example. If that problem is resolved, it will be done by the astronomers, working within a vastly different framework from that employed by the medieval philosophers or astronomers. Other questions have been reformulated in the light of the changes and advances that have taken place in the history of modern philosophy. The nature of divine attributes, for example, has now been recast as the problem of religious language; and discussions of the latter topic take place within a framework of concepts and methods provided by the recent work in logic and the philosophy of language. It may be of more than historical interest to see whether any of the medieval discussions of this particular problem can be reformulated within a more contemporary idiom, and if so whether they can help us toward a solution of *our* problem, which is no longer the question of the metaphysical substratum for any attribute we predicate of God but the question (among others) of what we are doing when we speak to or about God either in prayer or in religious discourse. I suspect that Gersonides' theory of divine attributes, or, as we say today, his account of religious language, might be of some contemporary interest. Moreover, it is not impossible that a medieval answer is precisely *the* answer to a question that we still ask. Contemporary philosophers are still discussing the alleged dilemma between divine foreknowledge and human freedom.[35] It may very well be the case that Gersonides' solution of this dilemma provides the safest route through its horns. In each case the adequacy of the answer will depend on how we formulate the question and on what kind of answer we expect. But in a sense all the great philosophers of the past anticipated this dialogue with future generations, just as their own works were often conversations with their predecessors.

Finally, perhaps the significance of Gersonides lies not so much in the

---

35. Nelson Pike, *God and Timelessness* (New York, 1970); Stephen Cahn, *Fate, Logic and Time* (New Haven, 1967).

answers he gave to specific philosophical-religious questions as in the general tenor and thrust of his philosophical program. Gersonides is the paradigm of religious rationalism in Judaism. In *The Wars of the Lord* we see a man who has taken seriously the fact that he has reason, who believes that this faculty is God-given, and who attempts to understand God with this instrument. Gersonides is the philosopher in Judaism who attempted to show that philosophy and Torah, reason and revelation are coextensive. There is only one domain of truth which both reason and prophecy can attain in their mutually different ways. Herein lies Gersonides' philosophical optimism: he sincerely believed that reason was fully competent to attain all the important and essential truths, especially those concerning man's ultimate and true perfection. These truths will turn out to be exactly those that are taught and revealed in Scripture. How could it be otherwise? Both reason and the Torah are God-given!

Here it will be helpful to compare Gersonides' philosophical optimism with the philosophical pessimism of Judah Halevi and the more moderate stance of Maimonides. Halevi drew a sharp distinction between the methods and conclusions of a philosophical approach to religion and the religion provided by revelation. Anticipating Pascal, Halevi saw the difference between the remote, intellectualized God of Aristotle, who eternally thinks of Himself, and the intimate, passionate God of Abraham, who intervenes and acts in history. The God of the philosophers is for him an abstraction, a *concept* that we reach after and through some kind of inferential process; the God of the Bible is a *person* whom the Israelites heard and with whom the prophets spoke. The former is a God we can perhaps describe; the latter is a God with whom we are acquainted. Hence, for Halevi philosophy and prophecy represent two radically different approaches to and styles of religion. Halevi rejected philosophy in favor of Torah.

Maimonides, on the other hand, was unable to make such a sharp distinction; for him it was too simplistic. Trying to give a more balanced judgment he set out to determine the exact limits of human reason in religion. Anticipating Kant, Maimonides believed that reason was not omnicompetent, that there were boundaries to its sphere of efficacy. In particular, there were certain questions, indeed the more crucial ones, that reason cannot answer at all or cannot answer decisively. For example, logic cannot resolve the venerable apparent dilemma between divine omniscience and human freedom; nor can philosophy provide a definitive demonstration that the universe is either eternal or created. On these issues we must have recourse to revelation. Thus, for Maimonides the domains of philosophy and prophecy do not coincide; the latter contains truths that the former lacks and cannot attain. Yet, unlike Halevi, Maimonides does not reject philosophy. Indeed, it is the proper method to understand the Torah, and without it our religious beliefs would be either erroneous, uncertain, or naive. Thus, the Maimonidean achievement is the Kantian program of a philosophical demarcation of the limits of reason in religion.

To a Halevi, Gersonides really doesn't have much to say, for they each represent radically different styles of religious thought. Halevi is a philosophical pessimist; Gersonides is a philosophical optimist. Adopting a phrase from William James, we could say that one is born either an optimist or a pessimist, and that's that. To Maimonides, however, Gersonides does have something to say. Why, he would ask, do you stop short? How do you know that reason has boundaries beyond which it cannot stray with impunity? Just because *you* have not found a proof for creation does it mean that no one can discover one? Why prevent others from undertaking the task? We see then in Gersonides a most vigorous and consistent defender of human reason in religion, the Jewish philosopher who employed philosophy without any a priori limitations in his attempt to understand Torah.

In appreciating this endeavor we must keep in mind two things. First, Gersonides' rationalization of Judaism was culturally bound by the philosophical-scientific traditions of the Middle Ages, specifically the Aristotelian-Ptolemaic cosmology. Obviously, this framework is obsolete, and to the extent that his answers presuppose this cosmology we cannot accept them. However, in this regard what is important is not so much the answer but the attitude and approach that the answer reveals. As we are often told, especially by philosophical pessimists, philosophical and scientific theories come and go. Indeed, the history of Jewish philosophy is in one sense the story of how the Jewish religion has been successively reformulated in terms of changing philosophical fashions. We have the Platonic Philo, the Aristotelian Maimonides, the Leibnizian Mendelssohn, the Kantian Hermann Cohen. What is important in this ever-changing story is, however, the common attempt to *understand Judaism philosophically*. In this history, Gersonides stands out as perhaps the one philosopher who truly believed that what makes man divine is his reason. It is not so much Gersonides' Aristotelian answers but his absolute faith in reason that counts.

Second, we must also realize that philosophy has in our century changed considerably, not only in terms of its different theories but more importantly in its self-conception. Philosophers no longer conceive of themselves as propounding truths about the world. This is in part the result of the rift between science and philosophy that has taken place. Whereas in the medieval curriculum science was part of philosophy, in our program of studies the two are kept distinct, and with good reason. It is physics that tells us what the universe is like, not philosophy. And with this change the role of philosophy in religion too must be reinterpreted. No longer can we optimistically say, with Gersonides, that philosophy can prove the teaching of religion. This optimism now seems naive and perhaps arrogant. Most contemporary philosophers of religion confine themselves to the clarification and analysis of religious concepts and propositions, not with proving them. Indeed, it is not altogether clear to us what religious truth is or whether religion makes truth-claims at all. Rather than demonstrating the claims of religion, philosophers are trying to understand what they mean and their function in religious experience. If we modify Halevi's language a bit, we can reformulate this current view about religion in terms familiar to the Jewish poet from medieval Muslim Spain. Religion is concerned with matters other than science. It is the latter's province and duty to discover truths about the universe. It is religion's business to teach us how to live in this universe. Only the most arrogant of the scientists pretend to do the latter; only the misguided and zealous of the religionists attempt to do the former. This was the truce that Spinoza tried to effect in the seventeenth century. There are still many who reject this kind of religious irenicism. Some do so in the fervid, indeed fanatical belief that their religion contains all the truth, that philosophy and science are wholly irrelevant in the important areas and questions of life; others, perhaps a dwindling minority, still believe that philosophy does have an important, indeed crucial role to play in religion, that religion cannot be divorced from reason. For these Gersonides is a guide.

· 3 ·

COMPOSITION AND STYLE OF
THE WARS OF THE LORD

Chronology of The Wars of the Lord

EVEN a superficial reading of *The Wars of the Lord* could give the impression
that this work was written at the height of Gersonides' intellectual
powers, perhaps in the latest period of his intellectual development and
philosophical career. But such an impression would be mistaken. In fact, the
final version of Levi's magnum opus was completed at the end of what one
could call his "middle period"—1329. But philosophical books do not spring
forth spontaneously from their creator's head. Twelve years earlier Levi had
already begun to conceive of and compose a philosophical-theological essay
on the problem of the creation of the universe.[1] This issue had vexed Jewish
philosophers since Philo; and it seemed to Gersonides that his predecessors,
even the illustrious Maimonides, had not successfully solved the problem.
A fresh examination, he believed, was in order. Yet, a few years later he
decided that an adequate treatment of this issue could not be achieved without
a more thorough examination of the natural sciences. After all, the problem
of creation, as it was conceived and discussed by the medievals, concerned
such topics as time, motion, the infinite, and the void. It would appear that
this critical point in Levi's literary career took place around 1321 or earlier.
For in his supercommentary on Averroes's *Epitome of the Physics*, completed
in June 1321, Levi mentions that he had already finished a draft of his essay
on creation but that he had not yet disseminated it. A month later he again
alludes to this essay in his commentary on Averroes's *Intermediate Commentary
on the Physics*, where he also describes it as not having been distributed to
others. In this latter work the "unpublished manuscript" on creation is referred to for the first time under the title "The Wars of the Lord," a phrase
occurring in Numbers 21:14, where a lost book describing some battles of
the ancient Israelites is mentioned. It would appear that Levi gave this title

---

1. Levi alludes to this essay at the end of Bk. 6, pt. 1 of *The Wars.*

to his own book because in it he defends the Torah against the false opinion of Aristotle that the universe is eternal. At this point, Levi halted any further work on this essay and kept it out of circulation until he felt more secure in the natural sciences. For the next several years he went back to his philosophical and scientific teachers, Aristotle and Averroes, made an exhaustive study of their writings, and eventually composed a series of commentaries on the scientific corpus of Aristotle. In some of these commentaries, allusions to *The Wars* are found, primarily with respect to topics in astronomy and cosmology, Levi's original concerns.

In 1325 Levi began to compose his first efforts in biblical exegesis. During this year he wrote the commentaries on Song of Songs and Job, two of his most philosophical biblical commentaries. At this juncture a second critical point in his writing of *The Wars* seems to have occurred. The original conception now seemed to Levi too narrow, and a more extensive and comprehensive treatise was needed. For in these two biblical commentaries Levi refers to discussions in *The Wars* concerning topics that go beyond the domains appropriate to a book on creation. For example, in the Commentary on Song of Songs (14d, 19c) Levi refers to corresponding discussions of the soul that are found in Book 1 of *The Wars*. In the Commentary on Job, Levi mentions *The Wars* at least eleven times, the references being to topics that eventually appear in Books 2, 3, 4, and 6 of *The Wars*. Evidently by now Levi had restructured his treatise so as to include a number of philosophical-theological problems other than the original issue of creation. There may have been at least two reasons for this change in plan. First, one of the more striking theses in Gersonides' cosmology in his claim that, although the universe was created, it is everlasting.[2] This thesis not only goes against one of the major theorems of Aristotle's cosmology, but also seems to differ from some traditional rabbinic aggadot.[3] Now either as the result or in support of this thesis, Levi came across an analog of a created but everlasting universe in a vastly different domain: the soul, or at least one part of the soul. After all, it was a fairly common view among medieval philosophers that the soul or one of its parts was immortal, although created. If the possibility of a created but everlasting substance had been granted on one level, there would be no logical reason for excluding the possibility on another level. Thus Levi was led to consider the whole problem of immortality of the soul, a problem that had received a special but troublesome formulation by Averroes.

---

2. See *The Wars*, Bk. 6, pt. 1, chap. 16.

3. Consider, for example, Rabbi Abahu's saying that God created and destroyed many worlds before this present universe was created (Genesis Rabbah 3; Maimonides, *Guide* 2.30).

But in the context of medieval philosophy the concept of the soul spawned a number of other issues. Moreover, Levi's study of Aristotle's *On the Soul* and *Parva Naturalia*, along with Averroes's commentaries on these treatises, stimulated his inquiring mind to consider related issues in psychology, such as the phenomena of dreaming, divination, and prophecy. Book 2 of *The Wars* was then written, but Levi did not stop there. For some cases of these three kinds of phenomena are in his view examples of supranatural communication to man. Levi was then led to consider the whole question of divine communication to and knowledge of man. Book 3 of *The Wars* followed, which is referred to in Levi's Commentary on Job. The derivation of Books 1–3 from the original monograph on creation is a good example of how philosophical problems are self-generating. By 1325, eight years after he had begun to compose an essay on creation, Levi had already completed one-third of a far more extensive philosophical treatise, while at the same time having finished commentaries on Aristotle's scientific treatises and on the Song of Songs and Job.

In October 1328 Levi composed a commentary on the Book of Ecclesiastes, another scriptural book that lends itself to philosophical exegesis. But during the period 1325–28 Levi had also written Book 4 of *The Wars;* for in the Commentary on Ecclesiastes (35a) he makes reference to this part of *The Wars*, as well as to his Commentary on Job. The latter two works both deal with the important theological issue of divine providence, a topic which presupposes and is intimately connected with the general problem of divine cognition, which was treated in Book 3 of *The Wars*. After writing both Book 3 and the Commentary on Job, Levi recast the latter in a more philosophical and nonexegetical form and the result was Book 4 of *The Wars*, which cites the Commentary on Job several times.[4] By October 1328 Levi had already finished Books 1–4 of a vastly different work having the original title, *The Wars of the Lord*.

Books 1–4 have thus been dated, although roughly and indirectly, from the dates provided by Levi himself in his supercommentaries on Averroes and in his biblical commentaries. In none of the closing remarks of Books 1–4 did Levi give the dates of their completion. But this is not the case with Books 5 and 6. All the parts of these two books are dated by Levi. As indicated in the chart below, these books were completed in less than three months! And these are the longest, most difficult parts of the whole treatise. Obviously these dates represent only the final versions of preliminary drafts. On the

---

4. On the relationship between these two works, see C. Touati, *Les guerres du Seigneur* (Paris, 1968), pp. 9–12.

basis of the direct dating provided by Levi and the dates found in his other writings that refer to *The Wars*, we can construct the following chronological chart of the composition of *The Wars*.[5]

> 1317: First draft of Book 6, on creation
> 1321: Draft of Book 6 completed but not circulated
> 1321–24: Preliminary versions of Books 5 and 6
> 1325: Books 1–3
> Before October 1328: Book 4
> November 24, 1328: Book 5, part 1
> November 28, 1328: Book 5, part 2
> December 5, 1328: Book 5, part 3
> January 2, 1329: Book 6, part 1
> January 8, 1329: Book 6, part 2

The Wars of the Lord took then approximately twelve years to complete.

Language and Style of The Wars of the Lord

In 1862 the first modern monograph on Gersonides' philosophy appeared, written by one of the pioneers in the history of Jewish philosophy, Manuel Joël, who characterized Levi's language and literary style as "tasteless and simple, to the point of unattractive prosaicness."[6] This view was accepted and even accentuated by Isaac Husik over seventy years later, when he described Gersonides' style as having "no use for rhetorical flourishes and figures of speech," his habit of presenting all the arguments for and against a view as "monotonous and wearisome," and his "lucubrations" as "bewildering" and "fatiguing."[7] Perhaps a different picture of Gersonides' style will emerge if it is placed in its proper historical and philosophical setting.

Not all philosophers have written philosophy as did Plato, who, as the first major philosopher, wrote books of the highest literary quality, perhaps unsurpassed since. The Greek philosophical tradition established by Plato and Aristotle created a language that served as a medium for philosophical discourse for close to a millennium. Since Greek was a living language during this period, even Semites like Zeno of Citium and Lucian assimilated and became known as Greek philosophers. The medieval philosophers, however,

---

5. Touati, *Gersonide*, pp. 49–51.
6. M. Joël, *Levi ben Gerson (Breslau, 1862)*, p. 16. My translation.
7. Isaac Husik, *A History of Mediaeval Jewish Philosophy* (Philadelphia, 1948), pp. 331, 332, 353.

had to forge a philosophical language for themselves, for hardly any of them read Greek. Nor was the classical Greek language still alive or widely used. To some extent philosophers writing in Latin were the beneficiaries of Cicero's and Boethius's importation of Greek philosophy into the Roman world and their significant contributions in creating a Latin suitable for philosophy. But Jewish philosophers in the Middle Ages had no Cicero or Boethius. Either they wrote in Arabic (like Saadia, Maimonides), or they wrote in Hebrew, in which case they had to create ex nihilo a language for this purpose (like Abraham bar Hiyya). If one studies the earliest Hebrew specimens of philosophical literature and traces them from Abraham bar Hiyya through Judah and Samuel ibn Tibbon, one sees a definite growth and progress in semantic richness and syntactic ease. The watershed was attained when the translations of Averroes' commentaries by Moses ibn Tibbon and others were accomplished. By this time Hebrew had become an adequate, flexible, and precise linguistic medium for the expression of philosophical and scientific ideas. Gersonides was the inheritor of this achievement. He read Aristotle, Euclid, and Ptolemy in translations performed by a "school" of Jewish translators who rendered these basic "Great Books" into Hebrew from the Arabic.[8] These translations "preserved to a remarkable degree not only clear-cut analyses of the text . . . but also the exact meaning of . . . terminology and forms of expression." This characterization was given by Harry A. Wolfson to the Arabic-Hebrew translations of Aristotle, and it is generally true of many of the medieval Arabic-Hebrew translations of the Greek philosophers and scientists.[9] Out of these translations, and the commentaries and treatises written on them, there emerged a Hebrew philosophical language that was quite serviceable for the expression of philosophical ideas and arguments. Philosophy in Hebrew had come of age.

Now to some extent Joël and Husik were correct in their characterization of Levi's lack of literary grace and rhetorical flare. But, as they themselves admitted, Levi did not aspire to be a Plato, who was characterized by Mai-

---

8. No comprehensive study of medieval philosophical Hebrew terminology exists, analogous to the work of Gad Sarfatti on medieval Hebrew mathematical terminology. Yet there are a number of important monographs and essays on the philosophical language of several medieval philosophers. See Israel Efros, *Philosophical Terms in the Moreh Nebukim* (New York, 1924); "Studies in Pre-Tibbonian Philosophical Terminology," *JQR* 17 (1926): 129–64, 323–68. In most of Harry Wolfson's essays and books there are useful discussions of terminology; most helpful is his *Crescas' Critique of Aristotle* (Cambridge, Mass., 1929). Moritz Steinschneider's *Hebraische Übersetzungen* also contains information about terminology; Registers I–IV should be consulted. The various Hebrew editions of the *Corpus Commentariorum Averrois in Aristotelem*, published by the Mediaeval Academy of America, all contain valuable glossaries of terms.

9. Wolfson, *Crescas' Critique of Aristotle*, p. 7.

monides as a writer of obscure parables.[10] Philosophy in Levi's eyes demands a precise, clear, and direct style. The aim is to communicate ideas, and the language must be able to convey these ideas in the simplest, most efficient way. Levi himself tells us in the Preface to *The Wars* that he wants to write a book that will be comprehensible and clear. Unlike Maimonides, whom he does not single out specifically but who is, I believe, in his mind, Gersonides does not intend to write an *esoteric* treatise, containing all sorts of enigmatic allusions, parables, or intended ambiguities. The aim of a philosophical treatise is, he says, clarification, not perplexity. Thus Levi's style is admittedly "simple," but that is the way he wanted it.

Husik complained of the unrelieved monotomy of Levi's arguments and analyses and the paucity of "rhetorical flourish" in Levi's style. In the history of modern philosophy we have perhaps a better example of such a style, although the critic of it is the author himself. Kant apologized for his not giving enough examples in his *Critique of Pure Reason;* to have done so, he explains, would have lengthened an already overly long book.[11] Gersonides was not as stingy as Kant. Although *The Wars of the Lord* is primarily a book of philosophical arguments and analyses, it is not lacking in examples, analogies, or even a story here and there. Philosophical argument is frequently interspersed with quotations from Scripture or rabbinic literature, which vary the pace of the exposition. Admittedly, Levi tends to be prolix, even verbose. But, as in the case of Kant, sometimes repetitiousness has a virtue: when the argument or idea is difficult, repeating it, especially in different contexts, sometimes helps us to understand it. Levi was no Plato, but neither was he a Heidegger.

---

10. Maimonides, Letter to Samuel ibn Tibbon, contained in *Kobetz Teshuvot HaRambam v'Iggerotav*, ed. A. Lichtenberg. (Leipzig, 1859) Part 2, page 28d.
11. Immanuel Kant, *The Critique of Pure Reason*, preface to the first edition.

· 4 ·

ON TRANSLATING *THE WARS OF THE LORD*

The Critical Apparatus

ALTHOUGH Charles Touati's critical edition of the Hebrew text of *The Wars* has not yet appeared, he has already provided much valuable information about the various manuscripts and the printed editions of the book. Presented here is a listing of the manuscripts; a detailed description of them is found in Touati's French translation of Books 3–4 of *The Wars*.[1]

Paris: Bibliothèque Nationale
  MS. Hébreu 721. Complete, except for Gersonides' own Introduction.
  MS. Hébreu 722. Complete. This manuscript was used for the printing of the first edition of *The Wars* (1500). It is defective in many places.
  MS. Hébreu 723. Complete. A good text. This manuscript was used by me in the translation and it is referred to in the critical apparatus by the letter *P*.
Paris: Bibliothèque de l'Alliance Israélite Universelle
  MS. 73. Complete.
Oxford: Bodleian Library
  MS. Pococke 376 (Neubauer, *Catalogue of the Hebrew Manuscripts in the Bodleian Library*, Oxford 1886, no. 1286). Complete. This is also a good manuscript and was used in my translation. In the critical apparatus it is referred to as *B*.
  MS. Michael 252 (Neubauer, no. 1287). Lacks part 3 of Book 5 and all of Book 6.
  MS. Michael 253 (Neubauer, no. 1288). Lacks Books 1–4 and Book 5, parts 1–2.
  MS. Canonici Orientales 74 (Neubauer, no. 1289). Quite defective.
  MS. Huntington 53 (Neubauer, no. 1290).
  MS. Marshall Or. 41 (Neubauer, no. 2426.3).
  MS. Neubauer, no. 1903,2. Very brief.

---

1. Charles Touati, *Les guerres du Seigneur*, pp. 31–36. His *La pensée* updates this list with two additional manuscripts and a fragment (p. 76, n. 123).

Cambridge: University Library
   MS. Add. 502.
   MS. T.S.G. 159. Geniza fragment of five folios.
Rome: Bibliotheca Vaticana
   MS. Urbinate 28. Excellent manuscript. In the critical apparatus it is
   referred to as *V*.
Rome: Biblioteca Nazionale Centrale Vittorio Emanuele II
   MS. Ebr. 26.
Parma: Biblioteca Palatina
   MS. 3209 (De Rossi, *Codices Hebraici*, Parma 1803, no. 135). Complete
   and good.
   MS. 2447 (De Rossi, no. 460). Complete.
   MS. 2448 (De Rossi, no. 621).
   MS. 3153 (De Rossi, no. 1069).
   MS. 3030 (De Rossi, no. 1342). Complete.
   MS. 3458.
Venice: Biblioteca Nazionale Marciana
   MS. 14.
Turin: Biblioteca Nazionale
   MS. XXI (A.II.1). This was the only manuscript that contained *all* of
   The Wars, including the astronomical part 1 of Book 5. Unfortunately
   it was destroyed by fire in 1904.
   MS. CVIII (A.II.26). Quite defective.
   MS. CXXXIII (A.V.13). Quite defective.
Florence: Biblioteca Medicea Laurenziana
   MS. LX. Complete and good.
Mantua: Biblioteca Communale
   MS. Ebr. VII.
Naples: Biblioteca Nazionale
   MS. Ebr. III: F, 4
Munich: Bayerische Staatsbibliothek
   MS. Heb. 18.
   MS. Heb. 94. This manuscript contains 3 distinct copies of *The Wars*,
   one of which is complete (folios 1–140).
   MS. Heb. 73.
   MS. Heb. 125.
Leiden: Bibliotheck der Rijksuniversiteit
   MS. Warner 13.
Jerusalem: Hebrew University Library
   MS. 4:666.

PRINTED EDITIONS

Riva di Trento 1560. This is the editio princeps of *The Wars*. The printing press in this northern Italian town was founded in 1558 under the sponsorship of Cardinal Christofolo Madrucci. The Hebrew books were printed and edited by Rabbi Joseph Ottolenghi and Dr. Jacob Marcaria, who was the particular editor of *The Wars* and who supplied an introduction to the text as well as some textual correction.[2] Nevertheless, the text is quite defective; frequently whole sentences are missing.

Leipzig, 1866. This edition virtually duplicates the 1560 edition, with all the latter's mistakes. It is referred to in the critical apparatus by the letter *L*.

Berlin, 1923. A reprint of the 1866 edition.

A photo-offset of the 1560 edition was published in Jerusalem in 1966.

TRANSLATIONS

Although no other complete translation of *The Wars of the Lord* exists, there are several partial translations, which are listed below in chronological order.

Die Kämpfe Gottes von Levi ben Gerson, trans. Benzion Kellermann (Berlin, 1914, 1916). This is a German translation, containing notes and some textual variants, of Books 1–4. It is not reliable and was severely criticized by Isaac Husik in "Studies in Gersonides," *JQR*, n.s.7 (1916–17): 553–94, and 8 (1917–18): 113–56, 231–68.

Les guerres du Seigneur, livres III et IV, trans. Charles Touati, École Pratique des Hautes Études-Sorbonne, Sixième Section: Sciences Économiques et Sociales, Études juives 14 (Paris, 1968). This is an excellent French translation of Books 3–4, containing useful introductory and supplementary material, notes, and corrected readings.

Providence in the Philosophy of Gersonides, trans. J. David Bleich (New York, 1973). This is an English translation of Book 4. It also contains a useful introduction.

Gersonides On God's Knowledge, trans. Norbert M. Samuelson (Toronto, 1977). This is an English translation of Book 3, containing a lengthy and informative introduction and explanatory notes to the translation.

---

2. Joshua Bloch, *Hebrew Printing in Riva di Trento* (New York, 1933), pp. 10–11; David W. Amram, *The Makers of Hebrew Books in Italy* (Philadelphia, 1909), chap. 12.

Prophecy in Gersonides, trans. David W. Silverman (unpublished Ph.D. dissertation, Columbia University, 1973). This is a translation of Book 2 with a useful introductory essay.

The Creation of the World According to Gersonides, by Jacob Staub, Brown Judaic Studies, 24 (Scholars Press, Los Angeles, 1982.) Contains a translation of Book 6, part 2.

What Kind of Translation? Ideally, the translator of a classical or medieval philosophical work should have a critical edition of the text before him; otherwise he will find himself in a difficult position, especially if it is evident that the printed editions are defective. Fortunately for the present translation, Charles Touati is currently preparing a critical edition and has already made the necessary analysis of the extant manuscripts and determined the superiority of three manuscripts: Bodleian Library, Pococke 376; Paris, Hébreu 723; and Vatican, Urbinate 28. On his advice, a complete study of these manuscripts was made and the translation was done on the basis of these three manuscripts as well as the printed editions. On occasion some other manuscripts were consulted, and where such consultation yielded a result, the additional manuscript is cited in a footnote. Since the printed editions are defective, frequent use was made of the manuscripts to correct the text. Not rarely whole sentences or long clauses that are found in the manuscripts are omitted in the printed editions. Frequently the reading in the printed edition is defective grammatically or orthographically, and it is not unusual for such divergences to yield significant differences in the meaning of the argument. Fortunately the three manuscripts are in frequent agreement, with the Vatican and Bodleian texts being most similar. Where no unanimity in manuscript readings exists, a choice obviously has to be made. And at this point the work of the translator becomes especially difficult and crucial. How does he decide among divergent readings?

Occasionally Levi himself provided the answer. His habit of repeating himself is an invaluable aid, for sometimes he repeats the same point or argument later in the chapter or in a different chapter, and here the manuscripts often do not diverge. The latter passage then clarifies the former difficulty, though unfortunately this aid was not always forthcoming. Levi's other habit of self-quotation also proves to be helpful in establishing the text. Sometimes a citation from *The Wars* appears in another work in the correct or a more intelligible version. Wherever this was the case, a footnote directs the reader to the corresponding passage in the other work. Where the passages were citations from his commentaries on Averroes, the original passages were checked and compared with the Latin translations, where available, of Averroes's commentaries. Outside aid was occasionally provided by authors who cited Levi in their works: Crescas, Abrabanel, Abraham Shalom, and Judah Moscato, to mention a few, quote Levi extensively. Sometimes they have a reading that proved to be helpful.

Yet often no clues either from Levi or from others were provided. But here the translator of philosophy may have an advantage over the translator of other kinds of materials. In the work of an author like Levi, who delighted in argument, logic plays a very large role. There were passages in which the direction or sense of the argument required, for example, a negative particle; otherwise, the argument would be obviously invalid and the whole course of Levi's analysis or exposition would be aborted. In such a case I adopted the manuscript reading with the negation. But logic was not always a tool that could be used to decide among variant readings, and in such instances I simply had to surmise what I thought was the "authentic reading." This practice, known to biblical critics as well as classical scholars, is admittedly hazardous, but it is unavoidable. The principle governing the choice among divergent readings was philosophical comprehensibility: I chose whatever reading made most sense out of or in Levi's argument. Naturally a certain element of subjectivity enters the picture at this point, but this is unavoidable in philosophical translation. In many cases footnotes explain the choice of readings. Instances in which the text of the printed edition has been corrected are indicated by superior lower-case letters, in alphabetical sequence. The manuscript readings are listed in the critical apparatus at the end of each book of the treatise; only rarely have I taken the liberty of suggesting an emendation of the text not supported by a manuscript reading. Wherever this is done, an explanation is provided.

What about the translation itself? "Traduttore traditore" is an old and almost trite apology used by translators. This is particularly true of philosophy. Anyone who consults modern English translations of Plato or Aristotle will see how even the most competent classical scholars differ significantly in their understanding of such philosophers.[3] And they have critical texts to work from! How much more difficult it is when the text concerned has not yet been definitively established. Philosophical ideas are not easily communicated, and the arguments used to support or prove these ideas inherit the initial difficulty. Sometimes a literal rendition of a philosophical text results in obscurity or even nonsense; sometimes it is awkward to the point of incomprehensibility. On the other hand, too much freedom in translation falsifies the text. As usual, striking the proverbial happy medium is not easy.

---

3. Compare, for example, any three modern translations of Aristotle's *Metaphysics* or Plato's *Republic*.

In this work I have tried to be as faithful as possible to Gersonides' philosophical intentions, taking a certain amount of liberty (I hope not too large) with his language. Levi's style is, as Husik rightly pointed out, prolix. He frequently uses expressions that, if translated literally into English, would result in tedious redundancies. He is also fond of saying, "as I have already said." Some shortening of his style was in order to facilitate the readability of the overall argument. In addition, Levi is not consistent in his use of philosophical terminology: different terms are used interchangeably to connote the same item. For example, for the Aristotelian notion of an immovable mover of a heavenly sphere, Levi uses indifferently: *meniy'a ha-garam ha-shamayimi, sekhel nibdal, zurah nibdelet,* and *sekhel nifrad.* Analogous uses of synonyms in English appear in the translation, especially where the repeated use of one expression would be tedious. Levi, however, was not always prolix, and sometimes there are gaps in his exposition or argument that one wishes he had filled up with a cross-reference. In these cases I have taken the liberty of inserting in brackets the needed reference or phrase that provides continuity or facilitates comprehension.

No translation of a philosophical text whose provenance is a vastly different age and philosophical culture can be an exact replica of the original. Yet I have tried to retain the overall Aristotelian flavor of Levi's language, despite its virtual disappearance from current philosophical work. Fortunately many of Aristotle's terms are still entrenched in our language, even if we no longer use them in the way Aristotle intended or understand them as philosophical terms at all (e.g., 'quality'). However, this fidelity to Aristotle's linguistic and conceptual framework was not always possible. Certain words and concepts were especially difficult to translate into English. The common device of translating some of these terms by using their standard Latin equivalents was not adopted, this being, after all, an English translation. Moreover, since the Latin term would in most cases require an explanation, it seemed more appropriate to find an English term and, if necessary, provide an analogous explanation.[4] Wherever a term proved to be especially difficult, I have frequently provided notes explaining my particular rendition. Additional notes have been supplied explaining most of the technical terminology found in the text and showing their derivation from or equivalence to the appropriate Greek, Arabic, and Latin terms.

There is a very revealing letter written by Maimonides to Samuel ibn

---

4. The most notorious example of this was the term *muskal*, which has been traditionally rendered into Latin as the singular *intelligibile* or in the plural *intelligibilia*. See *The Wars,* Bk. 1, chap. 1, n. 5.

Tibbon, as the latter was preparing his translation of the *Guide of the Perplexed*, in which Maimonides expresses his philosophy of translation. The key passage reads as follows:

> First I want to mention to you one general principle. Anyone who wants to translate from one language to another and intends to translate one word by another word and to preserve the exact order both with respect to sentences and to words will find it troublesome and his translation will be doubtful and quite inaccurate. Such a method is inappropriate. Rather, the translator should first understand the subject matter [in question]; then he should render and explain what he understands of that topic in the language [of the translation] and explain [it] well. It will be impossible for him not to transpose the order and not to render one word by many words or conversely, or to add or subtract words, such that the matter under consideration will be clear and comprehensible in the language of the translation.[5]

This piece of advice was not in fact adhered to by Samuel, whose translation of the *Guide* is quite literal and faithfully follows the word order and sequence of the Arabic original, so that it frequently lacks felicity of expression and sometimes even clarity. Maimonides' principle allows the translator a certain measure of freedom, whereby he is permitted to find the most appropriate linguistic form for the philosophical idea expressed. In my translation of *The Wars of the Lord* I hope I have not abused Maimonides' principle; indeed I have tried to move in the direction of Samuel, without, however, following in his footsteps entirely. My underlying and persistent aim has been to make Gersonides' philosophy understandable to a modern reader of medieval philosophy.

---

5. Maimonides, *Letter to Samuel ibn Tibbon*, 27b. The passage cited is my translation.

PART TWO

SYNOPSIS OF
THE WARS OF THE LORD
· BOOK ONE
IMMORTALITY OF THE SOUL

THE first major topic that Gersonides discusses in *The Wars of the Lord* is one of the more difficult issues both in medieval philosophy in general and in Jewish theology in particular: the immortality of the human soul. It is not at all easy to give a clear-cut and definitive answer to the question, What is the traditional Jewish concept of immortality? The difficulty in answering this question is aggravated by the fact that Jewish eschatology is a complex of several different ideas, whose historical and theological relationships are not altogether perspicuous. One gets a good feel for the difficulty by reading Maimonides' last major essay, *Ma'amar tehiyyat ha-meytim* (Treatise on resurrection),[1] in which he tried to straighten out the various threads in the complicated network of ideas that make up the fabric of Jewish eschatology, such as resurrection, immortality of the soul, and the days of the Messiah. Although Gersonides does attempt to fit his philosophical ideas on immortality into the rabbinic tradition, his main concern is first to sort out and analyze the philosophical tradition on this issue, and then to formulate his own theory on the basis of philosophical argument. Accordingly, it is this philosophical tradition that is the focus of his discussion; hence a brief explanation of this tradition is in order.[2]

The medieval philosophical framework for the topic of immortality was Aristotle's psychology and in particular one extremely difficult and notorious passage in Aristotle's treatise *On the Soul*. In that passage Aristotle suggests that human thought exhibits two aspects, one passive and the other active. The human mind is initially passive, or receptive; but it is energized and put into action by some intellectual power, which is itself essentially active. This latter point, as we shall soon see, became one of the major points of

---

1. Maimonides, *Ma'amar tehiyyat ha-meytim* (Treatise on resurrection), ed. Joshua Finkel (New York, 1939), a new translation of which by Abraham Halkin is forthcoming (JPS, 1984).

2. For a useful summary of this topic see Isaac Husik, *A History of Mediaeval Jewish Philosophy* (Philadelphia, 1948), Introduction.

disagreement in medieval discussions of this topic. Since this passage was so crucial to the whole subject, it will be worthwhile to cite it here:

> And in fact mind as we have described it is what it is by virtue of becoming all things, while there is another which is what it is by virtue of making all things: this is a sort of positive state like light: for in a sense light makes potential colors into actual colors. Mind in this sense is separable, impassible, unmixed, since it is in its essential nature activity. . . . When mind is set free from its present conditions it appears as just what it is and nothing more: this alone is immortal and eternal (we do not, however, remember its former activity because, while mind in this sense is impassible, mind as passive is destructible), and without it nothing thinks.[3]

It is not an exaggeration to describe this passage as "obscure." Indeed its obscurity was responsible for the almost endless number of commentaries and treatises written by the ancient and medieval commentators on this topic. At least two questions about it can be raised at the outset: (1) What is this "other mind" that is responsible for the intellectual activity of the human mind? (2) Which mind is immortal and eternal? Although many other issues were raised in the subsequent literature on this problem, these two questions functioned as the foci of the medieval theory of the immortality of the soul.

Most of the later discussion, especially its terminology, of this topic is based on the interpretation given to this passage by the Greek commentator of Aristotle's works, Alexander of Aphrodisias, who was active at the close of the second century C.E. For Alexander the human intellect is a passive receptor of information, i.e., a disposition; accordingly, he characterizes the human mind as the potential, or material intellect.[4] The mysterious "other intellect" in the above passage from Aristotle is interpreted by Alexander as a separate, eternal substance that is active in nature; hence he calls this entity "the Agent Intellect." Moreover, he characterizes this intellect as *divine*; indeed he virtually identifies the Agent Intellect with God. The third feature of his theory is the notion of the acquired intellect. This is the sum total of intellectual cognitions attained by an individual throughout his lifetime. Or,

---

3. Aristotle, *On the Soul* 3.4.430a. 14–25. Translation of John A. Smith from *The Basic Works of Aristotle*, ed. Richard McKeon (New York, 1941), p. 593.

4. The term 'material' connotes here the receptive features of the mind in analogy with the receptive aspects of matter in Aristotle's *Physics*. For further elucidation see the text and notes, Bk. 1, chaps. 1–3.

it is the material intellect perfected and matured.[5] Within this conceptual framework Alexander then advances the thesis that the material intellect qua disposition is mortal; it is mortal because it is a power of the human body, and hence is subject to the same conditions of corruptibility which the body suffers. On the other hand, the acquired intellect is able to transcend these limitations and attain a level of survival after the death of the body. That is, under certain conditions the acquired intellect is immortal. We shall discuss this point in some detail later.

The second philosopher discussed by Gersonides who made a major contribution to this theory is the fourth-century Greek commentator on Aristotle, Themistius. Themistius rejected Alexander's notions that the material intellect is a mere disposition rooted in the bodily structure of the organism. Instead he argued that the material intellect is a substance of which this disposition is predicated; that is, the material intellect serves as a substratum for this disposition. But as a substance, the material intellect is an ontologically independent entity, which for Themistius means that it is capable of existence independent of, or separate from, the body; that is, the material intellect is essentially incorporeal, although it is accidentally and temporarily concretized in individual human bodies. Since it is substantial and incorporeal, the material intellect is eternal. Moreover, contrary to Alexander's claim, the Agent Intellect is not identical with God. Indeed Themistius suggests that the Agent Intellect is identical with the material intellect.[6]

The stage has now been set for the third major protagonist in this philosophical drama: Averroes. Although several of his Muslim predecessors such as Al-Farabi, Avicenna, and Avempace had contributed to the earlier dialectic between Alexander and Themistius, it was Averroes's doctrines that furnished the cues for much of the late medieval debate over this issue and for Gersonides' discussion in particular.[7]

Gersonides and more modern commentators have understood Averroes's

---

5. The latter is probably the more accurate characterization of the acquired intellect. The former is the way Gersonides understands Alexander's notion of the acquired intellect. It is worthwhile noting here that Gersonides had no firsthand knowledge of any philosophers other than Aristotle, Averroes, and Maimonides; perhaps even his knowledge of Aristotle was through Averroes. His expositions of the views of Alexander and others have to be understood in this light. See Julius Guttmann, *Philosophies of Judaism* (New York, 1964), p. 248.

6. Octave Hamelin, *La théorie de l'intellect d'après Aristote et ses commentateurs* (Paris, 1953), pp. 38–43.

7. The best recent work on Averroes's doctrine of the Agent Intellect is that of Alfred Ivry: "Averroes on Intellection and Conjunction," *Journal of the American Oriental Society* 86 (1966): 76–85; idem., "Towards a Unified View of Averroes' Philosophy," *The Philosophical Forum* 4 (1972): 87–113.

ideas on this topic as a synthesis of the views of Alexander and Themistius. But as Gersonides' own discussion will show, it is more accurate to say that Averroes's theory of the material intellect is the logical consequence of Themistius's doctrines shorn of some of their less attractive or more objectionable aspects. At least this is the way Gersonides understood Averroes.[8] From Themistius, Averroes accepted the notion that the material intellect is essentially a substance, not a disposition. Indeed many of the essential features attributed to this substance by Themistius are taken over by Averroes. This means that for Averroes too the material intellect is more a substance than a disposition, more form than matter, incorporeal rather than corporeal. And, most importantly, the material intellect is in reality identical with the Agent Intellect.

We now have the most significant feature of Averroes's doctrine, which has turned out to be a development of the theory of Themistius. The Agent Intellect exhibits two aspects or modes of existence. On one level it is transcendent, existing by itself as a separate intellect, although not identical with God. On another level it is "attached" to individual human beings, and on this level it is the material intellect. In other words, the material intellect is the Agent Intellect embodied in man. Thus the Agent Intellect has both transcendent and immanent aspects or careers. But since the Agent Intellect is one, so is the material intellect one, for they are identical. To be sure, there are many individual men who are intellectually active. But it is one and the same material intellect in all men that is the subject of this intellectual activity. The individuation of human cognitive activities, as Themistius already suggested, is only accidental or temporary. It is possible in this life and certainly after death that the material intellect will "lose" all its idiosyncratic expressions exemplified in individual men and "return" to its pristine form as the Agent Intellect. The dematerialization of human life or the suppression of the material conditions of human life "detaches" the material intellect so that, undisguised, it appears as it really is—the Agent Intellect. Immortality consists then in the elimination or disappearance of the individuating features of human life, which are attributable to and derive from the body. A preview of this state is possible in this life when our cognitive activities have reached such a level of perfection and intensity that we have, so to speak, become "pure intellects." In such a state we have become "at-

---

8. It is important to observe here that Gersonides did not know Averroes's major work in psychology, the *Long Commentary on Aristotle's* On the Soul. For this reason, and perhaps others, Gersonides' understanding of Averroes should not be identified with Averroes's ultimate beliefs. Our exposition is a description of Gersonides' Averroes, not the real Averroes, whoever he may be.

tached" to the material intellect qua Agent Intellect. That is, that which has disguised the material intellect's true identity has been removed or has disappeared, and we have become one with the Agent Intellect. Clearly, on this view there is no such thing as individual immortality, for the individuating conditions of our ordinary and mundane life, which are derivable from matter, are absent. All are one in the one Agent Intellect.[9]

Having presented the views of these three protagonists and the arguments in behalf of these theories, Gersonides proceeds to examine critically these theories and arguments, with the aim of developing his own doctrine out of a dialectical engagement with these three philosophers.[10] Gersonides' own theory of immortality consists of several steps or theses. He first criticizes the Themistius-Averroes theory of the material intellect as an eternal, incorporeal substance, and thus opts for Alexander's more naturalistic view of the material intellect as a psychological disposition, or capacity, residing in the human body. Gersonides virtually accepts all of Alexander's arguments for the notion that the material intellect is nothing over and beyond this psychobiological capacity for knowledge.[11] This "Alexanderian" view of the human intellect, however, leads to the view that the Agent Intellect, which is admitted by all to be an eternal substance and a separate intellect, is *not* identical with the material intellect, which is, as we have seen, only a disposition and subject to corruptibility and death. Indeed, for Gersonides, the material intellect is sharply differentiated from the Agent Intellect, which is *wholly* transcendent. Unlike Alexander, however, Gersonides does not identify the Agent Intellect with God.[12] The Agent Intellect has for him two chief functions: (1) it energizes the material intellect in human cognition, and (2) it is the agent of generation of phenomena here on earth.[13] Not only does Gersonides differ in this respect from Alexander on the question of the Agent Intellect, but he will also differ from him on the nature of human immortality.

---

9. Maimonides briefly alludes to such a view and according to some interpreters actually subscribes to it. Maimonides, *Guide* 1. 74, 7th method; see S. Pines's Introduction to his translation (Chicago, 1963), cii–ciii, and C. Touati, *La pensée philosophique et théologique de Gersonide* (Paris, 1973), p. 441, n. 26.

10. Gersonides briefly mentions and discusses a fourth view that he attributes to certain "modern" thinkers, who have been taken by some recent commentators to be Christian theologians of Gersonides' day (Guttmann, *Philosophies of Judaism*, p. 249; Touati, *Gersonide*, p. 404). Since this view is but a minor variation on a theme by Themistius, we can ignore it here. Further comment on it is given in the text (Bk. 1, chap. 5).

11. See below, Bk. 1, chaps. 3–5.

12. Bk. 5, pt. 3, chaps. 5–13.

13. Bk. 1, chap. 6; Bk. 5, pt. 3, chaps. 1–4.

But before we take up this latter point, we must briefly discuss the nature of Gersonides' critique of the Averroist identification of the material intellect with the Agent Intellect, which will then set the stage for the denouement of this philosophical drama.

The theological argument against the identity of the material intellect with the Agent Intellect and against its corollary, the unicity of the material intellect, is simply that, if according to this thesis there would be no differentiation among individuals when immortality is achieved, then immortality would be gratuitous and human life pointless. In religion the doctrine of immortality is almost always associated with the doctrine of reward and punishment: immortality is seen as a prize for those who merit it. In the philosophical version of this doctrine the qualifications for immortality were redefined to a considerable extent, especially in the philosopher's insistence that intellectual perfection is at least a necessary condition for the attainment of immortality. But if immortality is a state that has to be *earned*, then there will be some who will *not* earn it. Indeed, there will be some who earn it to *a greater degree than others*. For although "all Israel has a share in the World-to-Come," there are exceptions, as the Mishnah quickly points out, and there are those who have a greater share in the World-to-Come. These are the righteous, who by virtue of the quality of their moral life have earned either a greater share or a higher level of existence in the World-to-Come. After all, it is the righteous only who gaze upon the glory of God.[14] But if immortality is such that there is no differentiation among those who attain it, then we have a view that is not only inconsistent with traditional religious belief but one that results in an injustice to those who have lived more virtuous lives on earth and hence deserve more of the supernal benefits.

Moreover, something even worse follows from this doctrine. If the material intellect is identical with the Agent Intellect and if there is really only one such intellect, then everyone will attain immortality. For on this theory immortality consists of the union, or conjunction, with this intellect such that all individual differences disappear and are erased. This would mean that the kind of life lived here on earth *does not matter*. The fool as much as the wise man, the wicked as well as the saint would all attain this blessed state of conjunction. But this undermines the whole concept of immortality and renders it otiose.[15]

---

14. Berakhot 17a. Both Maimonides and Gersonides use this rabbinic dictum in their philosophical interpretations of immortality.

15. See below, Bk. 1, chap. 4. It is interesting to note in this connection that Spinoza, who insists on the intrinsic value of virtue, that virtue is its own reward, nevertheless maintains that immortality is individually differentiated. See Spinoza, *Ethics* 5, Prop. 38; Harry A. Wolfson, *The Philosophy of Spinoza*, 2 vols. (New York, 1969), 2:318–19.

So far the argument has been theological. It would be open to the claim by the defender of the Averroist doctrine that no matter what the ordinary man on the street believes, immortality is not individually differentiated. And if some injustice seems to be attendant upon this doctrine, it is a trifle, not to be considered at all in the light of the reward. After all, if I am completely satisfied and sated, what does it matter if someone else, no matter how stupid or wicked, is equally satisfied and sated? At this point Gersonides' argument against Averroes turns philosophical. He now considers various difficulties to which Averroes's theory is subject as a theory of cognition. In other words, the identity of the material intellect with the Agent Intellect fails to account for various epistemological phenomena.[16]

It fails because it cannot account for the obvious individual differences in knowing among people. Underlying all the various criticisms leveled by Gersonides against Averroes is this common motif. An adequate theory of knowledge ought to account for not only how people know, but also why people do not know; i.e., it ought to explain error and ignorance as well. A follower of Alexander's reading of Aristotle would say that, since Abraham and Isaac have different material intellects, i.e., different cognitive dispositions, there is no problem. Indeed individual differences in cognition are to be expected according to this theory. Nor do changes in the cognitive achievements of any one particular individual over time present problems for this theory. After all, it takes time for a habit, or disposition, to be developed, and such dispositions can be strengthened by intellectual exercise or weakened by the lack of it. But if there is only one material intellect that is shared by or embodied in *all* human beings, as Averroes claims, these problems seem to be unavoidable.

Actually, this difficulty is reducible to a more basic issue: if the material intellect is one, how can we attribute to it contrary and incompatible properties? But this is precisely what we are doing when we say that A knows some proposition p, whereas B does not know p! Since A and B have the same intellect, they should know or not know the same things at the same time. Or, consider any individual knower A. He is knowledgeable with respect to p but not with respect to a different proposition q; whereas individual B knows q but not p. Yet each has the same intellect! Or, A is capable of knowing several things, i.e., he is potentially a knower of p, q, and r, but at a particular time he knows only p. On the other hand, B is also capable of knowing p, q, and r, but at that particular time he knows only q. In this

---

16. It is important to remember that this whole hypothesis was introduced by Aristotle as an account of the process of knowing.

case one and the same intellect knows actually *and* potentially p at the same time; but this is absurd, since according to Aristotle, one and the same thing cannot sustain contrary properties at the same time.[17]

In addition to these epistemological difficulties, attendant upon the thesis of the unicity of the material intellect, the Averroist doctrine is subject to several serious metaphysical problems as a result of the Averroist theory of the identity of the material intellect with the Agent Intellect. First, the main role of the Agent Intellect is to actualize the intellectual capacities of human beings. But according to Aristotle, that which actualizes something with respect to a particular property must not only have this property in actuality but must be distinct from that which it actualizes.[18] And since the Agent Intellect as material intellect is embodied in these human beings, this alleged identity would mean that the Agent Intellect would be actualizing itself! Second, the chief epistemological characteristic of the Agent Intellect is, for Averroes, self-knowledge, whereas the main cognitive function of the material intellect is knowledge of things in nature. Thus one and the same thing has been defined differently, which is absurd. Third, if the material intellect is identical with the Agent Intellect, then how do we account for the process of its diversification in the almost infinite number of human beings? Some other agent must be responsible for this transformation. Fourth, far from being a mere accidental change, the multiplication of the material intellect in human beings represents a radical departure from the nature of the Agent Intellect. For the Agent Intellect is supposedly an incorporeal, i.e., "separate," entity, a pure intellect. Now in the medieval theory of individuation, incorporeal entities are differentiated only by species, whereas corporeal entities are distinguished by their material differences. For example, two human beings are distinguished by their size or eye-color; but two angels can be differentiated only by their different functions, or natures, each such nature constituting a distinct species.[19] Now how is this separate intellect to be individuated when it is manifested in many men? If it is differentiated by virtue of the fact that each individual body in which it is found is different from every other body, then it is differentiated materially, i.e., by the fact that each of its material subjects differs numerically from other subjects. But this means that this intellect is no longer an incorporeal, or separate, substance. For one of the defining features of an incorporeal substance is that it is not individuated according to subjects. In other words, if there are

---

17. Aristotle, *Metaphysics*, 4.4.
18. Aristotle, *Physics* 3.2–3; 5.1; 7.1.
19. Maimonides, *Guide* 1.74, 7th method, and 2.6: Genesis Rabbah 50.

incorporeal substances, each one would be a unique substance, not replicable or belonging to a species. Indeed, on this theory an incorporeal substance either is a unique member of a species or is not a member of a species at all. A corporeal substance, on the other hand, not only falls into a particular species but is replicable. And this is precisely what happens if we say that the material intellect is differentiated by the subjects in which it is manifested.

The upshot of Gersonides' criticism of Averroes comes to this: if the material intellect is one, then we cannot make sense out of some basic epistemological facts; if it is many, then we cannot explain how it is many and at the same time claim that it is an incorporeal, separate, and eternal substance.

The final act in this drama consists of the resolution of the original questions posed in the first act: is man immortal and wherein lies his immortality? By now it is fairly clear that Gersonides has opted for Alexander's theory of the soul. But remember that this theory has a strong naturalistic flavor, and that one of its consequences is the intrinsic corruptibility of the material intellect. It would seem that if this is the case, immortality is an illusion. But this is only an apparent consequence of the theory. For we have yet to account for the notion of the acquired intellect: the material intellect in so far as it has achieved intellectual perfection via its cognitive acquisitions. For both Alexander and Gersonides human immortality consists precisely and only in this intellectual attainment. Nevertheless, they differ on how this attainment is achieved and on its precise nature.

As Gersonides interprets Alexander, the latter was the first to teach the doctrine that human immortality is attained through the conjunction of the material intellect with the Agent Intellect, which for Alexander was identical with God.[20] The theory of conjunction in its Alexanderian form means that, although the material intellect is inherently corruptible and thus mortal, under certain conditions the acquired intellect can become immortal. For in so far as it has cognition of the Agent Intellect, the acquired intellect becomes immortal through this apprehension. Conjunction then for Alexander means the union of the acquired intellect with the Agent Intellect through the

---

20. Throughout his discussion of this point Gersonides generally attributes to Alexander the view that it is the material intellect that becomes immortal through conjunction with the Agent Intellect, and that this conjunction is achieved by the apprehension of the Agent Intellect by the material intellect (Bk. 1, chap. 8). However, this is not altogether accurate. Alexander actually holds that it is the *acquired intellect* that becomes immortal. In the subsequent exposition I shall formulate his position in his own terminology; but the reader should realize that Gersonides uses a different mode of expression in his exposition of Alexander's doctrine. See Husik, *Mediaeval Jewish Philosophy*, p. 333, and P. Merlan, *Monopsychism, Mysticism and Metaconsciousness* (The Hague, 1962), pp. 16–20.

cognition of the latter by the former. Cognition of things in the world of generation and corruption, i.e., the world of nature, is not sufficient to guarantee immortality. Indeed, for Alexander all the knowledge we acquire of this world is really irrelevant to the attainment of immortality, since it is subject to destruction when the body dies. It is only by virtue of our knowledge of the Agent Intellect that we can attain immortality. This thesis is shared by Themistius and Averroes, although Alexander does not teach their doctrine of the intrinsic identity of the material intellect and Agent Intellect. Thus in Gersonides' mind, Alexander, Themistius, and Averroes all maintain that immortality is attained through the apprehension of the Agent Intellect, which means some kind of union with this eternal and incorporeal substance.

Despite his Alexanderian leanings, Gersonides rejects this theory.[21] He argues that the Agent Intellect cannot be apprehended by man in such manner that immortality is achieved. For him immortality is attainable, but it is not achieved through union with the Agent Intellect. In Gersonides' theory it is the acquired intellect that is immortal.[22] It is immortal not by virtue of a cognition of the Agent Intellect but by virtue of certain features of the concepts that constitute the nature of the acquired intellect. However, before we develop Levi's account of immortality, let us see why he rejects the theory of conjunction.

Gersonides' rejection of this theory is based on a more strict or literal interpretation of the phrase "apprehending the Agent Intellect." It is important to recall here that in Aristotle's account of cognition the mind becomes virtually identical with the object known. This is a consequence of the notion that the mind is a receptacle for the forms or concepts of the objects known. It is as if the form or concept of the object "fills up" the mind.[23] Now if we are to take the doctrine of conjunction at face value, we ought to say that when the material or acquired intellect apprehends the Agent Intellect, it becomes *identical* with it. But this means that it ought to apprehend *all* that

---

21. Although occasionally in his writings, including *The Wars of the Lord*, Gersonides does speak affirmatively of a union or conjunction with God or the Agent Intellect, these passages have to be taken with a grain of salt. As the subsequent discussion will show, he rejects this doctrine. Where he sounds as if he does accept it, he should be construed as maintaining that *in some sense* the human intellect can apprehend *in part* the same thing that is apprehended by or is contained in the Agent Intellect. Certain passages in his biblical commentaries support this interpretation: e.g., in his 9th lesson to *Parshat Vayishlaḥ* he says that man cannot apprehend the *essence* of the Agent Intellect (Commentary to the Torah 42a); in the 8th lesson to *Parshat Shemot* he says that man cannot apprehend the Agent Intellect *completely* (ibid. 56a; Touati, *Gersonide*, p. 437, n. 13).

22. This is, as we have noted, the authentic view of Alexander.

23. Aristotle, *On the Soul* 3.4–5, 7, especially 431a, 431b18.

is known by the Agent Intellect! That is, the doctrine of conjunction leads to the conclusion that man is as knowledgeable as the Agent Intellect. Common to many medieval philosophers was the view, found in Alexander as well, that the Agent Intellect serves as a locus for some, if not all, of the forms of created things. In other words, the Platonic Forms, which were left "homeless" by Plato, were now located in some supernal intellect. One of the earliest proponents of this view was Philo, whose Logos serves as a home for the Platonic Forms.[24] Gersonides rejects the claim that the human intellect can have the same intellectual content as the Agent Intellect. For no matter how perfect any man becomes in his cognitive powers and attainments, his intellect will still not have mastered all that can be known of the world about him. There will always be concepts and propositions that elude man's cognitive powers. Moreover, not only is human knowledge essentially incomplete, it is also essentially inadequate in so far as it can never apprehend the inherent unity of all that is known by and is comprised in the Agent Intellect. That which is known by the latter constitutes a rationally ordered *system* of concepts and propositions. At best we can understand only part of this system and grasp some of its intrinsic logic and unity. But *complete* apprehension of this system is impossible for man. Hence the human intellect cannot attain conjunction or union with the Agent Intellect.

In what then does human immortality consist? Man is immortal in so far as he attains the intellectual perfection that is open to him. This means that man becomes immortal only if and to the extent that he acquires knowledge of what he can in principle know, e.g., mathematics and the natural sciences. This knowledge survives his bodily death and constitutes his immortality. But how is this possible if, as Gersonides admits with Alexander, the acquisition of knowledge is a process and hence is subject to generation? After all, one would normally say that a man's knowledge dies with him when his brain dies. In what sense then can Gersonides say that this knowledge survives the death of the body? The answer lies in Gersonides' theory of universals.

For many medieval philosophers the question of universals was epistemological, as well as metaphysical, in character. They wanted to know what the ultimate foundation for our knowledge is. Since the empirical objects of knowledge, such as individual dogs and men, are continually changing and

---

24. Harry A. Wolfson, *Philo*, 2 vols. (Cambridge, Mass. 1948), 1, chap. 4. Indeed, one could see the medieval doctrine of the Agent Intellect, especially as developed by Gersonides, as a variant of the Philonic Logos.

are subject to generation and destruction, they do not possess the requisite stability to be the foundation for our knowledge. The medieval philosopher accepted the Platonic-Aristotelian assumption that knowledge and truth require some permanent foundation in reality. Yet most of them subscribed to the Aristotelian principles that, first, knowledge consists of universal propositions that are grounded in something universal in nature and, second, there is no such thing as a separately existing universal entity. Thus, although reality consists of individual men, dogs, and roses, the sciences of anthropology, zoology, and botany consist of general propositions about their species or natures. Herein lies the medieval problem of universals.

Now, although Gersonides argues that in some sense we derive our knowledge from particular objects perceptually apprehended and that universal propositions about these objects constitute a science, this knowledge is ultimately "grounded" in a permanent system of general concepts comprised in the Agent Intellect. This system is often called by Gersonides "the rational order of the terrestrial world." It is like a blueprint for our earth. Corresponding to this blueprint in the Agent Intellect are our own cognitions, whose truth and reality derive more from this plan than from the objects of sense, from which we initially acquired our data. Indeed these objects of sense exhibit this order and derive their structure from the Agent Intellect.[25] Our knowledge is then a composite of perceptual data and the stimulation of the Agent Intellect.[26] Since the rational order contained in the Agent Intellect is incorruptible—for the Agent Intellect is incorruptible and this order emanates to it from God—our cognitions of this order as it is exemplified in nature are also incorruptible. Accordingly, the acquired intellect, the total intellectual capital of our minds, is immortal by virtue of the fact that its contents are ultimately grounded in the rational order comprised in the Agent Intellect. Although our bodies and their physical functions will eventually decay and die, our intellectual acquisitions will survive their death, for they do not share in the conditions of corruptibility characteristic of the body.

Since immortality consists in the incorruptibility of the acquired intellect, we have a clear answer to the question that vexed some of Gersonides' predecessors, i.e., whether immortality is individually differentiated. For in so far as the cognitive capital of each individual varies, so does the acquired

---

25. *Wars of the Lord*, Bk. 2, chaps. 4 and 6; Bk. 5, pt. 3, chaps. 1–3.
26. Ibid., Bk. 1, chap. 10; see also Gersonides' *Commentary on Song of Songs* 2b, and his *Commentary on Ecclesiastes* 30b.

intellect of a particular person differ from the acquired intellect of another. Hence the immortality enjoyed by Maimonides is significantly different from that enjoyed by someone with less education. Although "all Israel has a share in the World-to-Come," it doesn't follow that the portion is equal for everyone.[27]

It would seem that Gersonides' theory of immortality is a blend or synthesis of Platonic as well as of Aristotelian-Alexanderian elements. On the one hand, he believed that the immortal feature in man has to do with his knowledge and that knowledge is concerned with universal, incorporeal entities. With the Middle Platonists, such as Philo, Gersonides located these incorruptible entities in some supernal intellect that transcends man. This is the Platonic legacy. On the other hand, he learned from Aristotle that, although knowledge may have an ontological foundation in incorruptible and permanent entities, it is *aquired*. No one is born with the theorems of Euclid in his head. Gersonides did not believe in innate, or preexistent, knowledge, any more than did Aristotle. Moreover, he agreed with Alexander's reading of Aristotle's *On the Soul*: the material intellect is essentially a biopsychological disposition for knowledge, not an independent, substantial entity; and as a disposition of the organism it is subject to decay. What remains is man's intellectual acquisitions in so far as these are grounded in and correspond to the "rational order of the universe" as found in the Agent Intellect.

Gersonides now raises the following point: what differentiates the knowledge acquired by any person during his lifetime and the enjoyment he derives from it now, from his knowledge and enjoyment of it after his body dies? First, while the human intellect is attached to a body, its cognitive acquisitions are gradual and accumulative, requiring an extended period of time for their development and perfection. Once this bodily attachment is dissolved, the intellect is able to contemplate all its cognitions simultaneously; i.e., *all* these intellectual acquisitions are apprehended in an everlasting intuition, not subject to change, interruption, or interference. Second, although this intellectual immortality has the virtue of continuity, it is limited: the immortal acquired intellect cannot be increased. With the dissolution of the body the intellect can no longer obtain new cognitions, since, as we have seen, the perceptual faculties are for Gersonides the occasions for the acquisition of knowledge. This intellectual enjoyment which constitutes immortality is

---

27. Bk. 1, chap. 13.

limited then to that which has been acquired during man's corporeal existence.[28]

In understanding Gersonides' theory of immortality one should recall the
Aristotelian picture of God contemplating Himself.[29] At the highest level of
intellectual activity the knower and that which is known are numerically
identical. In God's case this is *always* the case; in man this condition is only
intermittently realized while his intellect is attached to a body. But after
death the human mind is identical with its intellectual acquisitions. Immortality then is an *imitatio dei* in so far as the human cognitive state has become,
as far as possible, assimilated to the divine cognitive condition. For Gersonides immortality is not a mystical union of the human intellect with God or
even with the Agent Intellect; this would be asking for too much. Instead,
what we can hope for is the survival of what is truly human, what elevates
man above the animals: his knowledge. At the same time, however, what is
truly human is also divine. For man was created in the divine image, which
means for Gersonides that he was endowed with an intellect. The perfection
of this gift is his immortality.

---

28. The opposing view was held by Thomas Aquinas, who claimed that the soul can acquire
new knowledge in its disembodied state. However, Aquinas's theory is based upon a different
conception of the intellect and the soul, which accounts for his view that the soul is capable of
new knowledge after the death of the body. See Aquinas, *Summa Theologiae* 1, question 89;
Harry Blumberg, "The Problem of Immortality in Avicenna, Maimonides and St. Thomas
Aquinas" in *Harry A. Wolfson Jubilee Volume*, 3 vols. (Jerusalem, 1965), 1: 180–85.

29. Aristotle, *Metaphysics* 12.9.

PART THREE

THE WARS
OF THE LORD
LEVI BEN GERSHOM
(GERSONIDES)

INVOCATION[1]

$\mathbf{B}$Y the word of God the heavens were made [Ps. 33:6]; the work of a consummate craftsman [Exod. 28:6], whose activity[a] is perfect [Deut. 34:4]. By His light, in which He wrapped Himself as with a garment [Ps. 104:2], they [the heavenly bodies] have light;[2] and He brings forth to light that which is hidden [Job 28:11]. Through His will[3] the heavens were made beautiful; His hand has created a bounteous body [Job 26:13].[4] He raised and lifted it, exalting it greatly over all other bodies. He has established the heavens on its base [Ezra 3:3] like a molten mirror [Job 37:18];[5] He has made it firm, stretching and spreading it out as a tent to dwell within [Isa. 40:22]. It is so firmly fashioned that it will not change. No other body can be compared to it with respect to its essence and everlastingness; nothing can be likened to its beauty [Ezek. 31:8].

With wisdom God has established the earth [Prov. 3:19] on its foundations [Ps. 104:5]. He stretched over it the line of confusion and the plummet of emptiness [Isa. 34:11]; He placed a perfect measure for darkness and the

---

1. In this opening prayer Gersonides takes fragments from various biblical verses and weaves them into a "psalm" of his own invention. Since these phrases have been taken out of their original places, their meanings have changed and are determined by their new contexts. In translating this prayer I have been assisted by Professor Norman Bronznick of the Hebraic Studies Department of Rutgers University.

2. Genesis Rabbah 3: 2–4; Midrash on Psalms 27; Pirke de–Rabbi Eliezer, 3 (Friedlander edition).

3. Gersonides understands the term *be-ruḥo* as meaning by His will (Gersonides, Commentary on Job 26:13).

4. In medieval philosophical Hebrew the term *geshem* connotes 'body'. Gersonides construes the word *ḥolelah* in the phrase *ḥolelah yado* as 'create' (ibid.).

5. In his Commentary on Job (37:18) Gersonides notes that the heavens are transparent like mirrors made of glass.

NOTE: Superior lower-case letters indicate where the text of the printed edition of Leipzig, 1866, has been changed. The sources of the variants are to be found in the Critical Apparatus at the end of Bk. 1.

shadow of death [Prov. 11:1 and Job 28:3].[6] His hands formed the dry land [Ps. 95:5] in order that He accomplish His work, as it is this day [Gen. 50:20] upon the face of the inhabitable world [Job 37:12]. And to satisfy every living thing with favor [Ps. 145:16] He brought forth the fruit of the earth.

All the bright lights of the heavens [Ezek. 32:8] He brings forth for loving-kindness to do whatever He commands them [Job 37: 12–13]. He establishes them as His government upon the earth [Job 38:33]; He makes their signs as signs [Ps. 74:4] although there is no one among us who knows their true operations [Ps. 74:9].[7] Through them it is arranged that every earthly crea-ture—fish, creeping things, birds, man, and animals—acquire their souls.[8] God is the source of life for each living thing. Even though traps are set [Jer. 5:26] for them individually, their species arise again through His generosity [Isa. 32:8].[9]

God chose for Himself a rational creature [i.e., man] among the entities composed [of matter and form]. Man alone shines in the light of the coun-tenance of the King of Life [Prov. 16:15][10] by virtue of the excellency of dignity [Gen. 49:3] that God has given him through knowledge and by the

---

6. These biblical phrases are given philosophical meanings in Gersonides' commentaries. The passage from Isa. 34:11 *ve-natah ʿaleha qav tohu ve-ʾabney bohu* refers to the basic cosmological principles of primary matter—*bohu*—and remote, i.e., the most general, form—*tohu* (Gersonides, *Commentary on Genesis*, 9c; *The Wars*, Bk. 6, pt. 2, chap. 4). the phrase *ʾefel zalmavet* from Job 28:3 also connotes primary matter (Gersonides, *Commentary on Genesis*, 9d; *Commentary on Job*, ad loc.).

7. In the passage *ve-ʾim ʿeyn itanu yodeʿa ad mah* the phrase *ad mah* is not transparent. Literally, it means "how long." But so understood the phrase would suggest that we do not know for how long the heavenly bodies function as signs. This contradicts, however, Gersonides' insistent claim that the orbits of the heavenly bodies are immutable and everlasting (*The Wars*, Bk. 6, pt. 1, chap. 16, and pt. 2, chap. 12). I suggest therefore that we construe *ad mah* as connoting the essence, or operations, of the heavenly bodies, or their purpose. This is consistent with Gersonides' conviction that a complete and accurate astronomy is not within our capacities.

8. In this verse Gersonides alludes to the medieval Aristotelian doctrine that the heavenly bodies play a part in the generation of earthly creatures by preparing (*hekhin*) the internal temperaments of each organism. Each level of life—plant, animal and man—exemplifies a different type of soul (*nefesh*). The heavenly bodies arrange or prepare the temperaments of the earthly creatures to receive their respective souls, which ultimately emanate from God through the movers of the heavenly bodies, the Separate Intellects, the most important of which in this context being the Agent Intellect. This theory is elaborated and developed in Bk. 5, pt. 3.

9. This verse appears to allude to Gersonides' theory of providence, according to which general providence reigns throughout nature, especially among nonhuman organisms. Only wise and righteous humans merit individual providence (*The Wars*, Bk. 4).

10. In his *Commentary on Proverbs* 16:15 Gersonides understands this passage as referring to the acquisition of immortality through intellectual perfection.

understanding placed in his heart. From mankind God has chosen for Himself a kingdom of priests and a holy nation [Exod. 19:6]. They turn upward [Hos. 7:16] and walk upright [Mic. 2:3]. In His perfect Torah [Ps. 19:8] He told His people the power of His deeds to give them access among the angels[11] [Zech. 3:7] [and] through it [the Torah] the soul becomes wise.[12]

Praises are appropriate to God according to all that great good which He has given us [Isa. 63:7], in bestowing us with knowledge that is pleasant to our souls [Prov. 2:10]. Through His eternal pleasure [Ps. 16:11] everything exists. His being is most awesome; who can withstand it [Joel 2:11]? The understanding of the wise cannot comprehend Him. Abundance of praises cannot equal Him [Job 28:17]; God is above all blessing and praise [Neh. 9:5]. How can He be compared to a tumultuous noise [Ezek. 1:24]? When a man comes near[b] to bow unto Him [2 Sam. 15:5] He is pleased by him who lifts up a still voice. In this way every soul should praise[c] [Him] [Ps. 150:6].

---

11. In the third chapter of Zechariah the prophet speaks of the high priest and his renewed position as the leader of the nation. If the high priest is faithful to God, he will be granted a status comparable to that of the angels. Since in the preceding verse of this poem Gersonides has spoken of the whole of Israel as a kingdom of priests, he now transfers the privilege bestowed upon the high priest to the whole nation. It is also worth noting that some of the traditional Jewish commentators, such as David Kimhi and Malbim, interpret this verse from Zechariah as alluding to immortality of the soul. Gersonides too may be interpreting the passage in the same way.

12. The phrase *bah behkimah* is difficult. I take the particle *bah* to refer back to *le-nafsham*, so that the whole phrase means that the soul becomes wise, and hence immortal, by virtue of the Torah.

INTRODUCTORY REMARKS

HAVING given our praise and thanks to God and having asked Him to direct us in His way, I would like to examine in this book several important yet difficult questions on which many crucial doctrines relevant to man's intellectual happiness are based. First, is the rational soul immortal when it has achieved some perfection? If it is immortal, are there different levels of human immortality?[a] This question is important but very problematical, and the errors concerning it severely prevent man from achieving his true happiness. Second, when a man is informed by dreams or divination or prophecy of future events, is he informed of them[b] essentially or accidentally (i.e., without an efficient cause)? If there is here an efficient cause, what is its nature and how is this communication accomplished?[c] No matter how these questions are answered, there are many difficulties in this question. Third, does God know existent things? If He does, how does He know them? Here too there are many difficulties and confusions, no matter how we answer these questions. Fourth, is there divine providence over existent things? If so, in which way, and does it extend over the human species and its individual members? Fifth, how do the movers of the heavenly bodies move these bodies, and how many movers are there, as far as we can know? And how is this motion accomplished by them? And[d] how are these movers related to each other and how is God (may He be blessed) related to them? This question is very complicated. Sixth, is the universe eternal or created? If created, in what way has it been created? This question is also very difficult. Indeed, upon it rest many principles that direct us in some way toward our intellectual and political happiness.

It is clear then that a man examining this topic[1] is engaged in no small task. For the value of the inquiry depends on the value of the subject of the inquiry; and there is no more important topic than this one, for the universe in its entirety is by far more important than any one[e] of its parts. Moreover,

---

1. It would appear from the subsequent discussion that Gersonides is referring here to the problem of creation. As noted in the Introduction, Gersonides' first draft of *The Wars* was devoted entirely to this question. It may be that this paragraph was part of Gersonides' original introduction, which he incorporated into his final and more comprehensive version of *The Wars*.

the differences on this question have resulted in differences on many other important issues. For this reason this question is a fundamental principle for many other things. And it is clear that the true understanding of principles is exceedingly valuable, since it leads to a true understanding of those ideas that come after these principles; just as an error in principles is serious because it gives rise to errors in those beliefs which are based on the principles, especially when these beliefs are ideas that guide us toward our intellectual and political happiness, as is the case in this particular question. Therefore, the earlier[f] thinkers of repute spent a good deal of time on this question, since because of its importance they naturally desired [to know the answers]. It is important to realize that on this question we cannot derive proofs from that which is prior[g] to the world, e.g., from[h] the First Cause; for our knowledge of the essence of the First Cause is very slight. Hence, we cannot make it a premise from which we can construct proof for this question [of creation]. Indeed, the kind of proof available to us in this inquiry is the a posteriori proof, which is based on phenomena posterior to this generated[i] entity [the universe], if it is the case that the world is generated.[2]

We have also appended to these questions two difficult problems of a religious nature. The first concerns signs and miracles. How are they possible? Through whom are they performed? Who is the agent? [The problem here is:] What happens to our religious beliefs [in these matters] when our philosophical views are conjoined with it. The second [is the question]: Is there [some kind] of promise [or testimony] by virtue of which we can determine who is a real prophet, as we see in the encounter of Jeremiah with Hananiah ben Azzur?[3]

Now it is without doubt essential that the reader of this book be familiar with the mathematical sciences, the natural sciences, and metaphysics. Of

---

2. Gersonides is ruling out the possibility of proving creation by arguing from some propositions about God, who is, even on the eternity thesis, prior to the universe, at least in the sense of being the First Cause of its motion. If we wish to prove that the universe is created, we must utilize data posterior to the world in the sense that they presuppose the latter's existence. From such data (e.g., time and motion) we can argue "back" to the world and show that it must have been created. Such a proof is then a posteriori.

This idea of proof goes back to Aristotle, who distinguished two kinds of argument in scientific inference: (1) a proof that begins with the causes of phenomena and moves toward the effects, showing how the latter are derived from the former (the "a priori" proof); (2) the proof that begins with the effects and moves backward to their causes (the "a posteriori" proof) (Aristotle, *Posterior Analytics* 1. 2. 13). Aristotle regarded the former as superior to the latter (ibid. 1. 27; *Metaphysics* 1. 1–2). In the medieval Hebrew philosophical terminology this logical contrast was expressed by the terms *mofet muḥlat* and *mofet re'iyah*. (Isaac Husik, "Studies in Gersonides," n.s. *JQR*, 7 (1916–17): 556–57; Gersonides, *Commentary on Song of Songs*, 3d.

3. Jer. 28:1.

the questions mentioned so far, some belong to the sciences, others to metaphysics,[j] and others require a knowledge of mathematics [including astronomy]; for example, the problem of the number of movers of the heavenly bodies depends on the determination of the number of the heavenly bodies that are moved by them, and this latter question belongs to the science of mathematical astronomy, as Aristotle has explained in Book twelve of the *Metaphysics*.[4] Moreover, whether the universe is[k] eternal or created is a question that can be determined by considering either the essence of the world or[l] its particular accidental features, physical or mathematical, or its efficient cause, if [indeed] the latter [alternative] is open to us. Now it is not our intention to discuss in this book the modes of arguments[5] by virtue of which these things [in the sciences] have been verified. For if we were to do so, our book would encompass all or most of the sciences. Rather, we shall assume as principles that which has been actually demonstrated in those sciences. In addition, the reader should not expect from us a complete treatment of these principles in terms of which that which we intend to affirm can be verified. We shall provide some brief argumentation [only], since these principles are evident to the reader of this book. We want to be[m] as brief as possible, since verbosity on these matters will distract the reader. There are places where we have supplied lengthy proof and where the reader would think that the matter has [already] been proved by others; [in such places] we have added something new or introduced a new method of presentation which might facilitate its true comprehension. [Finally,] the kinds of proof that are employed in this book are evident from the preceding remarks: some of them will be necessarily mathematical, others scientific, and others philosophical [metaphysical], according to the nature of the problem at hand.

We recognize that there are many reasons why it might seem proper to refrain from examining these questions. First, because of the various difficulties [pertaining to these problems], this inquiry is extremely difficult. All the more so when it turns out that our predecessors have not treated most of these questions philosophically, and what they do say philosophically about them is[n] false, as will be demonstrated in our book. In addition to this factor, a further complication arises from the disturbances[o] of time that prevent any thought.[6]

---

4. Aristotle, *Metaphysics*, 12. 8.

5. *Meqomoteyhem*. The term *maqom* in medieval philosophical Hebrew often connotes 'argument' or 'mode of argument', corresponding to the term τόπος in Aristotle's logic. As Wolfson notes, the term strictly connotes the locus or nerve of the argument, cf. Harry A. Wolfson, *Crescas' Critique of Aristotle*, pp. 390–91.

6. Gersonides may be referring here to the difficulties suffered by the Jews in France during the early part of the fourteenth century.

Second, without doubt many people will reject our[p] ideas because they find in them something unfamiliar to them by virtue of opinions they hold, which do not derive from philosophical or religious requirements but which they have inherited. However, we are not concerned with these people; for it is sufficient for them to believe, not to know. We are concerned with those who are deeply perplexed by these questions and who are not satisfied with what is merely said about the secrets of existence but with what can be conceived[q] [about them].

Third, I think that because of envy, which shall never disappear, some will attribute to me arrogance and rashness in investigating the question of eternity or creation of the world.[7] For, perhaps they[r] think that the intellect of a sage cannot reach the truth on this topic, except if he is a prophet; all the more so when they have seen that earlier scholars of stature from our nation (e.g., the glorious jewel of the sages of our Torah, Moses ben Maimon) have not investigated this question in the way [that we propose]. From this they have concluded the impossibility of arriving at the truth on this question by means of philosophy. For if this were possible [they say] it would not have escaped the earlier sages.

Now this argument is very weak. It does not follow that what was not known by the former sages will also not be known by their successors. For in time the truth will be forthcoming, as Aristotle says in book two of the *Physics*.[8] Were this not so, a man would not [for himself] investigate any science[s] but only accept what others have taught him.[t] But if this were the case, there wouldn't be any science at all—which is utterly absurd. Moreover, if what we say on this matter is right, that which was thought to be shameful on our[u] part will turn out to be praiseworthy, i.e., if we have achieved what our predecessors have not. If what we say turns out to be wrong, then we will be blameworthy, but for this reason only.

It has been alleged that only a prophet can attain the truth on this matter. Perhaps, they say, what a prophet obtains through prophecy is inaccessible to a wise man who uses only reason. Indeed, they do say that in fact this matter [the creation of the universe] was explained to the prophet by a prophecy; from this they conclude that it is not accessible to human reason by itself.[9] This objection, however, can be easily disposed of. A prophet is necessarily a wise man. Thus some of the things that are known by him are peculiar to him as a prophet, e.g., most of the things he predicts that will

---

7. Husik, "Studies in Gersonides," p. 558.
8. Aristotle, *Physics* 2.2; *Metaphysics* 2.1.
9. Husik, "Studies in Gersonides," pp. 558–59.

occur at a particular time; other things he knows simply because he is wise, i.e., the things that are known by him about the secrets of the world. The difference between a prophet and a wise man, however, lies merely in the [relative] ease with which the prophet obtains [his knowledge]. For the knowledge of the prophet is generally greater than the knowledge of a wise man who is not a prophet. Therefore, prophecy is joined with wisdom [but] not [in the sense] that what is to a wise man a derived cognition is to the prophet a primary cognition, as some people have maintained.[10] If this were the case, the knowledge of the wise man would be more perfect, since he knows the thing by means of its causes, whereas the prophet does not. But this is absurd.[11] It is possible that there are things that a wise man who is not a prophet cannot apprehend, but which can be known by a wise man who is a prophet *insofar as he is wise.*

Given this explanation of the matter, i.e., there is some knowledge that both the prophet and the wise man can possess, you will find that in the books of the Prophets there are things that can be proved philosophically, as the unity of God, which is mentioned in the Torah, and the Secrets of the Divine Chariot,[12] which are mentioned in Ezekiel and Isaiah, (may they be blessed with peace). Indeed, there are many other ideas of lesser philosophical importance that are found in the words of the Prophets, so that they are comparable to the first principles among the philosophers. For example, it is said, "And God saw all that He had made, and found it very good,"[13] and "His deeds are perfect."[14] And the Torah shows the necessity of water and cultivation for plants, e.g., "Because the Lord God had not sent rain upon the earth and there was no man to till the soil."[15] The Torah also

---

10. *Muskal rishon*: 'undemonstrable or intuited principle'; *muskal sheni*: 'derived, or demonstrable, principle'. According to Maimonides, a prophet differs from a philosopher in his ability to know certain propositions intuitively, i.e., without demonstrative proof (*Guide* 2.38). Such propositions are called 'first cognitions', whereas propositions that are derived by demonstration are 'second cognitions' (Maimonides, *Treatise on Logic*, chap. 8). On this view the prophet would differ from the philosopher in that his knowledge is *intuitive*, whereas the philosopher's knowledge is primarily *deductive.*

11. Knowledge of causes is superior knowledge (cf. Aristotle, *Posterior Analytics* 1.2).

12. *Ma'asey merkabah.* The doctrine of the Divine Chariot originally referred to the esoteric interpretation of the theophanies described in chap. 6 of Isaiah and in Ezekiel. To Maimonides this esoteric doctrine is identical with metaphysics (*Guide*, pt. 1: intro. and chap. 33; and pt. 3: intro. and chaps. 1–7). Cf. Leo Strauss, *Persecution and the Art of Writing* (Glencoe, Ill., 1952), pp. 41–42.

13. Gen. 1:31.

14. Deut. 32:4.

15. Gen. 2:5.

relates the rising of vapors from the earth: "A flow would well up from the ground";[16] and there are many similar passages [relating philosophical or scientific truths]. Indeed, such pieces of knowledge are unique since they are not prefaced with the phrases "and God said," "and God spoke," or "and the word of God came to me," etc. [suggesting that they are not cognitions unique to prophecy]. And if with such philosophical knowledge is found indication suggesting that it is prophetic [in origin], then this is because both kinds of knowledge are intertwined. Now if the matter is as we have suggested, it is evident that the doctrine of creation, which is mentioned in the Torah, may be one of those ideas that can also be proved by the philosopher.

If someone objects that perhaps this doctrine is one that cannot be philosophically demonstrated, we reply that until a proof is forthcoming that shows the impossibility of such a philosophical demonstration, this is not a valid objection against us. Nor is that which Maimonides (of blessed memory) pronounced concerning the impossibility of knowledge on this topic a valid criticism, unless the[v] absurdity of what we shall affirm with respect to one of the possible alternatives on this question will have been demonstrated, as has been [just] mentioned.[17] Indeed, it can be shown in several ways that the philosophical verification of this doctrine is possible. For we find among the community of[w] philosophers throughout the ages a natural desire to attain the truth on this question, as Aristotle and Maimonides (of blessed memory) have both related. [Indeed], we ourselves have perceived [this desire] in the accounts of all the inquirers [on this topic] that have reached us. Now a natural desire cannot be for something that is unattainable, all the more so if it is unattainable by any investigation. In conclusion, the aforementioned arguments do not preclude completing our investigation of this topic as best we can. For human happiness is achieved when a man knows reality as much as he can, and it becomes more noble[x] when he knows the more superior things than when he knows only the things of inferior rank and value. For

---

16. Gen. 2:6.

17. In the preceding sentence Gersonides argued that unless a proof exists showing the undecidability of this question by philosophical means, the gates of inquiry are not closed to him. The reservations of Maimonides in particular are then inappropriate. For his claim that neither creation nor eternity is provable, and hence revelation must be appealed to, is just a claim. In fact, Maimonides only invalidated Aristotle's proofs for eternity and expressed some reservations with respect to *some* of the Kalam proofs for creation. He did not, however, offer a proof for the undecidability of the whole question! And until such a proof has been achieved Gersonides is free to pursue his research. Indeed, in the next sentence Gersonides attempts to show that there is a real possibility of discovering the answer to this question.

My translation of this passage, which is based on the readings found in the Vatican and Bodleian manuscripts, differs from that of Husik, "Studies in Gersonides," p. 560.

this reason we desire to have a little knowledge of the former things rather than much knowledge of the latter. This will be proved in greater[y] detail in Book one of this treatise, God be willing.[18]

Moreover, it is not proper for someone to withhold what he has learned in philosophy from someone else. This would be utterly disgraceful. Indeed, just as this entire universe emanated from God for no particular advantage to Him, so too is it proper for someone who has achieved some perfection to try to impart it to someone else. In this way he is imitating God as best he can.

It is also clear that none of the perfect ones should fault me for entering into these difficult inquiries. Rather, I should be praised for attempting to arrive at the truth in such profound questions, even if only for my effort, not my success. All the more so should I be praised for that which I have achieved (as far as this is possible) in these questions, as shall be apparent in the sequel. Nor should any one of my readers, whom I love and want to help, contend with me simply because he likes[z] to argue; for this might be a cause of his not understanding what I am saying. It is also right that he grant me the premises that he grants my opponent, whether he be a non-believer in religion or someone who rejects any of these opinions because of some sensual desire. But if he is a believer in religion, this [i.e., granting the same premises] is even the more proper, since these topics are such that many religious doctrines are based on them, as shall be apparent in the sequel (God be willing). Indeed, I have been very hesitant in writing a treatise on these questions, for I know the ways of those who are fools but wise in their own eyes, especially on these profound topics. Nevertheless, my strong desire to remove the obstacles that block the man of inquiry from attaining the truth on these questions leading to human happiness has led me to undertake this project.

I have decided to mention all the possible[a1] opinions on a given issue of the various problems I shall discuss and the arguments for and against them. For in this way many principles involved in these questions will be established for us,[b1] and it will be easier to determine the true from the false so that the truth in these matters will be achieved in an indubitable manner. Doubt arises on a given matter when we have contrary views concerning it; but when the inquiry will be completed and the[c1] true will be sifted out from the false, the doubts in this matter will vanish. Since there have been many false opinions among our predecessors on these matters, and we have [there-fore, in our] investigation contended with them in order to refute these views

---

18. Bk. 1, chap. 13.

in every possible way, and yet everything that we have been able to demonstrate is the view of our Torah, we have accordingly entitled our book "The Wars of the Lord." For we have fought the battles of the Lord in so far as we have refuted the false views of our predecessors.

The reader should not think it is the Torah that has stimulated us to verify what shall be verified in this book, [whereas in reality] the truth itself is something different.[19] It is evident, as Maimonides (may his name be blessed) has said, that we must believe what reason has determined to be true. If the literal sense of the Torah differs from reason, it is necessary to interpret those passages in accordance with the demands of reason. Accordingly, Maimonides (may his name be blessed) explains the words of the Torah that suggest that God (may He be blessed) is corporeal in such a way that reason is not violated. He, therefore, maintains that if the eternity of the universe is demonstrated, it would be necessary to believe in it and to interpret the passages of the Torah that seem to be incompatible with it in such a way that they agree with reason.[20] It is, therefore, evident that if reason causes us to affirm doctrines that are incompatible with the literal sense of Scripture, we are not prohibited[d1] by the Torah to pronounce the truth on these matters, for reason is not incompatible with the true understanding of the Torah. The Torah is not a law that forces us to believe false ideas; rather it leads us to the truth to the extent that is possible, as we have explained in the beginning of our commentary on the Torah.[21] Accordingly, it is our practice in these discussions to begin with an exhaustive philosophical inquiry into the question at hand, and then to show that what we have philosophically discovered concerning the question is compatible with the Torah. With respect to some of these problems the Torah itself has, in its marvelous way, directed us toward the truth. Indeed, this should be the case, since the Torah is intended to guide its adherents to human perfection as far as it is attainable, as we have explained in our commentary on the Bible.[22] Thus, since there are here many profound problems, whose solutions are extremely difficult to achieve, it is fitting that the Torah guide us in the attainment of their true solutions.

It is obvious from the preceding that our investigation is necessarily concerned with controversial topics. It is incumbent upon us, therefore, to

---

19. That is, the reader should not think that Gersonides' main purpose in this book is to defend certain theological doctrines even if they are not substantiated by reason.
20. Maimonides, *Guide* 2.25.
21. Gersonides, *Commentary on* the Torah, 2a.
22. Ibid.

explain the rationale behind our ordering of these topics. Yet if we were to give the reason for [the order of] each particular discussion, duplication[e1] would result for those topics that we have ordered[f1] according to the same principle. Accordingly, we have thought it proper to adopt a certain method, according to which the rationale for the order will be made apparent. In this way we will not have to mention the reason for every topic.[g1] It is as follows.

Know that the order of presentation is very useful for the reader in his attempt to obtain the goal intended in the particular inquiry. This is so, we believe, for seven reasons: some of these reasons concern the necessary order within the subject itself and [the necessary procedure to be adopted by] the inquirer, or just the latter; some of them relate to the most preferable [order] either in the subject or for the inquirer, or in both. [Let us consider these reasons individually.]

First, there are things such that the knowledge of some of them precedes by nature the knowledge of the others. This is true in one science; for example, the priority of knowledge of the premises to the knowledge of the conclusion implied by them. And it is true with respect to two sciences; for example, knowledge[h1] of mathematical matters precedes by nature knowledge of matters in the natural sciences, although the one subject [mathematics] is more general than the other [natural sciences]. For the mathematician investigates body in the abstract,[i1] whereas the natural scientist investigates body not only in the abstract[i1] but also in so far as it is in motion. Thus in one science there are things that precede in order and by nature other things; and with respect to several sciences some precede in order and by nature others.[23] This type of priority is necessary both with respect to the subject matter and with respect to the inquirer.

---

23. This paragraph is difficult if the reading of the manuscripts and of the printed editions is retained. This reading is as follows:

כי יש ענינים קודמת ידיעת קצתם בטבע לקצת כקדימת ידיעת [אמתת VB] ההקדמות לידיעת התולדה המתחייבת מהם [בעצם V] וזה אם בחכמה אחת אם [ואם L] בשתי חכמות כמו שהענינים הלמודיים תקדם ידיעה בהם [ידיעתם L] בטבע לענינים הטבעיים ואם הנושא האחד יותר כולל מהאחר וזה כי הלמודי יחקר בגשם במוחלט [מוחלט L] והטבעי יחקר גם כן בגשם במוחלט [מוחלט L] אלא שהוא יחקר בו מצד שהוא מתנועע ולזה היו בחכמה אחת ענינים קודמים קצתם לקצת בסדר ובטבע והיו קצת החכמות קודמות בסדר ובטבע לקצת.

As it stands this reading does not provide *in sequence* an example of natural priority in one science or area of inquiry. Hence the conclusion of the argument beginning with the term ולזה is really incomplete. However, if we take the clause beginning with כקדימת ידיעת ההקדמות and place it after בחכמה אחת, we get a strict parallelism in the argument, with an example of natural priority within one science and an example of natural priority relative to two sciences.

The notion of natural priority needs some comment. Aristotle distinguishes various senses of priority (*Metaphysics* 5.11). In the *Posterior Analytics* 1.2, Aristotle claims that the more universal

Second [there is] the priority of the more general to the more specific. By virtue of this priority the premises that are employed to prove the more general theorems are [logically] prior, i.e., their predicates are essentially predicated of their subjects, and thus duplication [of proof for the more specific theorems] is avoided.[24] This kind of priority is, as it were, intermediate between that which is necessary from both respects [the subject and the investigator] and the most preferable from both respects, although it is more like the former.[25]

Third, it is clear that an author does not write for himself, but to impart [his knowledge] to someone else. It is therefore necessary that he try to present his material in such a way that the reader will achieve the intended purpose of the book. For this reason it is necessary for the author to begin the discussion with the easier material, even if that which comes first [in presentation] does not make known in an essential way that which comes afterwards.[26] This kind of priority is the more preferable with respect to the subject but necessary with respect to the reader for whom the book was intended; for in this manner the reader will accustom and educate himself in that science so that the difficult will become easy. Those authors, however, who do not follow this procedure but increase obscurity either because of poor organization or opacity of language so that the easy becomes difficult, defeat the purpose for which they have written their books. They have actually increased the perplexity of their readers as well as not having given them anything worthwhile; unless[27] it was the intention of the author to conceal [his ideas] from the masses so that only a few would understand [his

---

is *naturally prior* to the less universal in the sense that in the order of being the universal is prior, i.e., more fundamental, and hence more knowable as such than the particular, although the latter may be more knowable relative to us. In the case of one science the axiom or premise of a proof is considered more universal, since from it the special case or theorem is derived. The conclusion is dependent upon the premise, and in this sense, Aristotle suggests, the premise is *naturally* prior (*Metaphysics* 5.11.1019a2–4). In the case of two distinct sciences we can say that one is more universal than, and hence naturally prior to, the other, if it treats the same subject from a more abstract or general perspective than the other. Whereas mathematics, for example, studies extension in general, physics studies extended bodies in motion, which is a particular feature of extended bodies. Physics is then more specialized than mathematics (Aristotle, *Physics*, 2.2; *Metaphysics* 6.1; Gersonides, *Commentary on Song of Songs*, 3c–d).

Husik too sensed a difficulty in the ordering in this paragraph, but he proposed a different emendation (Husik, "Studies in Gersonides," pp. 562–64). His proposal, however, doesn't provide an example of natural priority in one science.

24. Aristotle, *Posterior Analytics* 1.4–5.
25. Husik, "Studies in Gersonides," pp. 565–67
26. Aristotle, *Posterior Analytics* 1.2.
27. Literally "By God, unless"—an Arabic idiom.

words], because such ideas would, if understood, cause harm to the masses.[k1][28] Occasionally the author intentionally adopts this device when he suspects that [his book] contains flaws or weaknesses. Therefore he employs obscure or eloquent language and introduces things to surprise the reader greatly, so that the defects of the book will be hidden from him because of the effort that is expended on understanding the [obscure] language and the ideas; especially since the author has intentionally concealed from him [some ideas] and attracted him toward that[l1] which will surprise him. But this is not our intention in this book! We wish that the amplitude of our language, as well as its explanation and proper order, make our[m1] intentions, together with their profundity, explicit to the reader.[29] Opacity of language (omeq ha-lashon) or faulty arrangement should not hide the defect and weakness of our intention. For this reason we have not employed rhetorical flourishes or obscure language; the profundity of the subject, together with the right organization and clear language, are sufficient. There is no need to add obscurity of language and bad organization.[30]

Fourth, when it is necessary for an author to speak about different things that are not cognitively related [or are not evidence for each other] but which do have a real or natural order, such as the priority of the number one to the number two or the priority of the triangle to the square, it is proper to present these things in their real[n1] order. It is for this reason that the author should not omit[o1] anything from them and that the places where these problems are [treated in] the book[p1] should be easily known [to the reader]. This kind of priority concerns the more preferable order with respect to the subject and the inquirer.

---

28. Cf. Maimonides, *Guide* 1, preface; Averroes, *On the Harmony of Religion and Philosophy*, trans. G. Hourani (London, 1961).

29. The expression *harhabat leshonenu u-be'uro* is difficult. Usually the phrase *harhabat lashon* or *harhabat ma'amar* means figurative, metaphorical language. In his translation of Maimonides' *Guide*, Pines renders this phrase as: "an extension of the meaning of the expression" (Maimonides, *Guide* 2.1, p. 244 in Pines's translation; J. Klatzkin, *Thesaurus Philosophicus Linguae Hebraicae*, 4 vols. [Leipzig, 1928], vol. 1, pt. 2, ad loc.). However, this does not seem to be Gersonides' meaning in this context. A few sentences earlier he explicitly says that he will use plain language in his exposition, and in general his practice fulfills his promise. Toward the end of his preface this phrase occurs again—*yarhib bo ha-be'ur*—with the connotation of detailed exposition or fullness of explanation, perhaps to the point of repetitiveness. Thus Kellermann translates this phrase as "ausführlich." B. Kellermann, *Die Kämpfe Gottes von Levi ben Gerson*, 2 vols. (Berlin, 1914), 1:13.

The term *harhabah* appears to derive from the Arabic *ittisā'*, which can in this context be translated as "vagueness of expression" (H. Wehr, *A Dictionary of Modern Written Arabic* [New York, 1971], ad loc.) or as "amplitude or sufficiency." I adopt the latter.

30. There is no mention in the printed editions or in any of the manuscripts consulted of the kind of order this reason exhibits.

Fifth, sometimes the author requires the use of one premise to prove several different propositions. If it is the case with respect to one of these propositions but not to the others that this premise seems true and evident, it is necessary that the author deal with this proposition first, even if it might be more difficult from another aspect than the others. This kind of priority pertains to the order necessary for the inquirer.

Sixth, when it is necessary for the resolution of a particular question to establish one part of a disjunction of contradictories and to disprove the other part, it is proper for the author to disprove the latter before he proceeds with the former, if this is at all possible. This is analogous to the procedure of the physician, who tries to remove the malady before he brings about a healthy constitution.

Seventh, when an author realizes that some of his discussions explain things that are strange to the reader because of the opinions with which the latter is familiar and habituated from youth, so that the reader is upset by them even if he finds no logical inconsistencies in them, and hence for this reason would be prevented from obtaining knowledge from the rest of the book—then the author should arrange his material in a way that is appropriate to what he wants to convey to his reader. [That is,] he should present first the material that is not so strange to the reader; in this way the author will wean him away gradually from his [intellectual] heritage, so that his former opinions will not prevent him from obtaining the truth on that question. This kind of tactic is similar to that employed by physicians of the body and of the soul, and it is necessary to use such a tactic because of the disposition of the patient. The author too [is often in the same position] when the disposition of his reader is such that on a particular topic it is in a sense diseased, although he doesn't realize it but thinks that he is sound and not in need of any therapy or the advice of physicians. Such an ill person must be introduced gradually[q] to the therapy, so that he doesn't experience too strong a stimulus. Therefore, when an author realizes that the reader has corrupt[r] opinions, whose contraries he is about to establish, he should uproot them step by step. Since he can succeed in this undertaking only if he has the consent of the reader, for he has no physical means to persuade him and the reader actually doesn't want to be disabused of these ideas, the author must use for [this process of] uprooting those principles all the means available that are not too strong. In this way the malady will be removed and the patient will be cured. Hence the author should try to dissipate that which nourishes those opinions before he actually uproots them. Even [in removing] this nourishment the author should adopt a definite order, i.e., the nourishment that the reader will miss the least should be removed first; and this should continue gradually without stop until all the sustenance that sustains this opinion will be removed. Then it will be easy for the author to uproot that opinion; indeed, the opinion might disappear by itself. And if it happens that the author turns the sustenance for that opinion into sustenance for the view that he wants[51] to establish, this is all the more [to his advantage]. This is like war, where one tries to diminish the allies of his opponent; and if one is able to persuade one of these allies to come to one's own side, one gains the ascendancy over his opponent in two ways: his opponent is thereby weakened, and he himself is correspondingly strengthened.[t1] This kind of priority concerns the more preferable kind of order to be adopted for the sake of the reader; [indeed] it approaches the kind of order that is necessary, as we have indicated.

Now that the various reasons for the ordering of subjects have been explained, the reader should not ask us to explain the reason why we have considered one question before other questions that are [in some sense] prior to it, or why in dealing with one particular question we have refuted one point before refuting another or proved one thesis before proving another. For the reader should be able to discern the reason for the arrangement that we have in fact adopted. It is clear from the reasons previously mentioned that it is possible, given two things, that one should be prior to the other from one point of view, but that the latter should be prior to the former from another point of view. With things of this nature it is imperative for the author to consider carefully which kind of order is the most appropriate in regard to these things. Hence the reader should not inquire concerning these things why we have treated this thing before some other thing, since [he thinks] that the other thing should be treated first because of one of the aforementioned reasons. We have in fact treated one particular subject first precisely because of one of these reasons: and it is obvious that if we had adopted the reverse order the same question would have been raised. It is imperative for the reasons mentioned above that the reader of a book not consider that which comes later in the book before that which comes earlier, if the author [of that book] is of the type that arranges his material according to the proper rules of ordering just mentioned. The necessity for a reader to consider that which comes first in a book before that which comes afterward constitutes an eighth principle of ordering. Sometimes an author relies, when it is possible, on what he has established earlier in treating something later in his book; hence he does not elaborate on it in that place. If he were to do so, his explanation would be repetitious and superfluous. If the reader begins with the later part, it can happen that he will not understand it at all or perhaps he will distort the meaning of the author. It is therefore necessary that you, my reader, if you want to understand this book, follow the order that we have ourselves followed; if you do not do this, you will be greatly confused on most topics. This confusion will be inevitable in the attempt to understand the profound mysteries and secrets of this book. The reader should realize that this book was not composed carelessly, that what is found in it is the result of a thorough investigation, so that no doubt[u1] remains [on any of the topics] included in this book. In addition, many difficulties that have plagued the sciences generally will be dissipated in this book, as will be clear to the reader who is familiar with the sciences and has recognized the difficulties in them. In this way, the basic principles of the Torah will in their entirety have been established.[v1] It is therefore clear that it is not proper for any of our readers to alter anything included in this book either with respect to its order, its content, or its proper explanation; for to do so might misrepresent our intentions.

The first six parts of this treatise are as follows: Book one—the immortality of the soul; Book two—the communication of knowledge about future events; Book three—God's knowledge of things; book four—Divine Providence[w1]; Book five—the heavenly bodies, their movers, the mutual relations among these movers, and the relation between God and these movers, as far as can be determined by the human intellect; Book six—the creation of the universe. We have also included a discussion of miracles and of[x1] the signs and the tests for a prophet.[31]

We have here explained the purpose and utility of this book, the meaning of its title, its order, the necessary [arrangement] of its parts, and its value. This is what we have intended [in this preface].

---

31. In the printed editions this sentence is appended to the preceding one; in the manuscripts it is placed as a distinct sentence. The latter procedure makes better sense of the opening phrase of this paragraph: והנה חלקי זה הספר הראשונים.

· BOOK ONE ·
IMMORTALITY OF THE SOUL

CONTENTS

CHAPTER I

THE VIEWS OF OUR PREDECESSORS ON THE ESSENCE OF THE HUMAN SOUL

S INCE the intellect is the most fitting of all the parts of the soul for immortality—the other parts are obviously perishable together with the corruption of the body because they use a bodily organ[a] in the exercise of their functions—it is necessary that we inquire[b] into the essence of the human intellect before we investigate whether it is immortal or not, and whether if it is immortal, in what way it is immortal. For human immortality[c] and human happiness are accidental qualities[1] of the intellect, and it is not proper to investigate the accidents of a substance before we know the essence of it, since without the knowledge of the latter no knowledge of the former is possible. Since philosophers have differed widely about the essence[d] of the intellect, it is also fitting that we make a preliminary survey of their views. Whatever truth we find we shall accept; and in whatever we find to be false we shall point out the truth that lies in its refutation. In this way we can disabuse our readers from erroneous opinions to which they have adhered, so that they will not be hindered by these ingrained and habitual opinions from attaining the truth in this matter.

There have been three main views on this topic among our predecessors. The first view is that of Alexander,[2] according to whom this disposition, i.e.,[3] the material intellect, is in a subject, i.e., in the soul in its entirety or

---

1. *Masigim; lāḥiqa*: 'accidental properties of a substance'. Maimonides, *Guide* 1.21; Anne-Marie Goichon, *Lexique de la langue philosophique d'Ibn Sina* [Paris, 1938], p. 363.

2. Alexander of Aphrodisias was a late second-century–early third-century Greek commentator of Aristotle whose works were quite important in Arabic philosophy. Cf. P. Merlan, *Monopsychism, Mysticism and Metaconsciousness* (The Hague, 1963), pp. 14–21, where extensive bibliographical material is to be found.

3. The term *bakhanah* and *isti'dād* correspond to Alexander's term ἐπιτηδειότης 'suitability'. The Latins translated it as *praeparatio* (Thomas Aquinas, *Summa Contra Gentiles* 2.68.) Since this term denotes a capacity, or power, of the soul Alexander called it the *hylic*, or material, *intellect* (ὑλικὸς νοῦς), since matter is, for the Aristotelians, the source of potentiality. Moreover, since the material intellect is for Alexander nothing but a power, it is akin to prime matter, which is nothing but the power to receive the forms of corporeal substances. Cf. Alfred Ivry, "Moses of Narbonne's 'Treatise on the Perfection of the Soul': A Methodological and Conceptual Analysis," *JQR* 57 (1967): 276, n. 16.

in one of its parts only, like the imaginative soul or the phantasms that are found in it, and this intellect is nothing but a disposition. The second view is that of Themistius and his followers, who maintain that this disposition is a separable intellect that is neither generated nor corruptible.[4]

The third view is that which is found in Averroes's commentary on Aristotle's *On the Soul*, where Averroes advances the doctrine that this disposition is actually the Agent Intellect itself; but in so far as it attaches itself to the human soul, it is a disposition and has a potentiality for knowledge of terrestrial phenomena, i.e., these are cognitions[5] that are derived from sensible objects outside the mind; e.g., as in such propositions, "All living objects have sensation," or, "All men are rational," etc. Considered in itself, however, it knows its own essence and not terrestrial phenomena. [6]

There is also a fourth view that has been recently put forth, according to which this disposition is a separable intellect that is generated essentially [but] not from something else.[7]

---

4. Themistius was also a Greek commentator of Aristotle who flourished in the latter part of the fourth century C.E. Cf. O. Hamelin, *La théorie de l'intellect d'après Aristote et ses commentateurs* (Paris, 1953).

5. *Muskalot; ma'qulat; intelligibilia.* It has been a common practice to translate this chameleon-like term by giving the Latin equivalent. See F. Rahman, *Avicenna's Psychology* (London, 1952), pp. 19, 33–35; A. Ivry, "Averroes on Intellection and Conjunction," *Journal of the American Oriental Society* 86 (1966), p. 78; A. Hyman, *Averroes' Long Commentary on* De Anima, trans. in A. Hyman and J. Walsh, *Philosophy in the Middle Ages*, p. 315. The most literal English renditions would be: 'objects of thought,' 'objects of knowledge,' corresponding to the Greek νοητά (Plato, *Timaeus* 30C; Aristotle, *Nicomachran Ethics*, 1174b34). Wolfson gave a variety of translations for the term (H. Wolfson, *Crescas' Critique of Aristotle*, 247, 546, 547; ibid., *Philosophy of Spinoza*, 2 vols. [New York, 1958], 02:25, 46–47, 118–121.) Since one of Levi's concerns in Book 1 is to determine precisely what a *muskal* is, I shall generally use the literal phrase 'object of knowledge' so as not to prejudice what his answer will be. Occasionally, the connotation of this term is not so "open," and a less literal rendition is given that is appropriate to the context. Where *muskal* connotes an epistemological-psychological entity, such terms as 'cognition,' 'concept,' 'conception' will be used. The phrases *muskalot rishonot, muskalot sheni'ot*, are rendered respectively as 'axioms,' i.e. first principles, and 'theorems,' i.e. secondary principles.

6. Merlan, *Monopsychism*, and Hamelin, *La théorie de l'intellect*.

7. According to Julius Guttmann, the fourth opinion is the view of some of Gersonides' Christian contemporaries (Julius Guttmann, *Philosophies of Judaism* [New York, 1964], p. 219). For a general discussion of these different doctrines, consult Isaac Husik, *A History of Mediaeval Jewish Philosophy* (Philadelphia, 1948), pp. 332–40; "Anonymous Treatise on Beatitude and the Agent Intellect, in *Medieval Philosophy*, ed. John Wippel and Alan Wolter (New York, 1969), pp. 421–44; Thomas Aquinas, *On the Unicity of the Intellect against the Averroists*, trans. Beatrice Zedler (Milwaukee, 1968); idem., *Summa Theologiae* 1. q. 75, a. 2 and a. 6.

CHAPTER II

THE ARGUMENTS IN FAVOR OF THESE VIEWS

HAVING mentioned these views by our predecessors of the essence of the intellect, it is proper that we now examine the various arguments that have been either explicitly advanced in favor of them or that can be extracted from their writings. For when these arguments are understood, it will be easy for us to assess the truth of these views. This procedure will guide us in obtaining the truth on this topic; for when there are many principles that are used to support different doctrines on a given question, it will be easier to select[a] from them something that will lead us to the truth on this issue.[1]

Now Alexander's doctrine has been thought to be in agreement with the intention of Aristotle and with that which follows from his principles. With respect to what Aristotle himself intended [Alexander's view is consonant with that of Aristotle], since Aristotle himself called [the intellect] "the material intellect." This shows that for Aristotle this disposition is not in a separate intellect, but rather that there is something that is related[b] to the disposition as its matter.[2]

On the other hand [Alexander's doctrine is consistent with] what follows from Aristotle's principles; for Aristotle lays down as a principle with respect to this disposition (i.e., the material intellect) that it is not an actual entity. Because of this Aristotle compares it to the capacity possessed by a blank tablet for being written upon.[3] This latter point is necessarily true. For what is[c] potentially something else cannot [now] be that thing, since potentiality

---

1. As we shall see, Gersonides will use the arguments and principles of one doctrine against those of another in such a way that no new arguments will have to be found.

2. ילך ממנה מדרגת היולי ; this is a technical phrase literally equivalent to the Arabic locution, *nazala min shay manzala hayūlī.* Cf. Husik, "Studies in Gersonides", p. 522.

Alexander equates Aristotle's conception of the potential, or possible, intellect (νοῦς δυνάμει; *ha-sekhel ba-koah*) with his own notion, introduced by himself, of the material intellect (ὑλικὸς νοῦς; *ha-sekhel ha-hiyuli*). Unlike the agent intellect (νοῦς ποιητικός; *ha-sekhel ha-po'el*), which term is also Alexander's innovation, the material intellect is not separable in his view from the human person, and hence is not immortal. (Cf. Thomas Aquinas, *Summa Contra Gentiles* 2.62.)

3. Aristotle, *On the Soul* 3.4.

and actuality are opposing conditions. Since this material intellect[d] is in some sense potentially all the forms, it cannot be actually any of these forms. Moreover, if this [material intellect] were really some form, this form would prevent the intellect from receiving any other form, as has been explained in *On the Soul*. Thus, this disposition cannot be something that exists in actuality. This [condition, i.e. that this disposition is not something that exists actually] can indeed be conceived if this disposition be posited as a material intellect in the way described by Alexander. For if it were posited as a separate intellect, it is false that there could be a separate form that exists by itself [and] that it is not an existent thing. But when we posit this disposition to be in a subject in the manner described by Alexander, it is correct [to say] that a disposition is not any existent form, but is [just] the potentiality to become any of them. Nor is it absolute nothingness, for a potentiality is not sheer nothingness.

Moreover, from Alexander's doctrine no absurdity results from the fact that man is generated and corruptible. For the form by virtue of which a man is what he is [i.e., a man and not some other species] is in this sense generated along with the generation of a man and is in a sense corruptible with the corruption of this man. This is necessarily the case with a generable and corruptible thing, since whatever is generated and corruptible is generated and corruptible[e] with the form that is generated in it after its matter has been prepared to receive its form.

If, however, we accept Themistius' view that this form is separate and eternal, a serious and unavoidable absurdity ensues with respect to man's generation[f] and corruption. For when this form is construed in this way, either of two consequences follows: either the form of Reuben was preexistent in the matter from which he was subsequently generated, and then when the matter was ready and received the capacities for digestion and sensation, the soul manifested its activities; or the form came to him from the outside[g] upon birth.[5] That the soul came (by essential motion) to him [upon birth] is absurd, since it has been proven in the *Physics* that every moving object is a body. The former alternative, on the other hand, leads to either of two consequences: either the soul is moved and comes[h] when the matter itself is generated, or it is preexistent in the matter from which the former matter was[i] generated. Since it is false that the soul moves, it follows that it would be preexistent in the matter from which the [proximate] matter has been

---

4. Aristotle rejects the Platonic doctrine of independently existing forms. Cf. *Metaphysics* 1.6, 7.13–15, 13, passism.

5. The term *ne'eteqet* here can mean 'transmigration of souls'. Cf. Klatzkin, *Thesaurus Philosophicus Linguae Hebraicae* (Berlin, 1928) under העתק .

generated. But, by parity of reasoning, it would follow that it would be preexistent in a third matter and so on *ad infinitum*, such that all generated and corruptible matters have human intellects, which is utterly absurd.[6] The same kind of absurdity obviously results when we consider the corruption of a man, no matter whether the form is alleged to migrate or to remain hidden in the matter. Since this whole hypothesis [no matter how it is interpreted] is absurd, it is evident that this disposition is not separated, and hence not eternal.

It has been objected that this absurdity does not ensue from the assumption that this form is separate. For since it is separate, it is not connected with matter at all and hence neither migrates into nor is embedded preexistently in matter in order to manifest [subsequently] its activity in each human being. On the contrary, it is alleged that this form is one in number and that it exerts its activity upon each matter that is already to receive its activity, as is the case with the Agent Intellect.[7] Accordingly, the aforementioned difficulties do not arise. In reply, let us first note that conjunction[8] of the separate form with matter can be understood in two ways: (1) either accidental union, as the conjunction of the Agent Intellect with sperm and plant seeds, where it is not their proximate form;[9] or (2) essential union, as the conjunction of the Separate Intelligences with the celestial spheres of which they are their proximate forms, and the conjunction in us of the material intellect, which according to Themistius, is our proximate form. In the case of accidental union, it is thought that matter can be bereft of form. In the case of essential union, however, as for example the heavenly bodies, this is not at all possible, for the form gives life to these bodies throughout their matter, and without form[j] they would be dead bodies. Now when we characterize the form as separate, we mean merely that its activity is not dependent upon some corporeal organ, as is the case with the material forms, as is evident to anyone versed in the literature on this subject.[10] Moreover, even if we were to assume that the celestial bodies were bereft of a separate form, it would not follow that the matter possessed by man is also deprived

---

6. If any particular man is generated from matter that already is "besouled," and if this matter is generated from matter that is also "besouled," then every generable matter is "besouled".

7. Maimonides, *Guide* 2.12.

8. *Devequt; ittisāl.* This term can assume a variety of philosophical connotations, but in this context, indeed throughout Bk. 1, it has the meaning of union or conjunction with some other substance or thing. Cf. Goichon, *Lexique*, p. 434, par. 775.

9. Husik, "Studies in Gersonides," pp. 574–75.

10. Thomas Aquinas, *Summa Contra Gentiles*, Bk. 2, chap. 78.

of the material intellect. Indeed this can be shown to be impossible. This [alleged separate] form is affected essentially in diverse individuals and in diverse ways, so that in one man it is knowledgeable and in another it is ignorant, or it errs with respect to what is known by another man. Therefore, it is impossible for the form that in one man is knowledgeable to be identical with the form that in another is either ignorant or in error, for it is impossible for one form to be simultaneously right and wrong with respect to the same point. Hence, this form would have to be united with individual men in so far as they are numerically different forms. But now the previous difficulty reappears [i.e., the various difficulties that arise out of the union with matter]. The impossibility of its being separate can be shown from this in another way[k] (which shall be discussed later as well): Since plurality derives from the diversity of subjects, it can be shown that this form cannot be separate; for a separate form cannot be multiplied, as has been explained in the proper place.[11]

Moreover, it seems that the most idiosyncratic properties of material forms, in so far as the latter are material, are actually found in these forms, i.e., the material intellect. For material forms qua material are generated in their subjects as the result of substantial change,[12] and they are multiplied [or diversified] according to the number of subjects. The generation of this [material] form [the material intellect] is also consequent upon a change in the matter in which it is found, for the latter is first prepared so that it can receive the capacities for digestion and sensation before this form is actually manifested in it. Moreover, this form is individuated in so far as it is manifested by different subjects, so that, for example, this form of Reuben is numerically different from the form of Simon. If this were not so, one and the same form would be[l] both knowledgeable and ignorant at the same time on the same point; i.e., if it assumed that the intellect of a wise man is identical with the intellect of a fool. But this is utterly absurd. And so individuation of this form can be accounted for on Alexander's hypothesis; but this is not the case on Themistius's hypothesis, for separate substances cannot be numerically individuated, except if they differ as species, as has

---

11. Forms that are separate are ex hypothesi not individuated, or diversified, by matter or multiplied by subjects. The form then that is responsible for knowledge, or the act of cognition, cannot be separate; for this form *is* diversified according to the levels of knowledge of each subject. Hence, the separate form, which is not diversified by and multiplied in a subject, is not the form that is cognitive.

12. Aristotle recognizes four main types of change: substantial, change in place, alteration of qualities, and growth or diminution. The first involves a change in substance or form. Aristotle, *On Generation and Corruption* 1, passim.

been demonstrated by arguments proper to this subject.[13] Thus, the proofs that establish Alexander's opinion refute Themistius's doctrine.

Let us now examine the arguments in behalf of Themistius's view. First, it would seem that the independence of the human intellect from the weakening of the sensory organs due to old age supports the thesis that this disposition is separate. For if it were a material intellect [as Alexander maintains], its power would necessarily diminish together with the weakening of the body in old age. For example, just as our visual powers diminish with the aging of the body, so too would the intellectual disposition weaken if it is material. But the contrary is the case: our intellect improves[m] with age. Thus, it would be thought that this disposition is necessarily separate.

Second, the corporeal cognitive faculties[14] do not apprehend an infinite [collection], for they receive [i.e., apprehend] things as individuals in so far as they receive them in a material manner. For example, our visual capacity perceives a definite color of a particular object in a definite surface of that object, which has also a specific shape. This is so because the receptive power of this capacity is material, i.e., in perceiving this quality it receives an impression of it. Hence, that which appears to it must be definite[n] in surface and in shape. One doesn't see color in general; one perceives a particular color. But our intellect has the power to make judgments of infinite scope, since it can make universal propositions and definitions that have unrestricted range.[15] It would therefore seem that the material intellect is separate.

Third, it could be maintained that this disposition is a form [or substance] and not merely a disposition, as Alexander claims. For, although it is the nature of the material intellect to apprehend forms, it can also apprehend this disposition as bereft of any form, and hence it has the power to apprehend sheer privation, i.e., since it apprehends itself as deprived of forms. Accordingly, that which turns out[o] to have a disposition to receive the objects of knowledge [i.e., intelligible forms] is itself a form.[16]

---

13. Maimonides, *Guide* 1.74. 7th argument.

14. *Ha-koḥot ha-masigot ha-ḥiyulaniyot.* These powers are those that have their source in sensation, and include imagination and memory in addition to sense perception.

15. In logic, a universal affirmative proposition has an unrestricted extension. Similarly, a definition applies to an indefinite number of things which it defines.

16. As it stands this argument is not transparent. Munk gives a French translation of this argument as it appears in Averroes's *Middle Commentary on On the Soul:* "Ce qui prouve d'ailleurs que ce n'est pas une pure disposition, c'est que l'intellect hylique peut concevoir cette disposition vide de formes tout en percevant les formes; il faudrait donc qu'il pût percevoir le non-être, puisqu'il peut se percevoir lui-même vide de formes. Par conséquent, la chose qui perçoit cette disposition et les formes qui lui surviennent doivent être nécessairement quelque chose en dehors de la disposition." (Salomon Munk, *Mélanges de philosophie juive et arabe,* 2d ed. [Paris, 1955],

Fourth, in the case of the corporeal cognitive powers, the sensation is numerically different from that which is apprehended. For example, the color which the visual faculty receives in perceiving an object is not identical with the color that is in the object, just as the heat that is in a heated object is not the very same heat that is in the source of heat. This is true in so far as these qualities are received materially;[17] for an accidental quality that is numerically one cannot be in two subjects, all the more at the same time. But in this disposition we find that the act of apprehension and that which is apprehended are numerically identical; for that which is apprehended in this act is the very same thing that comes to us in the act of knowing, since that which is known is a common nature embedded in a particular object and such a nature is in no way plural. For example, the species man is one, although the individual nature [of man] can be multiplied.[18] Accordingly, it would seem that this disposition[p] is necessarily separate.[19]

Fifth, the corporeal cognitive powers seem to be [corporeally] affected in the act of apprehension, so that when we turn from an object that produces a strong sensation to one that is weaker than it, we cannot immediately perceive it as it truly is. For example, when we look at the sun and then turn to look at something else, we cannot [immediately] see the latter clearly. This is also true with the other sensory capacities and results from the fact that what they receive [i.e., apprehend] is in a sense received materially.[20] This is not the case, however, with this disposition in us. For when we turn from a difficult concept to an easier one, we apprehend the latter more quickly. From this it would seem to follow that this disposition is not material.

Sixth, since this disposition is that by virtue of which we are essentially

---

p. 447.) The last sentence in the French is much clearer than its analogue in the Hebrew, which doesn't make clear why the disposition to receive knowledge must itself be a form. I translate the French as follows: "Consequently, that which perceives this disposition and the forms which are received by it should necessarily be something outside of this disposition, [i.e., a form]." Actually, the opacity of the argument lies in the invalidity of the inference, as Gersonides himself will show in the next chapter.

17. An impression of color or heat is actually in the body.

18. That is, 'species', or 'natures' (*ba-tev'a bakollel*) are always unique, although they may have many instances.

19. Since the intellect, the act of intellect, and that which is known are identical and cannot be individuated, the human intellect must be a separate form. Cf. Aristotle, *On the Soul* 3.5; Maimonides, *Guide* 1.68.

20. Supra, n. 17.

constituted as a distinct species,[21] it is fitting that it be a [separate] substance. If, however, we construe this disposition as Alexander does, then it is neither a substance nor part of a substance; rather it would be an accidental feature of either the imagination or of the images themselves, or[q] of the soul as a whole, or of anything from them that can be assumed to be a subject [for this disposition]. But if it is construed as a separate intellect, then it is itself a substance and serves to distinguish us as a species. Nor is it possible for someone to say that although the disposition is not a substance, its subject, e.g., the imagination, is [a substance] and that this subject serves to distinguish us, as in the case of other dispositions that are considered distinctive because of the subjects from which they are derived. This suggestion has nothing in its favor, since the imagination does not distinguish us, as it is found in other animals.[22]

Seventh, just as the subject of the disposition of other things receives the form that results from the actualization of the disposition, so too is it the case with our disposition for receiving the objects of knowledge. Hence, since that which receives the objects of knowledge is an intellect, it is fitting that the subject of this disposition be also an intellect. It is not proper that the disposition and its subject be of diverse genera, i.e., that the disposition would receive the objects of knowledge independently of its subject, as would be the case in Alexander's theory. Indeed, Alexander[r] says this explicitly, i.e., this disposition receives knowledge without any involvement on the part of the subject, whether it be the imagination or the soul in general, or whatever other subject be postulated. If the disposition were intertwined with its subject, besides not being able to apprehend universal concepts— for its subject [the imagination] is of such a nature as to perceive only particular things[23]—the form that is its subject would prevent the disposition from receiving other forms, as has been explained in *On the Soul*.[24] These are, then, the arguments that support Themistius's view; they seem to serve as counterarguments against Alexander's theory.

Let us now consider Averroes's contention that this disposition is gener-

---

21. שנתעצמנו בה והיא הבדל לנו. The verb *nit'zem* connotes those properties or activities that make a thing what it is, i.e., its essential features. It corresponds to the Arabic term *tajauhara*. (Cf. George Vajda, *Isaac Albalag* [Paris, 1960], p. 100, n. 3; Goichon, *Lexique*, p. 52, par. 116). The term הבדל connotes the 'specific difference' (ἡ διαΦορά) that serves to distinguish the various species within a common genus.

22. Aristotle, *On the Soul* 3.3

23. Aristotle, *Posterior Analytics* 1.31.

24. Aristotle, *On the Soul* 3.4

able and corruptible, i.e., that when the Agent Intellect is united with us it becomes merely a disposition and that this union is generated in the generation[s] of each man and vanishes in each man's death. The arguments that support Alexander's view also support this thesis of Averroes. On the other hand, Averroes's view that this disposition is identical with the Agent Intellect is supported by the arguments of Themistius. Averroes has in some way[t] combined both of these views. There are other arguments that favor Averroes over Themistius besides those previously mentioned which support Alexander's and Averroes's theories and that refute Themistius's view. [Let us examine them individually.]

First, according to Themistius's view, it would follow that there would be a disposition in a separate substance, i.e., the disposition to receive knowledge. But this can be shown to be absurd. A capacity [i.e., a disposition] is necessarily a feature of matter and inheres only in it. When a capacity is present in a form, it is so only accidentally by virtue of the subject; in this manner we are entitled to say that forms receive other forms, as is explained in *On the Soul*.[25] For example, we could say that the nutritive soul [or form] has the disposition to receive the sensitive soul, since the subject of the former [i.e., the body] receives the latter by means of the former.[26] This difficulty [i.e., a capacity inherent in a separate form] is not germane to Averroes's doctrine, however; for he attributes this disposition[u] to the form only in so far as it is conjoined to us, but not as it is in itself.[v]

Second, according to Themistius, it would follow that our first perfection is eternal, i.e., the material intellect, whereas the ultimate perfection, which should be more noble, is generable and corruptible. For on this hypothesis the objects of knowledge are generated in the material intellect, and since they are generated they are destroyed, as Aristotle has argued in *On the Heavens*.[27] Averroes's view, however, avoids this difficulty; for according to his doctrine, man's ultimate perfection, which is attainable by this disposition, is the Agent Intellect itself, which is eternal, although generable only accidentally in so far as it is united with us. There is nothing to prevent this

---

25. Strictly speaking, it is not the form that receives another form but the subject, i.e., matter. Aristotle, *On the Soul* 3.4

26. In Aristotle's psychology there are three distinct types and grades of souls, or living functions: (1) nutritive, (2) sensory-motor, and (3) intellectual, each dependent in some sense upon the one below it on this scale. Aristotle, *On the Soul*, passim.

27. Aristotle, *On the Heavens* 1.12. Knowledge, or the objects of knowledge, ought to be eternal, not the individual mind. Themistius, however, inverts this grading.

intellect from thinking of itself at any time, since it continually thinks of itself in so far as it is not conjoined with us, as Averroes claims.[28]

Finally, let us consider the view of the moderns [mentioned in chapter one] that maintains that this disposition is both generated and separated. Alexander's third argument can be cited in favor of its generated character, as against Themistius's claim that it is eternal. Concerning its separated nature, the arguments of Themistius support this contention, whereas those of Alexander deny it.

These are the arguments we have found in the ancient writers that support these views and refute [the counter-theses], although we did not[w] find them [in their original form] adequately presented. We have now completed the presentation of these various views as best as we could, for in this way our examination of them will be more satisfactory. It is necessary that if someone wants to arrive at the truth on some disputed question that he try to defend each of the opposing theories as far as this is possible.[x] Then the absurdity of the view he [wishes] to refute will be more easily established. For if he refutes any one of these theories but does not first try to argue for it (as far as possible), his refutation of that view is not well-grounded. This is obvious.

---

28. Averroes, *Averrois Cordubensis Commentarium Magnum in Aristotelis De Anima Libros* (The Long Commentary on Aristotle's *De Anima*), ed. F. Stuart Crawford (Cambridge, Mass., 1953), Bk. 3, pp. 399–413. An excerpt from this work has been translated into English and included in Arthur Hyman and James Walsh, *Philosophy in the Middle Ages* (New York, 1967), pp. 314–24; consult Moritz Steinschneider, *Hebräische Übersetzungen* (Berlin, 1893) for information concerning Averroes's other works on this topic.

CHAPTER III

HOW THE ARGUMENTS FOR THESE VIEWS ARE MUTUALLY INCOMPATIBLE

H AVING cited the various arguments given by our predecessors (or which can be extracted from their writings) in favor of these different theories, of which some refute the claims of the others, it is proper that we now examine these arguments to determine which of them is a valid proof or disproof and which is not. However, there is no way to verify in a conclusive manner any one of these arguments. If we could, such a verification would take the form of either a proof in favor of a particular hypothesis or a refutation of its contrary hypothesis. The latter procedure, however, is not decisive except when the competing theories on this question are contradictories. Since these theories are not exhaustive[a], a refutation of one proves[b] neither that any one of the others is not true nor that one particular theory of the others is true.[1] The former procedure is very difficult to execute, i.e., to discover a direct proof in favor of one of these theories. For it can be easily shown from what we are about to mention on this topic that no one of these arguments in behalf of any of these theories has sufficient force, at least in its present form, to establish the desired conclusion, and that the existence of a proof[c] of this sort[d] in this exceedingly profound and difficult subject is not very likely. Therefore, I shall give up the attempt to determine which of these arguments is a valid proof *for* one of these theories, and concentrate instead upon determining which of these arguments are valid *refutations* of any of these theories. The latter procedure is useful and instructive in attaining the truth on the matter upon which we are now engaged. For when we have determined in this way which of these doctrines are false, it will be easier for us to find which of them is true, or if all of them are false, to develop a totally different theory.[2]

Now it is clear that Alexander's doctrine of the material intellect, in so

---

1. If hypotheses H_1 and H_2 are contraries, both cannot be true although both can be false. Hence a disproof of H_1 does not by itself prove H_2. If H_1 and H_2 are contradictories, however, then both cannot be true but one must be true. Accordingly, a valid refutation of one proves the other. Cf. Aristotle, *On Interpretation*, 7 and 10.

2. Aristotle, *Nicomachean Ethics* 8.1.

far as it is based upon Aristotelian principles, refutes the doctrines of Themistius and of the fourth view that has been recently advanced. The latter opinions claim that this disposition is a separate substance, either an intellect or the subject of an intellect. Accordingly, it is either mixed with a form or is itself a form. In any case, it would not be able to apprehend all forms, for a thing can indeed[e] be receptive to everything only if it is itself not any of them. In this way, for example, the eye can receive all colors and the sense of taste all tastes[f], i.e., in so far as they are none of the qualities they apprehend. For this reason, if the sense of taste itself had a specific taste quality it would not be able to taste all kinds of tastes. And so Aristotle claims that if this power [the intellectual capacity] were mixed with any particular form, this form would prevent the intellect from apprehending other forms; or if it does apprehend them it would do so incorrectly, as would be the case with the sense of taste, which, if essentially characterized by a particular taste quality, would not apprehend accurately other taste qualities.[3]

Someone might object that this principle vitiates Alexander's own doctrine. For if the subject of this disposition is the soul or a part thereof, as Alexander maintains, then the disposition would be mixed with one of the forms, i.e., the form of its subject. Alexander obviates this difficulty, however, by maintaining that this disposition receives the objects of knowledge without involving its subject. The subject is merely a condition of its existence, not of its receptivity for knowledge, as Averroes reports in his *Epitome of* On the Soul.[4]

[Now concerning this point] there are in nature[g] [different] levels [of receptivity]. There are things [sense qualities] that are truly and literally received by subjects having the capacity to receive them; i.e., the subject is affected in some way by the sort [of thing] that it apprehends. For example, the sense of touch in some sense receives the things that it feels; i.e., it literally and truly becomes hot or cold with a determinate degree of heat or cold, even if it is not of the same intensity of heat or cold which it feels. For if it were [of the same intensity as the intensity of the hot or cold object felt], its sensation of heat or cold would take time, since it is warmed or cooled over time. But this is absurd, since we see that as soon as we touch[h] something we feel it. Moreover, if it were required by virtue of this sensation that the sense organ be affected originally by the quality that it is about to perceive, it would be impossible to perceive it; for it apprehends this quality precisely

---

3. Aristotle, *De Anima* 3, 429a.13–28.

4. Gersonides, *Supercommentary on Averroes's Epitome of On the Soul*, Oxford, Bodleian Library, Oppenheimer Ms. 38 (Neubauer, no. 1373), fol. 247.

because of its indifference [with respect to the sense qualities of that type], as has been shown in *On the Soul*.[5]

Other [qualities] are received in a way that is intermediate between the way that involves a mixing with matter[i] and the way that does not involve such a mixing; for example, the perception of colors.[j] For the eye is itself not literally colored; hence, it can receive contrary colors at the same time, as has been explained in the proper place.[6] [On the other hand,] the eye is in some sense mixed with matter. It will not, therefore, perceive something perfectly after it has seen some object that is much brighter. The common sense is even less involved with matter in its mode of receptivity; for its apprehension is more spiritual.[7] Then comes the imagination: its mode of receptivity is more spiritual because it receives [things] with very little mixing with its subject. Hence, the imagination follows our[k] will.

Nature ultimately reaches [a level where] the disposition receives the things without any mixing at all with matter and the subject of the disposition. Indeed, this is the disposition [about which we are concerned]; i.e., the material intellect, as is evident from its very nature.[8]

---

5. In tactile perception, the organ receives the sense quality in such a way that it is physically affected by the quality. However, the received, or sensed, quality is not of the same degree of intensity as the quality in the object sensed. For example, if I touch a hot plate that is 200° F, my finger immediately feels heat, but the heat in my finger is not 200° F; if it were, it would have to *reach* that degree of heat *over time*. Yet we feel heat right away! In this argument Gersonides assumes that the degrees of any sensed quality constitute a scale all of whose points have to be crossed before any particular degree is reached. Moreover, if it were required that my finger be hot previously in order to feel the heat in the plate, then I would not feel the heat in the plate at all. It would be like a person with a high temperature walking into a sweat-bath. (See Aristotle, *On the Soul*, 2:11, 424a 1ff; Husik, "Studies in Gersonides," 586–588.)

6. Aristotle, *On the Soul* 2.11. 424a3–9.

7. *Ruḥanit; ruḥi*; Averroes, *Epitome of Parva Naturalia*, trans. H. Blumberg (Cambridge, Mass., 1961), pp. 14, 16, and 32.

In his discussion of the 'common sense' (ἀισθησις κοινὴ) Aristotle claims that this faculty requires no special sense organ (Aristotle, *On the Soul* 3.1). In this sense one could say that its operations are more spiritual. This is the term used by Thomas Aquinas to describe the way in which the sense organs are affected by sense qualities (Thomas Aquinas, *Summa Theologiae* 1. q. 78 a. 3). Unlike the case where a body absorbs heat from another body, a sense organ does not itself become the quality it receives. For example, the eye doesn't become red. The latter type of receptivity Thomas calls *immutatio naturalis;* the former *immutatio spiritualis.* The first level of receptivity distinguished by Gersonides would then be a case of *immutatio naturalis;* the second level would be a case of *immutatio spiritualis.* For both he gives the same examples as does Aquinas. Gersonides gives a more detailed account of this notion of "spirituality" in his *Commentary on* Song of Songs, introduction, p. 2d. Cf. Harry A. Wolfson, "The Internal Senses in Latin, Arabic and Hebrew Philosophic Texts," *Harvard Theological Review* 28 (1935): 69–70.

8. Aristotle, *On the Soul* 3.4; Husik, "Studies in Gersonides," pp. 588–89.

Now Themistius and the more recent[l] philosophers cannot avoid this difficulty in this way. For they claim that the intellect, which is the subject of this disposition, is that which [actually] receives the objects of knowledge. But it shall be soon demonstrated that on this hypothesis, i.e., the subject of this disposition is an intellect, it will be impossible to say that the disposition receives the objects of knowledge without any mixture with its subject.

Furthermore, Alexander's argument with respect to the generation and destruction of man is without doubt sufficient to disprove Themistius's doctrine [of the immortality of the material intellect], as we have already indicated in our initial presentation of this argument.[9] Averroes briefly mentions this[m] argument in his *Epitome of* On the Soul. He objects to Themistius and those who follow him, that a form of this sort [separable and eternal] cannot be a form by virtue of which[n] a generable and destructible body is perfected.[10] This is obvious according to our previous explanation.

Moreover, Alexander's criticism of Themistius that this form [the separate intellect with which Themistius endows all men] would be multiplied[o] according to the plurality of subjects is clearly a valid argument against Themistius's position and the position of the more modern thinkers, as we have indicated in the last chapter. Averroes's [position], however, is not touched by this argument, since he too admits that this disposition is diversified by accident in so far as the [separate] intellect is united with individual men, although in itself it is numerically one.[11] The claim, which we already have mentioned, that this disposition is material because its generation is a consequent of a substantial change [e.g., the birth of an individual man], just as in the case of all material forms, does not by itself completely refute Themistius's position. For he does not admit that it [this disposition] is generated at all! Therefore, he would not say that its generation is a consequent of a [substantial] change; rather he would say that this change occurs for the sake of the generation of material forms in man, such as [those involved in] the nutritive system, sensation, etc. In a similar way the view of the moderns can also be defended [against this argument].

Themistius's argument that the intellect is separate because it is strengthened at the same time when the sensory apparatus is weakening, can easily

---

9. Supra, chapter 2.

10. I follow Husik's emendation of the underlined phrase in this passage: כי מה שזה דרכו מהצורות הנה אין דרכו שישלם בו [בה L] He emends it to read: גשם הוה נפסד בהוויה גשם נפסד. Husik, "Studies in Gersonides," p. 598. Gersonides, *Supercommentary on Averroes's Epitome of* On the Soul, fol. 236.

11. There is only one material intellect, according to Averroes, although it may be accidentally conjoined with many individual men (infra, chap. 4).

be seen to be invalid. The material forms [e.g., sense images] weaken when their respective organs weaken, not because the form weakens at that time, as Aristotle has pointed out;[12] for the nature of a form is one and the same throughout all individuals of a species, since the form is the essence of a thing, and the essence does not admit more or less. [Weakening of a function], therefore, occurs because of the weakening of the organ through which this activity is performed. For example, if an old man were to have an eye like that of a boy, his vision would be like the vision of a young boy. Accordingly, since this [intellectual] capacity does not employ any organ in the performance of its functions (for it has been explained that it receives the objects of knowledge without any mixture of forms), the weakening of the body does not diminish its powers. Rather, the intellect's powers increase inversely with the weakening of the corporeal functions of the body. Hence the latter's activities diminish and the intellect's activity is greater than it was when the body's activities were stronger[p]. For their operations prevent this [intellectual] power from exercising its function, since the soul is a unitary system and thus cannot use optimally all its cognitions simultaneously.[13]

Nor does Themistius's argument with respect to the intellect's power to apprehend judgments whose scope is infinite refute Alexander's position and establish the separateness of the intellect. The corporeal cognitive powers apprehend particulars [i.e., particular sensations and images] because of the nature of their subject which receives this [kind] of cognition; for this [subject] necessarily apprehends an object with the latter's[q] accidental qualities by virtue of which it is a particular, since it is not of the nature of a body to receive a form bereft of the accidental qualities that make it a particular form. But this disposition does not receive what it apprehends by means of a mode of receptivity that is mixed with its subject, as has been just explained. Hence, what it apprehends is not necessarily particular, as is the case with the corporeal forms.[14]

Furthermore, Themistius's argument that since the material intellect can know this disposition as bereft of any other form just as it can know these

---

12. Aristotle, *On Memory and Recollection*, 1 450b1ff, 453b5; *On the Soul* 1.4. 408b19ff.

13. The conclusion of Gersonides' argument is missing. It would be that the inverse relation between wisdom and bodily weakening can be explained without recourse to the doctrine that the human intellect is a separate substance.

14. In Aristotle's epistemology sensation apprehends the particular, idiosyncratic features of a substance, whereas the intellect apprehends the universal characteristics of a substance, i.e., its essence. Thus, universal judgments about the essence of a subject are possible on epistemological grounds without recourse to the thesis that the human intellect is a separate intellect. Cf. Aristotle, *On the Soul* 2.5. 417b22–23.

other forms, and so this disposition must itself be some kind of form, is upon examination self-refuting and not a refutation of Alexander. For if this disposition were a form or if it were to have a subject that is a form as Themistius maintains, then when this capacity [of the material intellect] receives this form [i.e., the disposition or its subject] in knowing it, it would receive itself, which is utterly absurd; i.e., that something could receive itself. This[r] absurdity does not arise in our view that the separate intelligences know themselves; for we do not maintain that they *receive* themselves, since in *their* knowledge there is no receiving of some other thing that they did not have [previously]. However, the *material* intellect receives forms in knowing them and is perfected by them. Accordingly, this absurdity necessarily arises if Themistius's theory is adopted.[15]

Nor does it follow from the fact[s] that this capacity [of the material intellect] can apprehend privation—i.e., either that some feature does not belong to something or that something does not exist at all—that the[t] reason for this is that it apprehends this form [i.e., the disposition] bereft of forms and that otherwise it would not be possible for it to apprehend privation, since the latter is not a form, [whereas] it is the nature of this capacity to apprehend forms, as has been pointed out in this objection.[16] For [it can be argued] that every capacity that apprehends some[u] thing can also apprehend the privation of that thing, since the apprehension of the privation belongs necessarily to the capacity that apprehends the possession of that thing, not to something else. This is obvious. For example, vision apprehends color [essentially]; but it [also] has[v] the [power] to apprehend the privation of color, [albeit] accidentally. Because of this we can see the shape [of the object] in which the perceived particular color is found, since the color terminates at the shape [and vanishes].[17] Analogously, since the material intellect apprehends the forms [of objects], it apprehends [as well] their privations. And it is in this way that it apprehends this disposition, i.e., in so far as the latter is a privation.[18] In this respect the material intellect differs from the separate

---

15. Husik, "Studies in Gersonides," pp. 592–93.

16. That is, since the material intellect can apprehend the disposition as bereft of forms other than itself, it *must* apprehend this disposition *as a form;* for the intellect apprehends forms.

17. The Hebrew phrase used here reads כי אליה יכלה המראה ויעדר. Gersonides' discussion is based upon Aristotle's remark that the color of a body is in a limit or is itself a limit: τὸ γάρ χρῶμα ἢ ἐν τῷ πέρατί ἐκτιν ἢ πέρας. Aristotle, *On Sense and Sensible Objects* 3. 439a30–31; Averroes, *Epitome of Parva Naturalia*, p. 10. There is a difficulty in this passage: how are we to render ויעדר ? Does this verb mean that the color ends, so to speak, at the surface of the body and then vanishes, i.e., that there is no color beneath the surface of the body?

18. The disposition is ex hypothesi bereft of all forms.

intelligences;[19] for the latter know themselves and not anything else, whereas the material intellect knows other things essentially, but itself only accidentally. Since the apprehension of privation is not really a receptivity for this intellect [i.e., there is nothing to receive], it is evident that from our assumption it does not follow that it knows itself in the sense that it receives the very thing [that is known].[20] This is [indeed] the absurdity that is entailed by Themistius's theory.

Themistius's argument that with respect to this disposition the act of knowing and that which is known are identical—a fact that is not the case with the corporeal cognitive capacities—is not sufficient to refute the position of Alexander, as can be readily seen from what we have already said. In the case of the corporeal cognitive faculties the apprehension and that which is apprehended are not identical because an organ is employed by virtue of which the apprehension takes place. Therefore, their perception is always the perception of a particular object as particular, as has been explained. This disposition, however, apprehends [its object] by a mode of receptivity that is not mixed [i.e., without the body or a bodily organ]; hence, it is not necessary that it apprehend it as particular. Rather, it apprehends the universal nature which is not multipliable [i.e., replicable]. Consequently, knowledge and that which is known are identical.[21]

Neither is Themistius's argument that since the corporeal cognitive capacities are actually affected by some impression in cognition—whereas this disposition[w] is not—a valid refutation of Alexander's position, as can be easily shown. These corporeal cognitive capacities are so affected because they employ some kind of bodily organ that serves as a subject for them.

---

19. The separate intelligences are those intelligences that are not embodied; e.g., the unmoved movers of the heavenly bodies. Gersonides discusses the separate intelligences in Bk. 5, pt 3.

20. The material intellect knows privation by the same faculty that it knows the presence of a form, except that it apprehends the latter essentially whereas the former it apprehends accidentally. A separate intelligence knows itself essentially because it is separate form; a material intelligence knows itself accidentally because it is not a separate form. Hence, in knowing the privation of some property, the material intellect is knowing itself only accidentally, and therefore is *not* a separate form. Cf. Husik, "Studies in Gersonides," pp. 592–94.

21. The identity of the act of apprehension and that which is apprehended, which is a basic theorem of Aristotelian epistemology, does not entail that the intellect is a separable form, as Themistius claims. This identity results from the fact that intellectual operations are concerned with the apprehension of forms which as general natures are individually one, i.e., there is only one essence of man. In apprehending the form, the intellect, which was first bereft of all forms, becomes one with the apprehended form. The corporeal cognitive faculties (e.g., sense perception), however, perceive by some organ the accidental features of substances, features that vary from individual to individual, and therefore serve to individuate them.

This subject is in some way affected in so far as it is impressed with an image of the perceived object. But, as we have just seen, this disposition does not receive [i.e., apprehend] what it does by means of its subject; and it is for this reason that it is not necessary for this disposition to be similarly [affected].[22]

In this regard there are in nature different levels. There are certain kinds of corporeal capacities for affectibility[23] whose subjects are truly [literally] affected through their operations, as is the case with the capacities for affectibility in the primary elements and in the homogeneous compounds derived from them.[24] [On the other hand,] there are capacities[x] whose subjects are not literally affected, as in the sensory powers. The latter in fact exhibit levels of affectibility, as has been explained in *On the Soul*.[25] Finally, we ultimately come to a capacity whose subject cannot in any way be affected through its operation, as is the case with this disposition [the material intellect], according to Alexander's doctrine.

Similarly, Themistius's argument that this disposition serves to distinguish us [from other species, and hence is a form] is not a valid objection against Alexander's theory. Alexander does not maintain that this disposition is our form but that its subject is[y] our form in so far as the disposition inheres in it. This subject is something that exists in actuality, i.e., the soul or one of its powers. Now this soul or one of its powers may be found in some other animals, but in them it is not combined with this disposition. Thus, we can admit that this subject is our form insofar as this disposition inheres in it, without incurring the previous difficulty.

Moreover, Alexander's theory is not refuted by Themistius's argument

---

22. Aristotle, *On the Soul* 3.4. 429a15.

23. *Ha-koḥot ha-mitpa'alot ha-biyulaniyot*; in Arabic, *qūwa munfa'il*. The term *koaḥ mitpa'el* is frequently translated as 'passive power' (Maimonides, *Guide* 1.52, Friedlander translation). The concept goes back to Aristotle's categories of 'action' (ποιεῖν) and 'passion' (πάσχειν). The latter term has also been translated as 'suffering' and 'affection' (Loeb edition of Aristotle's *Categories* 4). Aristotle links the notion of πάσχειν to a specific capacity, or power, in the following passage: τά δὲ ποιητικὰ καὶ παθητικὰ κατὰ δύναμιν ποιητικὴν καὶ παθητικὴν (*Metaphysics* 5.15.1021a14–15). Similarly in *Metaphysics* 1.1046a11ff, a capacity for being affected by, or suffering, a specific quality or change is indicated ἡ τοῦ παθεῖν δύναμις. In the *Ethics* this power is referred to as δυνάμεις καθ ἅς παθητικοί (N.E. 2:5, 1105b24). In this present context we are concerned with an organic capacity to receive impressions, i.e., the capacity to be affected by some stimulus. It is this feature of affectibility that is central here, and I have so translated the word *mitpae'l*. Cf. Wolfson *Crescas' Critique of Aristotle*, pp. 165, 376–79.

24. *Mitdamey ha-ḥalaqim ba-murkavim*. The term *mitdamey ha-ḥalaqim* corresponds to Aristotle's notion of τὰ ὁμοιομερῆ, 'uniform parts' (Loeb edition of *Generation of Animals* 1. 715a11), of which blood, semen, and marrow are examples.

25. Aristotle, *On the Soul* 2.7–11; 3.13; *On Sense and Sensible Objects*, passim.

the subject of other dispositions receives the form that comes from the [actualization of the] disposition.[26] For someone might say that this disposition differs from all other dispositions precisely in this way [i.e., its subject does not receive the form that comes from the disposition]. Things that are within the same genus are not necessarily the same in all respects,[z] as is evident. Moreover, it is clear that a disposition in so far as it is a disposition requires a subject, since a capacity cannot exist in abstracto. Now if this is so, the following dilemma ensues: either its subject is a body, a soul, or[a1] an intellect. Whichever it is, it is necessary that the disposition receive what it receives without any mixture with its subject; for it is necessary that the disposition receive what it receives without any mixture with any form. But no matter which of these alternative subjects is assumed [to be the subject of this disposition], it would be necessary that the disposition receive what it receives mixed *with* [some] form. For a body necessarily has a form, and souls and intellects are themselves forms. Thus, it is evident that the subject of this disposition does not receive the form that comes from the [actualization of the] disposition, which is contrary to the conclusion of Themistius's argument.[27]

Furthermore, one of the arguments that has been adduced in behalf of Averroes's doctrine—the absurdity of a disposition[b1] without any matter—refutes Themistius's position, as we have already pointed out. It has, however, been objected that the existence of a separable disposition is no less impossible than the existence of separate forms for the heavenly bodies. Generally, a form belongs to the category of relations, i.e., it is related to matter just as the disposition is related[c1] to matter. But if there are forms [i.e., the separate forms of the heavenly bodies] that are not relational, then it is not impossible for the disposition to be not related to matter. This point has been mentioned by Averroes in the short essays wherein he attempts to remove this objection to Themistius's position.[28] Nevertheless, in saying that the forms [of the heavenly bodies] are separate we do not imply that they have no relation whatever to matter; indeed, these forms are the very perfections of these heavenly bodies. We call them "separate" because they accomplish their special function, i.e., cognition, without the use of any

---

26. Gersonides is referring here to Themistius's seventh argument in chap. 2. There Themistius argues that the disposition for receiving cognition is itself a separate form, or intellect.

27. Since on Themistius's view the disposition is already an intellect, or separate form, when it receives a new form, which is the product of its transition from a state of potentiality to actuality, this latter form would be mixed with itself; this is absurd, since it would make knowledge impossible.

28. Averroes, *Drei Abhandlungen*. First Essay.

material organ. If, however, we were to posit a disposition separate from matter, we would in fact sever absolutely the relationship between the disposition and that which is supposed to receive it. Moreover, the existence of separate forms [for the heavenly bodies] has been demonstrated, whereas there is no necessity to postulate the existence of a separate disposition.

Finally, Averroes's argument that on Themistius's theory our first perfection would be eternal but our ultimate perfection would be corruptible is not sufficient to refute Themistius's position in every respect.[29] On our hypothesis that the acquired intellect[30] is generated[d1] it doesn't follow that it is corruptible, as we shall prove later. However, this absurdity is entailed accidentally by Themistius's theory by virtue of his admission that the acquired intellect is corruptible; for he thought that the acquired intellect must[e1] be corruptible because it is generated and that Aristotle had demonstrated in *On the Heavens* that[f1] anything which is generated is corruptible.[31]

---

29. The first perfection is the material intellect, which for Themistius is eternal; the ultimate perfection is the knowledge obtained, which according to Averroes's reading of Themistius is corruptible since it is generated. Cf. chap. 2 end.

30. The 'acquired intellect': *ha-sekhel ha-niqneh*, *'aql mustafád*; νοῦς, ἐπίκτητος intellectus adeptus. The precise character of this dimension of the human intellect will be discussed by Gersonides in chapter 11. At this point it will be sufficient to describe the acquired intellect as the human intellect when it has reached a high level of knowledge. Merlan, *Monopsychism*, pp. 14–15.

31. Aristotle, *On the Heavens* 1.12; Gersonides will argue against the latter claim in Bk. 6, pt. 1, chapter 27.

CHAPTER IV

A COMPLETE REFUTATION OF SOME
OF THESE VIEWS

HAVING mentioned the views of our predecessors concerning the nature of the material intellect and having shown the absurdity of Themistius's position, it is proper to examine the remaining doctrines to see whether any one of them or a [completely] different theory is true. We shall begin our inquiry with the theory of Averroes, for his doctrine has been thought to be the most adequate explanation of the material intellect. We shall show, however, that if Averroes's doctrine is accepted, many absurdities inevitably ensue.

First, in this view, learning in the theoretical sciences whose goal is not action[a] would be pointless. For if they have no effect on human perfection, i.e., immortality of the intellect, it is clear that they have no utility at all. If they did have utility, it would be either for mental[b] perfection or for our material life; there are no other purposes. Now if they have no effect on our material needs, then they have no utility at all, since it has already been assumed that they have no effect upon the attainment of mental perfection. That they have no utility for our material needs is evident. Indeed, not only do they not contribute anything to our material needs but the pursuit of learning actually impedes the "good" life. It is quite often the case that those who pursue theoretical knowledge do not pay any attention to the corporeal pleasures of life and do not satisfy completely even those bodily needs that are absolutely necessary. If one were to object that the capacity for the apprehension of these[c] theoretical truths has been given us in order to acquire the principles of those practical arts that are necessary for the improvement of our everyday life, and hence it does have utility, he would ignore the fact that some theoretical skills are not directed towards practical employment at all. Moreover, if this objection were true, the practical skills would be superior to the theoretical skills, since they are the final end of the former. But this is contrary to our nature; for we find that men prefer theoretical inquiries over practical skills. And I myself find more happiness in the little I have achieved in the former than in my more numerous achievements in the latter. The proportion of pleasure that is found in the pursuit of theoretical studies is greater than that to be found in the pursuit of practical arts. Moreover, nature has endowed us, the human species, with the desire for theoretical knowledge rather than for the attainment of practical skills. All of these considerations indicate that our speculative capacity has not been given to us only for practical purposes. Accordingly, if the following hypothetical syllogism[1] be accepted, i.e., if theoretical knowledge has no effect upon human perfection, then it has no utility at all, then, we repeat, in Averroes's theory theoretical knowledge plays no role in the attainment of human perfection. For the unification with the Agent Intellect, which for Averroes seems to be the ultimate human perfection and is in some sense the truth as we shall see,[2] would on this view be achieved upon death, by any man, be he fool or sage. At that time the union of this[d] intellect with us would then cease and the material intellect would be completely identical with the Agent Intellect itself.[3] Accordingly, if the antecedent of this hypothetical syllogism is true [i.e., theoretical knowledge has no effect upon human happiness],

---

1. Normally the term *ha-beqesh ha-tena'i* means hypothetical or conditional syllogism, of which the medievals recognized two types: the conjunctive hypothetical syllogism—*ha-beqesh ha-tena'i ha-mitdabeq*—and the disjunctive hypothetical syllogism—*ha-beqesh ha-tena'i ha-mithaleq* (Maimonides, *Treatise on Logic* 7). The case before us is an example of the first type, which in scholastic logic was called the *modus ponens* (Horace W. B. Joseph, *An Introduction to Logic* [Oxford, 1916], pp. 335, 348, n. 1). In this argument, the major premise is a hypothetical statement of the form 'If *A*, then *B*'. The minor premise affirms the antecedent '*A*'. The conclusion then affirms the consequent '*B*'.

However, it was not unusual for the medievals to use this term to refer to the major premise of this argument as well as to the argument itself. For example, in the philosophical glossary that prefaces the commentary, *She'vil 'emunah*, to Saadia's *Book of Beliefs and Opinions* (Jerusalem, 1962) the term *beqesh ten'ay mitdabeq* is illustrated by the hypothetical proposition alone. The same is true here and in Book 2, chapter 6.

2. This parenthetical remark is puzzling, for although it is certainly true that for Averroes unification or conjunction with the Agent Intellect is the ultimate human goal, this is not the *summum bonum* for Gersonides, as he will argue in the later chapters of Bk. 1. Perhaps this phrase refers only to the contact the material intellect has with the Agent Intellect in the act of cognition, which Merlan calls "epistemological union," as distinct from "ontic union," or complete identification of the two intellects into one entity (Merlan, *Monopsychism*, pp. 18–29). Another way of construing this remark is to see it as an anticipation of Gersonides' theory of the acquired intellect and its immortality. For on this theory the acquired intellect is in some sense a partial representation of the Agent Intellect or an incomplete exemplification of the complete plan of the terrestrial world which the Agent Intellect comprises (infra, chaps. 10–13).

That Gersonides rejects the idea of conjunction is clearly evident in his *Commentary on the Torah*, where he says explicitly: "It is impossible for man to apprehend completely the Agent Intellect. . . . In this, some of the recent philosophers have erred, thinking that man could apprehend completely the Agent Intellect and become numerically one with it, and that herein lies human happiness . . . and human immortality" (56b; my translation).

3. According to Averroes's theory, as Gersonides understands it, when the agent intellect is manifested in men it is the material intellect. With death this manifestation of the material intellect ends and returns to its original and pristine state as the Agent Intellect.

then so is the consequent, i.e., the pursuit of theoretical knowledge is troublesome and vain. But this is utterly absurd; for if it were true, then nature would have endowed us with a faculty for theoretical inquiries[e] that would be for no purpose. Moreover, the natural desire we have for theoretical knowledge would also be superfluous; but this is absurd, since nature does not do anything in vain. Indeed, if this [hypothesis were accepted] not only would nature endow us with a faculty that has no use but which is also contrary to our[f] [very] being, as we have seen. But this is all contrary to nature; for it is evident that nature tries to endow beings with faculties that preserve their existence for the longest time possible and in the best way possible.[4]

Second, if the material intellect is [as Averroes maintains] really the Agent Intellect, and if the latter actualizes the former, as Aristotle has demonstrated, then the following absurdity results: something actualizes itself from potentiality to actuality. But this is absolutely impossible.

Third, on Averroes's theory one and the same intellect would possess knowledge of the sublunar world that is both actual and potential at the same time. For it has been explained that the Agent Intellect actualizes the potentiality of the material intellect that is manifested in us in the apprehension of these theoretical cognitions. It has also been proven[g] in the sciences that whatever brings out the potentiality in something other than itself has in actuality that[h] which is only potential in the recipient of its activity. In this manner it is possible for it to actualize this potentiality. For example, fire can make something that is potentially hot actually hot, since it is [now] actually hot. This principle has been verified, and difficulties that pertain to it have been solved in the sciences and in metaphysics. Hence, it is clear that the Agent Intellect actualizes the material intellect in the act of cognition by virtue of the fact that it possesses in actuality this knowledge, and that the material intellect receives this knowledge in so far as this knowledge is potentially in it. Now if the material intellect were identical with the agent intellect, as Averroes maintains, the same[i] objects of knowledge would be simultaneously actual and potential in the very same intellect. But this is absurd.

Someone might object that this absurdity does not follow. For [it can be argued], the objects of knowledge are in some sense present in actuality in the imaginative forms[5] and not in the Agent Intellect. The relation of the

---

4. Gersonides, *Commentary on* Song of Songs 6b; Aristotle, *On the Heavens* 1.4.

5. *Ha-ẓurot ha-dimyonot; ṣūra khayāliya*. This term connotes the sense images as preserved in the imagination or memory. Aristotle uses the term φάντασμα to denote such mental images. Aristotle, *On the Soul* 3.7. 431a15ff; Goichon, *Lexique*, p. 188, par. 372:11.

imaginative forms to the objects of knowledge we apprehend would then be analogous to the relationship between the object of sense to sensation, whereas the relation between the Agent Intellect and the objects of knowledge corresponds to the relation between light and the perception of color.[6] In this way the above absurdity would not arise.

The imaginative forms, I answer, are not sufficient to actualize this disposition in us, since they possess the objects of knowledge only potentially; i.e., when the corporeal features of the imaginative form are stripped away, it thereby loses its particular character, and the objects of knowledge, i.e., the general nature, which is potentially in the particular image, is now actual. This is explained by Aristotle in the *Metaphysics*.[7] It was for this reason that Aristotle had to introduce the Agent Intellect, whose job it is to transform these imaginative forms into actual objects of knowledge, whereas prior [to its activity] the latter are only potential objects of knowledge. It will be shown later that the Agent Intellect does in actuality possess this knowledge, as we have so far assumed; for it will be demonstrated that the Agent Intellect is the intelligible order for the things obtaining in the sublunar world. Hence it is necessary that the objects of knowledge be present in some sense in the Agent Intellect. Moreover, the Agent Intellect has a [power of] conveying information to man in dreams, divination, or prophecy[k] that is in no way possessed by the imaginative forms in us.[8]

Fourth, if the material intellect were identical with the Agent Intellect, it would turn out that two[l] things having different definitions would be numerically one. But this is utterly absurd. For, since the term 'apprehension' is used essentially in the definition of 'intellect' [and not merely verbally],[9] and because it is the nature of the material intellect to apprehend objects of

---

6. That is, the Agent Intellect is a medium, just as light is a medium.

7. *Metaphysics* 7.11. 1036b2.

8. Infra, bk. 2, passim.

9. Husik suggests the adoption of the reading of Paris, B. N., Ms. Hébreu 721: A₂. ההשגה לקוחה בדבר בגדר השכל . The underlined word בדבר is added. According to his interpretation this word has the force of contrasting a real, or essential, definition (בדבר) of some concept with a nominal, or verbal, definition (בשם) of it. In this context, this contrast requires us to discriminate between the kinds of apprehension involved in the two intellects under discussion. Isaac Husik, "Studies in Gersonides," *JQR* n.s.8 (1917–18):117; hereafter "Studies in Gersonides [2]."

Averroes makes the same point in a different context. In attempting to distinguish between divine and human cognition, he claims that the term 'cognition' in this context is homonymous. Gersonides takes this argument and uses it against Averroes in the subject under discussion. Averroes, *The Decisive Treatise Determining What the Connection Is Between Religion and Philosophy*, trans. G. Hourani, in R. Lerner and M. Mahdi, *Medieval Political Philosophy* (Ithaca, New York, 1972), p. 172.

knowledge pertaining to the sublunar world but not to apprehend the Agent Intellect, whereas it is the nature of the Agent Intellect to apprehend itself but not the objects of knowledge pertaining to the sublunar world (as Averroes points out in his discussion of the material intellect)—it is evident that the definition and essence of the Agent Intellect differ from that of the material intellect. But if we were to claim that the two are identical, then two things of different natures would be numerically identical, which is absolutely absurd. For it is impossible for them to be one in species; all the more so is it impossible for them to be numerically identical.

Fifth, Averroes's claim that the Agent Intellect does not know itself as a matter of accident because it is conjoined with us can be understood in two ways. Either it does not know itself at all so long as it is conjoined with us, and the cause of this lack of self-knowledge would then be external and accidental; or it knows itself continuously insofar as it is [considered in itself], i.e., essentially, but not insofar as it is conjoined with us. This [latter] interpretation would then be comparable to what is said of a builder when he is building, i.e., he is not building insofar as he is a man, since in the act of building the builder builds qua builder not qua man; for he builds insofar as he has an idea of the building not insofar as he is a man, since not every man is a builder.

Now if Averroes intends the first interpretation, let us put the following question to him: What is the cause that prevents the Agent Intellect from knowing itself except the transformation of its nature because of its conjunction with us? Or is it because human nature prevents it from having this kind of cognition, as Plato suggested in his metaphor of the Forms being hidden because of the immaturity of youth?[10] How is it possible for this intellect to be affected by human nature if it is a separate and self-subsistent intellect? And even if we were to admit that human nature frustrates this kind of cognition, how is possible that the Agent Intellect has, by virtue of this manifestation in us, the power to apprehend objects of knowledge pertaining to the sublunar world, a power that does not belong to its nature? Actually, it should not have any capacity because of this union save the capacity to know itself [which is natural to it], except that this union with us has blocked this knowledge, since this intellect has not been transformed by virtue of this union. Actually, it is not possible to explain this [lack of self-knowledge] without assuming that the Agent Intellect *has* experienced

---

10. *Be-leḥut be-'et ha-na'arut.* Cf. Averroes, *Epitome of Parva Naturalia*, p. 31; idem, *Commentary on Plato's* Republic, trans. Erwin I. J. Rosenthal (Cambridge, England 1956), p. 196; Aristotle, *On Memory* 450b1ff, 453b5ff.

substantial change as the result of this union. But this is impossible; since it does not change at all, for it is free from matter in every respect. Even if we were to grant the possibility of such a change, another difficulty of considerable weight arises: there would be no Agent Intellect to bring about this change, since the Agent Intellect has already changed by virtue of this union and has become a [mere] disposition; and it is impossible for it to have simultaneously its previous ontological status and the status which it has now acquired as the result of this change.[11] Moreover, it would follow that there is only one man at any given moment. For since there is only one Agent Intellect, when this intellect is changed so as to become the material intellect of Reuben, it would be impossible for the intellect of Simon to be generated from it except after Reuben's death, when it returns to its original state before the existence of Reuben, from which it then can be transformed into the intellect of Simon. But all of this is utterly absurd.

On the other hand, if Averroes intended the second interpretation, i.e., the [Agent] Intellect continuously knows itself but not in so far as it is united with us, several problems ensue from this hypothesis. First, there would be no point in the material intellect's pursuit of knowledge of the sublunar world, and its efforts to acquire such knowledge would be superfluous and futile. The reason for this is as follows: since [by virtue of its identity with the Agent Intellect] it now apprehends the essence of the Agent Intellect continuously, and since this essence is really the conceived order of the sublunar world and the form by virtue of which all the objects of knowledge pertaining to the sublunar world are a unified system (which is the most perfect expression of their existence), as shall be explained later, it thereby understands these objects of knowledge continuously and perfectly, and there would be no gain[m] in its effort to obtain this knowledge.

Second, on this hypothesis the material intellect would not require sense-data in its apprehension of definitions, i.e., conceptual cognition,[12] which

---

11. If the Agent Intellect is changed as the result of union, then there must be a cause of this change. But on Averroes's theory all changes are the effects of the Agent Intellect! What, then, changes the Agent Intellect?

12. Aristotle distinguishes between the cognition of essences or definitions (*hasagah ziyurit*) which is, if achieved, infallible and propositional knowledge (*hasagah 'imutit*) which affirms or denies a property of some subject, and hence is fallible (Aristotle, *On the Soul* 3.6. 430a26ff; *Metaphysics* 1051b15–30). Gersonides compares propositional knowledge with the type of perceptual judgment that, according to Aristotle, is fallible: when a sense faculty asserts a property that is not proper, or unique, to it—e.g., if on the basis of only visual perceptual data we judge that an object is sweet or hard. The proper object of vision is color, and perceptual reports based upon visual data about the colors of objects are usually correct; whereas such reports about other properties can be wrong (Aristotle, *On the Soul* 2.6).

knowledge is the peculiar characteristic of the material intellect, as Aristotle has pointed out. Propositional knowledge [however], involves two factors: intellect[n] and sensation. Thus, in the latter error results, just as error occurs in perception, when the sense faculty makes a judgment about a sensation that is not its proper object, e.g., when we judge that a yellow object which we see is sweet because we have perceived that honey is yellow and that it is sweet. That on this hypothesis the material intellect can dispense with sensation in its apprehension of definitions can be proven as follows: Since [ex hypothesi] it apprehends continuously the essence of the Agent Intellect, and since the latter already contains the definitions of things in the sublunar world, it is clear that the material intellect would not require sensation for the knowledge of definitions. But this is obviously absurd. That the Agent Intellect possesses this knowledge follows from the fact that it knows the rational order of the sublunar world, and that this order is a unified system. One who knows this order in its entirety knows also its several[o] parts, since it is impossible to know a compound without knowing its elements. Accordingly, the Agent Intellect contains a conception of rational order obtaining in all individuals. But this knowledge does not depend upon the existent particular[p] individuals as[q] is the case in our propositional knowledge; for example, when we say "All men are rational" or "All animals have sensation."[13] For the Agent Intellect does not acquire its knowledge of this order from the individuals [in the sublunar world]; rather these individuals acquire their existence from the knowledge that the Agent Intellect possesses of this order. Therefore, we have not said that the Agent Intellect possesses propositional knowledge of the same sort as acquired by the material intellect. Rather, it necessarily possesses knowledge of definitions, as we have explained; for such cognition is not contingent upon the individuals that exist [in the sublunar world].

Third, even though Averroes were to say that he means that the [material] intellect continuously knows[r] the Agent Intellect but not insofar as the latter is united with us, there is no way to avoid postulating a change in the Agent Intellect. For if the Agent Intellect does not change by virtue of this union, we would like to ask Averroes what nature has the Agent Intellect acquired by virtue of this union, so that it can apprehend objects of knowledge pertaining to the sublunar world, since according to its own nature it does not apprehend them? On this hypothesis, such knowledge necessarily accrues to the Agent Intellect insofar as it is mixed with our soul; accordingly, it

---

13. In the latter cases of universal judgments our knowledge is derived from the observations we have of particular individuals. Aristotle, *Posterior Analytics* 2:19.

would possess features that are common to the properties of the sensitive soul as well as to the properties of the Agent Intellect. That is, it would apprehend the objects of knowledge pertaining to the sublunar world that are composites of sensation and intellect, as has been explained by Averroes in his commentary on *On the Soul*. We would, therefore, like to ask Averroes to inform us what kind of composition has given rise to this [newly acquired] nature of the Agent Intellect. Is it the kind of composition where the constituent individuals still possess in actuality their original identity, i.e., composition by association? Or is it that kind[s] of composition wherein all the elements are completely mixed so that they do not in actuality retain their original identity, i.e., composition by blending?[14] If the former, then no new nature is thereby generated[t] from these elements; rather they possess the same nature as before. How, then, has the Agent Intellect acquired by this kind of composition a power not natural to it, i.e., the capacity to apprehend objects of knowledge pertaining to the sublunar world? This is utterly baffling on the assumption that this[u] new nature has been generated by this kind of composition, as has been just explained. If, on the other hand, the composition is that of a complete blending, then the material intellect would necessarily be different from the Agent Intellect; for the elements that have been blended together no longer exist in actuality after combination in the resulting blend, which is contrary to Averroes's assumption concerning this intellect. Moreover, the Agent Intellect would have changed essentially,[v] which is in no way possible. Since all of this leads to absurdities, Averroes's theory of the material intellect is clearly false.

Sixth,[15] if Averroes maintains that the material intellect is really identical with the Agent Intellect but that it has the power to apprehend the objects of knowledge pertaining to the sublunar world insofar as it is conjoined with us, the following dilemma ensues. Either insofar as it is conjoined with us it is numerically one, as Averroes himself claims—for the Agent Intellect, which is numerically one, has only two aspects: the aspect in which it is united with us and the aspect[w] in which it is not united with us. Or, insofar as it is conjoined with us it is numerically many. If it is alleged that the material intellect is numerically one when it is conjoined with us, then all the material intellects of all men would [actually] be numerically one, and

---

14. Gersonides is referring here to Aristotle's distinction between σύγκειμαι, and μίγνυμι (*Metaphysics* 7.14. 1039b6–7). In medieval Hebrew terminology, the former was given the name *harkabah shekhunit*, the latter *harkabah mizgit* (Wolfson, *Crescas' Critique of Aristotle*, p. 564).

15. This is the sixth of the objections to Averroes's general theory. The previous three objections were difficulties relevant to the fifth objection raised by Gersonides against the general theory.

these intellects would be attributed to them as one thing. From this the absurd consequence would follow that in the very same thing two contrary conditions would be simultaneously present. For the intellect of Reuben would know something, whereas the intellect of Simon would either be ignorant of it or be mistaken about it; so that the very same intellect would be simultaneously knowledgeable and ignorant with respect to the same question. Moreover, if this doctrine were true, I do not see why the intellect of Reuben does not use the sense-data apprehended by Simon. For when it is assumed that this intellect requires the senses in what it knows, it is evident that what is sensed by one man alone would be sufficient for [the presence] of the conception[x] of what is sensed in *all* men. But this is absurd.

On the other hand, if the material intellect is said to be many in so far as it is conjoined in us and by virtue of the particular relations it would have with individual men, several difficulties ensue. First, what was postulated to be separate is now not separate. The separate forms differ from other forms because they differ only qualitatively, whereas material forms differ among themselves both qualitatively and quantitatively. Qualitative diversity, for example, is illustrated in the sentence, "The form of a horse is different from the form of an ass." Quantitative diversity, for example, is illustrated in the sentence, "The form of this horse is different from the form of a second horse." Accordingly, since the material intellect can be diversified quantitatively (because it has been assumed that it is differentiated according to the diversity of the subjects of which it is the form), it is thereby not separate; for a separate form is not multiplied according to the diversity of subjects of which it is the form. But it has been alleged that the material intellect is identical with the Agent Intellect, which is separate. This [consequence] is absolutely false.

Second, on this hypothesis the Agent Intellect, which is numerically one, would now not only be many, but be infinitely numerous. For when the material intellect is identified with the Agent Intellect, and when on this hypothesis it is assumed that there are an infinite number of material intellects, the Agent Intellect, which [was thought to] be numerically one, now becomes infinite in number. But this is utterly false. There are many other absurdities that follow from Averroes's theory; but those that we have mentioned are worthy of notice and sufficient to show the absurdity of this position.

The aforementioned view of the more modern thinkers is also false, and its absurdity can be shown in many ways.[16] First, this view is self-

---

16. This view maintains that the material intellect, although a separate substance, is indeed generated, but not from anything else.

contradictory.[y] They maintain that this form is separate and generated.[z] Now since it is separate it is not capable of numerical differentiation [as has been demonstrated earlier]. If, for example, the form of Reuben which is now generated is the very same form of Simon who was existing before Reuben's birth, then the form of Reuben was actually existing before its own generation.[a1] Similarly, all human intellects would exist before their own generation. Then they would be nongenerated; but it has been assumed that they are generated. So the view is self-contradictory.

Second, this theory actually posits two different generations for each individual man, i.e., one generation for the individual intellect and another generation for the human body. But this is absurd, since one man is now actually two insofar as each of his parts exists independently and separately. A thing that is numerically one can be many in definition so long as the parts of the definition constitute a unit, i.e., one part is the completion of the other part of the definition and inheres in it. Thus, the individual is[b1] actually one although potentially many. This has been explained in the *Metaphysics*.[17] But when there is no unity between the parts of the definition [as in this case], the defined entity is actually two things. Themistius's theory also implies this difficulty, since it too maintains that the material intellect is separate and independently existing. Similarly, Averroes's theory is in a sense subject to this difficulty; for it maintains that the material intellect is identical with the Agent Intellect, which is separate and independently existing. Hence [on this identification] the material intellect would be separate and independently existing. And so the above[c1] absurdity results.

Moreover, it can be demonstrated in a different way that the hypothesis of the recent thinkers entails that something that is supposedly one is really numerically many. It is evident that from many generable things one object cannot arise unless there is a single process of generation for the whole group by virtue of which they become one[d1] thing. For example, in the case of fire and the other elements—each one of which is generated by itself—a single thing derives from them only if there is one process of generation for all of them together by virtue of which they become one thing, i.e., they are compounded[e1] and mixed together, and one thing is thereby generated from them. For an individual thing is generated by one process of generation, and whatever has one process of generation is numerically one. This is obvious. Hence, whatever is produced by many processes is itself numerically many.[18]

---

17. Aristotle, *Metaphysics* 7.12–14.

18. According to this hypothesis, the intellect and the body are distinct substances, having different origins. Gersonides argues that these substances are distinct individuals. Thus, any given person is actually two things.

Third, since this hypothesis claims that this material intellect is generated and exists independently [i.e., it is a substance], it entails that this intellect is some kind of form. But in so far as the intellect is, on this view, mixed with some form, it thereby fails to apprehend other forms; or if[f1] it apprehends them it does so[g1] incorrectly, as we have already pointed out. But this is clearly false, since it has been demonstrated that this intellect has the power to apprehend the truth. This difficulty arises also for Themistius, as we have already mentioned.[19]

Fourth, on this hypothesis sensation would be irrelevant to knowledge, so that we would know things without having perceived them, just as we know them by means of sense perception. For, how would it be possible for the sense-data to be relayed to the intellect if there is no unity between the intellect and the senses?[20] Would it be possible for me[h1] to know what you have apprehended when you have apprehended it?[21] This absurdity is also entailed by Themistius's doctrine, according to which this form [the material intellect] is separate and independently existing. Similarly, this absurdity follows from Averroes's theory; for from this doctrine it follows that this form [the material intellect] is separate and independently existing, as we have already mentioned.

Fifth, if the material intellect is separate and exists by itself[i1] [i.e., it is ontologically an independent substance], how is it that it cannot perform its function when the senses and the other perceptual faculties of the soul are simultaneously in operation? Would it be necessary that if you are engaged in doing something that I be thereby hindered in my[j1] work? The reason why [the senses and the intellect are so related that one faculty must be inoperative while another is functioning] is that the soul constitutes a unit, as Aristotle has pointed out.[22] But if it is claimed that there is no unity between the intellect and the other cognitive faculties of the soul, then there is no reason why the operations of the latter should prevent the former from functioning. Someone might object that this [functioning] does accrue to the material intellect, since it takes from the senses principles from which it brings forth[k1] what it knows.[23] This objection is absurd. For even if the

---

19. Supra, chap. 3.

20. On this theory, the intellect and the body are two distinct substances.

21. That is, since sensation is irrelevant, no principle of individuation is present to differentiate my knowledge from someone else's; for as pure minds we are all the same.

22. Aristotle, On the Soul 1.5. Cf. Averroes, Epitome of Parva Naturalia, pp. 27–28, 94, 101, n. 50a.

23. That is, the initial assumption that when the senses are at work then the intellect must be inoperative is now rejected. Although the thesis that the material intellect is separable from

intellect does possess principles acquired from the senses concerning a given problem, it is apparent that it cannot function while the senses are engrossed in their own operations. This difficulty is entailed by Themistius's theory of a separate, self-subsistent intellect and by Averroes's doctrine, from which it also follows that the intellect would be separate and self-subsistent,[l] as we have already pointed out.

Sixth, on this hypothesis it would follow that one intellect would receive simultaneously contrary conditions. For insofar as it is claimed that this intellect is separate and self-subsistent, all simultaneously existing human intellects are numerically one, since a separate form is not individuated by a plurality of subjects. Consequently [since it usually is the case that] the intellect of Reuben [or some other individual] knows the answer to a particular problem but the intellect of Simon [or another person] is either completely ignorant or in error, one and the same intellect would be simultaneously wise and stupid with respect to the same question. [But this is absurd.]

Seventh, this view asserts the contrary of Aristotle's principle that forms are generated only accidentally, i.e., in so far as the form is manifested in a subject [that is generated].[24] This position maintains, however, that this form is generated essentially.

Eighth, the generation of this form is either from a subject or ex nihilo. If the former, then the subject must have changed so that the former could be generated from it. But it has been proven that whatever changes is a body; hence the subject would be[m] a body. Now since it is evident that a body does not change into something that is not a body, it follows that this form would have to be a body or the possessor of a body, which is contrary to their hypothesis. If, on the other hand, it is claimed that this form is generated essentially ex nihilo—as is suggested by their language, for they call this generation "creation" (beri'ah)—this contradicts what Aristotle has demonstrated in Book one of the *Physics*, that every generation, essential or accidental, requires a subject.[25] Moreover, since ex hypothesi this form is generated after it did not exist previously, it necessarily existed potentially before its actual existence. But since a potentiality does not exist separately, it requires a subject in which it inheres. Thus, it is impossible to maintain that this form was generated from no subject. Now since it was previously proved that this form cannot be generated from a subject, it[n] is evident that this

---

the body is still maintained, it is now suggested that the material intellect employs sense-data for its knowledge.

24. Aristotle, *Metaphysics* 7.8.

25. That is, there is no creation ex nihilo (Aristotle, *Physics* 1.5). In Bk. 4, pt. 1. chaps. 17–18, Gersonides argues for this thesis in detail.

form cannot be assumed to be generated essentially either from a subject or ex nihilo. Hence, it is false to say that this form is generated essentially. There are many other absurdities, but those that we have mentioned are sufficient to refute this doctrine.

Since the doctrines of Averroes, Themistius, and the more recent thinkers correspond to the number of possible interpretations that can be given to the hypothesis that the subject of this disposition is a separate and self-subsistent[o1] intellect, and since it is evident from what we have established that all of these doctrines are false, the thesis that the subject of this disposition is an intellect is also false. That these doctrines correspond to the number of possible interpretations of this general hypothesis [i.e., that the subject of this disposition is a separate intellect] will now be shown. If the subject for this disposition is an intellect, then this subject is [related] to it essentially as Themistius and the recent philosophers maintain; or it is a subject [related] to it only accidentally, as Averroes suggests. Moreover, this intellect qua subject is either ungenerated, as Themistius and Averroes claim, or generated, as the more recent thinkers maintain. Now, since it is possible to construe these doctrines differently—e.g., if this intellect[p1] is the subject for this disposition only in an accidental sense, it could be construed as an intellect different from the Agent Intellect; or it could be suggested that this disposition has an intellect for its subject in an accidental sense but that it is generated, a view that has not been advanced by any of our predecessors— it is therefore necessary to prove in a general way that it is impossible for the subject of this disposition to be a self-subsistent intellect.

Suppose it were possible for the subject of this disposition to be a self-subsistent intellect [as Themistius, Averroes, and the recent thinkers maintain]. The following dilemma can now be put to them: either this disposition receives the objects of knowledge mixed with its subject, or it does not receive them in this manner. The former alternative has already been proven by Aristotle to be false; for it is impossible for it to receive the objects of knowledge in such a way that it is mixed with a particular form.[26] If, on the other hand, it receives them without admixture with its subject, the subject itself does not then apprehend the objects of knowledge. Now either the subject does apprehend or it doesn't apprehend [them]. If it doesn't, then we have a contradiction, i.e., an intellect that has no power of cognition.[q1] But if we say that it does apprehend, would that I knew *what* it does apprehend! Either it apprehends the objects of knowledge that the disposition embedded[r1] in it has received; or that which it apprehends is in some way

---

26. Aristotle, *On the Soul* 3.4.

related to these objects of knowledge as a form. If the former, then these objects of knowledge would exist in the subject both potentially and actually at the same time, which is absurd. If the latter, i.e., if that which it apprehends is that by virtue of which all the objects of knowledge received by the disposition are united, then this intellect would be either identical with the Agent Intellect (as shall be shown later in our discussion of the nature of the Agent Intellect), or it would be an intellect of even superior rank. In either case, it would possess this knowledge, for which it has the capacity to apprehend, in a perfect form; and it would[51] have a conception of each and every one of these objects of knowledge. Since it already has the disposition to receive these objects of knowledges in the form of concepts, it would turn out that it has simultaneously these concepts both potentially and actually, which is absurd. We have, therefore, demonstrated that all these absurdities are common to the three views that maintain that the subject of this disposition is a separate and self-subsistent intellect. It is quite clear then that it is absolutely false that the subject of this disposition is a separate and subsistent intellect.

CHAPTER V

AN EXPOSITION (AS BEST AS WE CAN PROVIDE) OF THE ESSENCE OF THE MATERIAL INTELLECT

NOW that we have demonstrated that the subject of this disposition is not an intellect, it is necessary to determine what is[a] its subject, since all capacities require subjects. This subject must be either a body or a soul, since there is no fourth possibility.[1] If we say that the soul is the subject of the material intellect, it would be so[b] only accidentally, since it is not the nature of forms to be the subjects of other forms.[2] Rather [when we say] that a form is a subject for another form [we mean] that the matter receives some forms via other forms.[3] This has been explained in *On the Soul*.[4] Accordingly, it follows that the body must be the subject for this disposition. Now, since the primary matter receives some forms in a primary manner [i.e., directly], as when it receives[5] an elemental form, and others indirectly, as for example in the case of a form of a thing of homogeneous parts made up from the elemental and secondary forms (i.e., it receives certain forms via other forms), and since it is clear that this disposition is not a form that the primary matter receives in the primary manner [i.e., directly], it is necessary that it is a form that the primary matter receives via other forms.

That this disposition is not one of the forms that is received by the primary matter directly can be demonstrated as follows. A form that is received in this manner is such that a compound body cannot be deprived of it, as has been

---

1. The third possibility—an intellect—has just been eliminated.

2. For Aristotle the soul of a living body is its form. Thus, to say that the soul is essentially the subject for this capacity is to say that a form is essentially the subject of other forms, since the material intellect is the power to apprehend the forms of other substances. But this claim has been shown to be false in the preceding chapters (Aristotle, *On the Soul* 2.1–2).

3. Cf. Husik, "Studies in Gersonides [2]," p. 121. Matter is the universal substratum of all change, including substantial change. Aristotle, *Metaphysics* 7.7, 8.1; *On Generation and Corruption* 1.3–4.

4. Aristotle, *On the Soul* 2.1–2.

5. Although the manuscripts have either בקבולו or בקבול , Husik suggests emending the text to כקבולו . Since the two letters ב and כ are often difficult to differentiate in medieval script, the emendation is plausible. It is adopted here since in the next clause the word כמו is used. Cf. Husik, "Studies in Gersonides [2]," p. 122.

explained in *On the Soul*.[6] For example, it is impossible for a compound body not to have one of the elemental forms, i.e.,[c] hot, cold, dryness,[d] or moisture; for these bodies receive the other forms by virtue of these [elementary] forms. But if this disposition is a form that is directly received by the primary matter, all compound bodies would then have minds—which is utterly false.[7]

Since it has been shown that this disposition must be a form that is received by the primary matter via other forms, one of the following alternatives must be true: either it is a form that the primary matter receives[e] before it receives the imaginative soul; or it receives the former after the latter. If the former alternative is accepted, then this disposition serves as a matter for the imaginative faculty, since the forms that come first serve as matter for those that come afterwards. But since that which serves as form is inseparable from that which is related to it as matter, as has been explained in *On the Soul*,[8] it would follow from this hypothesis that all animals having imagination would also have reason—which is completely absurd. Many animals do have imagination, but it would be manifestly false to say that they have reason. There is no point in going into this in detail. It would be absurd for a form to be present in a given species with none of the activities which should[f] derive from this form actually deriving from it. Hence, it must be that the body is the subject of this disposition via the imaginative faculty.[9] If it is assumed that the imaginative faculty is a part of the sensitive faculty, the body would then be[g] the subject of this disposition via the sensitive faculty, and hence the latter could be said to be the subject in some sense for this disposition. Now it is evident from Aristotle's discussion of this disposition that its receptivity for the objects of knowledge is a receptivity that is unmixed with its subject.[10] Its subject is necessary for its existence, not for its cognitive operations, as Alexander [maintains]. Since this form [disposition] is a form that the primary matter potentially receives, and since all such forms are generated, this particular form is therefore generated. The question whether this disposition is immortal after achieving cognitive perfection, or corruptible like the other material forms, will be discussed later.

---

6. A form that is received directly by a compound body is one that it cannot do without. Gersonides seems to be referring to Aristotle's initial definition of soul in Bk. 2 of *On the Soul*, especially chap. 1.

7. If the material intellect were a form that is received by matter directly, then the latter would never be free from it, as in the case of the elemental forms. Hence, *all* bodies would have this form and have minds, which is of course false. Cf. Husik, "Studies in Gersonides [2]," p. 123.

8. Aristotle, *On the Soul* 2.1.

9. That is, the second of the above alternatives is true.

10. Aristotle, *On the Soul* 3.4.

CHAPTER VI

AN EXPOSITION (AS BEST AS WE CAN PROVIDE IN THIS PLACE) OF THE ESSENCE OF THE AGENT INTELLECT

HAVING explained the nature of the material intellect, it is now fitting that we investigate whether it is immortal after having achieved[a] intellectual perfection. In his *Epitome of* On the Soul and in his shorter essays, Averroes has argued that if the material intellect is immortal, it is so only by virtue of its union with the Agent Intellect. Since the analysis of this union, no matter if it is possible for us or not, is impossible so long as we[b] do not know the nature of the Agent Intellect, it is necessary that we discuss the latter question. We shall not mention the opinions of the ancients, for we have not seen any writings by them on this topic.

It is evident that whatever has been brought forth from a state of potentiality to actuality requires the activity of an agent that has in actuality what the recipient has only in potentiality. The truth of this principle has been established and all doubts concerning it have been removed in the sciences of physics and metaphysics.[1] Hence, since it is clear from the nature of the material intellect that is has potentially the knowledge of the plan and order of the sublunary world, it is necessary that this order be known in some sense actually by the Agent Intellect. We have said "in some sense"[c] so that it is not required that this knowledge be the same in the agent as it is in the recipient when the latter [begins] to be actualized. For example, the form of a chair in the carpenter's mind is not identical with the form of the actual chair.[2] It is therefore necessary that we determine the manner in which the Agent Intellect does possess this knowledge.

Since the Agent Intellect imparts this knowledge to the material intellect successively [i.e., not all at once], it follows from what has preceded either that the Agent Intellect possesses *all* this knowledge, or that the material intellect is informed by a[d] plurality of agent intellects corresponding to the number of objects of knowledge it is capable of apprehending. The latter

---

1. Aristotle, *Physics* 3.1–3; *Metaphysics* 9, passim.
2. Aristotle, *Metaphysics* 9.8.

alternative is utterly absurd. An activity is one in an essential way only insofar as it derives from one agent, unless of course there is an ordered relation of agents each subservient to the other, as in the case of the master-craft which has under it several [different] subordinate crafts. In the latter case, each activity derives from one agent, i.e., the master-craft; for it is the latter who directs all the subsidiary crafts. For example, the carpenter cuts all the boards from which a ship will be made, and the boat-builder uses them in making the boat. In actuality, however, it is the master-craft that is the [real] agent in this matter, since it directs all the subservient activities in such a way that the product resulting from the latter will be in accordance with the [plan] of the master-craft. For example, the boat-builder directs the carpenter in such a way that the boards are cut so as they can be made into a boat.[3] Consequently, since the actualization of the material intellect with respect to the objects of knowledge for which it has the capacity [to apprehend] constitutes one activity—for this actualization is the very goal of the material intellect, and the true goal of something that is one [i.e., the material intellect] is itself one in number—the realization of this activity in the material intellect derives from one agent. And so it is necessary that the Agent Intellect possess complete knowledge [of the sublunary world]. And since the Agent Intellect also imparts to the material intellect the various relationships among these objects of knowledge—i.e., some forms are the perfections of others ultimately leading to one form that is the perfection of all of them, as, for example, the form of man, which is received by the primary matter by means of other forms which it is capable of receiving, is the very perfection of the latter forms—the Agent Intellect must know all of these plans as an ordered and unified totality. And it is in this sense that they constitute a unity in the Agent Intellect.[4]

This point can be demonstrated in a different way. If these various objects of knowledge were not united in the mind of the Agent Intellect, the latter would be many, since these objects of knowledge would be many and they constitute the very essence of the Agent Intellect; for it has been proven that

---

3. For the metaphor of the master-craft and the subordinate crafts, see Aristotle, *Metaphysics* 1.1 and *Nicomachean Ethics* 1.1.

4. Gersonides conceives of the Agent Intellect as exemplifying the various formal structures and arrangements that the terrestrial world manifests. Indeed, the terrestrial order exists in the Agent Intellect in a more perfect way, especially since in the Agent Intellect this order is unified and complete. This notion has Philonic overtones, reminiscent of the Philo's concept of the Logos. Philo, *On Creation of the Universe*, 2–5; Harry Wolfson, *Philo*, 2 vols. (Cambridge, Mass. 1948), 1, chap. 9.

the intellect and that which is known are identical.[5] But it has been previously demonstrated that the Agent Intellect must be[e] one in number, which is contrary [to the conclusion of this hypothesis]. Hence, it is evident that the Agent Intellect knows all these plans insofar as they exist in it as a unity; and in this way it is itself one. The material intellect, however, receives these objects of knowledge from the Agent Intellect with difficulty because it needs the senses [for its cognition]; hence, it happens that it does not apprehend them as an ordered system of plans but in a diffuse and disordered way.

One might object to our theory of the nature of the Agent Intellect saying that it does not follow from the role of the Agent Intellect in bringing about knowledge in the material intellect that it itself possesses this knowledge. It might be possible to argue that the relationship between the Agent Intellect and this knowledge is *not* like the relationship between the form in the mind of the teacher and the form acquired[f] by the pupil, or like the relationship between the object of sense and the form obtained from it by the senses.[6] Rather, the correct relationship is that which obtains between light and the visible objects: the former makes the latter, which are potentially visible, actually seen but without the colors [themselves] being actually in it. The Agent Intellect too makes the imaginative forms, which are potentially the objects of knowledge, actual objects of knowledge. It is not necessary, however, that the Agent Intellect itself possess these objects of knowledge.[7]

Our reply is as follows. If the Agent Intellect transforms that which is potentially knowable in the imaginative forms into an actual object of knowledge—that is, the general nature which is embedded in the image along with all the material features that make the image particular—without itself having cognition of this object of knowledge, this must happen either[g] by its endowing the image [itself] with a nature [i.e., power] of making intelligible to the material intellect the general nature [or universal] embedded in the image; or[g] by its endowing the material intellect [itself] with the power to apprehend the general nature embedded in the image. If we assume that the Agent Intellect endows the image with this nature[h] [or power], to make intelligible the general nature[i] embedded in the image—just as the light makes visible that which is potentially visible when it shines upon the latter—I would like to know the precise change that takes place in the general nature embedded

---

5. Aristotle, *Metaphysics* 12.7; Maimonides, *Guide* 1.68, especially Narboni's commentary ad loc.

6. The latter cases are often used by the Aristotelians in this context. Cf. Aristotle, *Metaphysics* 9.5–6; *Physics* 8.5; *On the Soul* 3.4.

7. Averroes, *Drei Abhandlungen*, 2d essay; idem, *Long Commentary on De Anima*, in Hyman and Walsh, *Philosophy in the Middle Ages*, p. 323; Aristotle, *On the Soul*, 3.430a 16–17.

in the image by virtue of which it becomes an [actual] object of knowledge. For[j] it doesn't seem possible to account for this change in a reasonable manner, even if one is prepared to concoct a theory out of thin air. Moreover, the material, or accidental features [of the image] can also be by themselves objects of cognition in so far as they are considered apart from their subject; for they can be understood as distinct essences, since every accidental quality can be apprehended in some way.[8] Hence, it is not possible to maintain that a nature [i.e., power] is given to some part of the image, i.e., the general nature which is known in it, by virtue of which the material intellect can pick out from the image the general nature; for there is nothing in the image [that] cannot be apprehended by the [intellect[k]].[9] Now since this hypothesis is false, it is evident that it cannot be maintained that the Agent Intellect endows the image with a nature[l] [or power], by virtue of which the general nature, which is embedded in the image along with corporeal features [i.e., accidental properties], is transformed such that the material intellect can[m] apprehend it.

It is also demonstrable that the Agent Intellect cannot endow the material intellect with a nature [or power] to apprehend this object of knowledge in this image. If this were possible, either this nature would be the same for every[n] object of knowledge that it knows; or the Agent Intellect would endow the material intellect with a specific nature for each of the objects of knowledge. If this nature is the same for the apprehension[o] of all the objects of knowledge, it would follow that the material intellect would not be able because of this [power] to pick out the general nature in the image from all

---

8. Redness, an accidental property, is as much an object of knowledge as the concept of a substance, man.

9. This clause is difficult, and the difficulty is aggravated by the discrepancies of the manuscript readings, which are listed below:

Leipzig, and Bodleian 376:

וזה כי אין שם דבר בה ולא יתכן בה שיהיה מושכל

Paris 723: וזה כי אין שם דבר בה לא יתכן בו שיהיה מושכל

Vatican 28: וזה כי אין שם דבר לא יתכן בו שיהיה מושכל

I have adopted the reading of the Vatican manuscript, since it fits the argument. Gersonides claims that the sense-image of a thing cannot by itself explain cognition of the general nature, or form, of that thing. The Agent Intellect must itself possess or exemplify this form. In the previous sentence it is maintained in behalf of this claim that since every sense-image exhibits the accidental features of a thing, e.g., the redness of some rose, and that since these features can be apprehended in some sense, i.e., as general characteristics, there would be no way for the material intellect by itself to differentiate the essence, or general nature, of the rose from any of its accidental features. The image is, so to speak, "too rich." In the sentence which begins "Hence . . ." Gersonides concludes that the image itself is not sufficient to account for knowledge of the general nature, and he repeats the reason in the clause, "for there is. . . ." Cf. Gersonides, *Commentary on the* Megillot, 2c–d, 10c, 15b, 33b.

the accidental features, since each one of the latter features would be [by virtue of this power] an object of knowledge. It would turn out then that the intellect would apprehend the image as it is [i.e., in all its particularity].[10] If [on the other hand] the Agent Intellect gives the material intellect different natures for each object of knowledge, it would turn out that one and the same agent gives to one and the same recipient different natures. But this is absurd. Moreover, it would be utterly false to maintain that the material intellect is given such a nature [or power] to receive the objects of knowledge; for if it had such a power it would thereby be a form, and such a form would prevent it from receiving these objects of knowledge, as has been explained. But this is contrary[p] to the initial hypothesis. It is therefore evident that it is impossible for the Agent Intellect to give either the imaginative form or the material intellect such a nature [without the Agent Intellect itself having the objects of knowledge]. Accordingly, it is clear that if the Agent Intellect is responsible for making what is potentially knowable in the imaginative form actually known, it accomplishes this by abstracting the general nature from all the accidental properties of the image. In so far as it abstracts this nature, it knows it, unless its process of abstraction is merely accidental. But if its abstracting is merely an accident, the correct apprehension [of these natures] would occur infrequently by means of this abstraction.[q] This is, however, absurd.

It should be clear from our analysis that it does not follow that the Agent Intellect apprehends the accidental qualities with which the general nature is associated. For it is quite possible to abstract something from another thing and [just] know the abstracted thing[r] alone. This is obvious. In this way the sense of vision perceives the color of a body[s] without [necessarily] seeing all the other properties of that body.

Furthermore, the Agent Intellect makes knowable things for which there are no imaginative forms in which they would be potentially knowable. Averroes mentions [this kind of cognitive communication] in his [commentary] upon [Aristotle's] *Parva Naturalia*; and this is indeed the case, as we shall show in the second book of this treatise; for this is the cognition received by man from the Agent Intellect in dreams, divination, or prophecy.[11] Con-

---

10. In the Aristotelian epistemology the particular features of an entity are strictly speaking not known by the intellect. The latter apprehends the essence or nature of the thing, not its idiosyncratic features. Thus, in zoology we study the general properties of the species, not the particular features of an individual member of the species. Aristotle, *Posterior Analytics* 1.24, 31; *On the Soul* 2.5; Thomas Aquinas, *Summa Theologiae*, 1., q. 86 a.l; Gersonides, *Commentary on the* Megillot 30b.

11. Averroes, *Epitome of Parva Naturalia*, pp. 39–53.

sequently, it is evident that this kind of knowledge is not transmitted by the imaginative form alone, but requires that the Agent Intellect actually possess the knowledge of which it informs the material intellect.

[Nor is the analogy with light correct.] Light makes colors, which were formerly only potentially visible, actually visible merely accidentally. It does so by preparing the transparent medium [air] so that the colors [will be visible] in some sense in it. Then [the medium] will be able to stimulate the visual faculty to receive the colors.[12] The sense of sight cannot apprehend its objects without a medium, as has been explained in *On the Soul*. Since the medium does not receive the impression of color except if it is clear, and it is the light that makes it clear, it is evident that the light is not in this context the [real] agent, but only that which prepares the medium to be active. The Agent Intellect, however, is an agent essentially. For the agent for an intellect must itself be an intellect, and this means that the Agent Intellect is an agent in so far as it possesses [the knowledge] of the plan and order [of the terrestial domain]. Hence, it necessarily[t] possesses such knowledge in the manner that has been explained.

Moreover, since the agent responsible for the [existence] of all beings in the sublunar world must possess the knowledge of the order [obtaining in this world]—just as the craftsman must have an idea of the order obtaining among the things he is to create—and since it is necessary, as we shall show, that this agent be the Agent Intellect (whose existence has been proven in *On the Soul*), it follows that the Agent Intellect possesses the knowledge of the order obtaining in the sublunary world. It does not follow from this merely that the Agent Intellect has knowledge of the sublunary world; rather, it possesses it in a perfect form, i.e., in a unified manner. Again, this is analogous to the way in which the craftsman comprehends the boards, bricks, and stones, from which the house is to be constructed, not merely as materials but as elements in a total framework, the form of a house, of which the materials are parts. This is the most perfect aspect of their existence.

That this is the case I shall now prove. The primary matter is affected by the Agent Intellect in such a way that it receives the various perfections by gradations; i.e., it receives some of them via others and some for the sake of others, so that ultimately the final perfection is attained for which it was potentially receptive. To this perfection all the others are subordinate. It is clear, therefore, the whole process of generation in the primary matter is a unified affair, since one goal is set for it. Accordingly, the agent responsible for these perfections must know them as a unitary system; in this way the

---

12. Aristotle, *On the Soul* 2.7. 419a13; Husik, "Studies in Gersonides [2]," pp. 127–28.

whole generation is directed towards its goal. Again, this is clearly analogous to the craftsman who makes the bricks for the house as well as the house; his knowledge of the plan involves the way in which these bricks are going to be used as materials[u] in the house, and it is for this goal of building the form of a house that he makes them. Accordingly, the Agent Intellect, on my hypothesis, knows the order of the sublunar world in the most perfect way, i.e., as a unitary system.

That the agent responsible for the existence of the things in the sublunar world is[v] the Agent Intellect, whose existence has been proven in *On the Soul*,[13] can be demonstrated as follows. It has been shown in chapter sixteen of the *Book of Animals* that there is an agent at work in the [generation of] plants and animals and that this agent is an intellect. Aristotle calls it "the soul that emanates from the heavenly bodies," which, he says, is a divine power, and an intellect.[14] Many of the modern philosophers have called it "the Agent Intellect." The seed [alone] is not sufficient to generate a soul because it consists of homogeneous parts and it is not [an intrinsic] part of the organism such that we could say that in it resides [some] animate power; for it is merely the last residue of the nutriment, as has been explained in the *Book of Animals*. Now it is possible that in the seed there is [some kind] of heat which is similar in certain ways to the natural heat of the generated organism, i.e., the proportioned heat,[15] which may emanate from the heavenly bodies via the rays of the sun and of the other heavenly bodies, as Aristotle has mentioned.[16] But it is not possible for the seed to possess the

---

13. Aristotle, *On the Soul* 3.5.

14. The *Book of Animals* consisted of three Aristotelian biological treatises: *Generation of Animals*, *History of Animals*, and *Parts of Animals*. Gersonides is referring here to *Generation of Animals* 2.3. 736b28–29. Cf. M. Steinschneider, *Hebraische Übersetzungen*, p. 143.

Gersonides' reference to Aristotle's characterization of this intellect as the soul that emanates from the heavenly bodies is not clear. In the passage from *Generation of Animals* Aristotle maintains that in the process of organic generation there is an external intellectual factor that can be said to be divine. But there is in that passage no mention of the emanation of this intellect from the heavenly bodies. In Bk. 5, pt. 3, Gersonides will examine the precise nature of the Agent Intellect, and he will argue that this intellect does emanate from all the heavenly bodies. Perhaps he is running ahead of himself here by identifying the Agent Intellect with the intellect referred to by Aristotle in *Generation of Animals* and by attributing this view along with his own theory of the Agent Intellect to Aristotle. Indeed, in the next sentence he mentions that the "modern thinkers" explicitly make this identification. Perhaps he is including himself under this rubric.

15. The concepts of natural heat (*ha-ḥom ha-tib'i*; ἡ τῆς ψυσέως θερμότης), animate power (*koaḥ nafshi*; δύναμις ψυχῆς, and proportioned heat (*ha-ḥom ha-meshu'ar*; θερμότης σύμμετρος play important roles in Aristotle's biology, especially in his embryology (Aristotle, *Generation of Animals*, passim). Gersonides discusses these notions in greater detail in Bk. 5, pt. 3, chap. 3, where explanatory notes on these technical concepts have been provided.

16. Aristotle, *Generation of Animals*, 2.3, 737a3–4.

formative power[17] to form[w] and create the limbs [of the body] in the marvelous and wise way which men have wearied themselves in trying to understand fully. For the heat of the seed cannot accomplish this unless a divine power, i.e., an intellect, is joined with it, as Aristotle has mentioned according to what we have found in that which has been translated from his language [Greek] for us by the Christians.[18] This is so because this power performs its operations without the use of an instrument,[19] since the seed has no instrument because of its homogeneous nature. This power also performs its operations in [the generation] of the limbs without using a specific instrument. [On the other hand,] parts of the limbs are generated in the organism from [a single] chief limb[20] of that organism and from the other limbs according to their various relationships [with each other]. For example, the part of the

---

17. *Ha-koaḥ ha-mazayyer*. This term seems to correspond to Galen's δύναμις διαπλαστική (Galen, *On the Natural Faculties* 1.5–6). Gersonides discusses this power in Bk. 5, pt. 3, chap. 3. In the *Commentary Kol Yehudah* to Judah Halevi's *Kuzari* 5:21 there is a citation from Gersonides' discussion of this topic and further elaboration upon it. For Aquinas's discussion of this topic, see his *Summa Contra Gentiles* 2.88–89.

18. This passage is especially vexing, and not only because of the textual variants. Over forty years ago Jacob Teicher used this passage to argue that Gersonides knew Latin well enough to use at least Latin translations of Aristotle and perhaps consulted other philosophical works in Latin as well. (Jacob Teicher, "Studi preliminari sulla dottrina della conoscenza di Gersonide," *Rendiconti della Reale Academia Nazionale dei Lincei*, ser. 6, vol. 8 (1932), p. 504.) A similar claim has been made more recently by Shlomo Pines, although it is based on a different kind of argument. (Shlomo Pines, "Scholasticism after Thomas Aquinas and the Teachings of Hasdai Crescas and His Predecessors," *The Israel Academy of Sciences and Humanities Proceedings* 1 (1966), no. 11.)

However this claim is ultimately decided, it cannot be supported by this passage alone. Teicher's argument is weakened by his failure to translate one crucial word in this passage לנו In the phrase in question, במה שהועתק לנו מלשונו מן הנוצרים, the term לנו indicates that a translation from the original Greek was made for Gersonides. Although it is possible that, as Teicher claims, Gersonides could have read this passage in a Latin translation, it is just as possible, indeed even more likely, that some Christian scholar translated the relevant passage in Aristotle into Provençal, the one language that can be safely said to have been a lingua franca for Gersonides and his Christian colleagues. There is no compelling reason to infer from this passage alone that he himself read a Latin translation of the Greek. My argument has been supported recently by Charles Touati in his *La pensée philosophique et théologique de Gersonide*, p. 38; cf. I. Husik, *A History of Medieval Jewish Philosophy* p. 326.

19. In this discussion and in subsequent discussions throughout the book I usually translate the word *keli* as 'instrument'. This word corresponds to Aristotle's ὄργανον which is usually translated as 'instrument' or 'organ'. Since the latter term has in English a special reference to certain parts of the animal body, it is not always applicable in the specific context in Gersonides' argument. Hence, I use the more general term 'instrument', which is to be construed as connoting some kind of auxiliary or intermediary device that is employed by an agent in the performance of some activity.

20. In animals with blood, the chief (or first) limb is the heart. Aristotle, *Generation of Animals* 2.4. 740a3ff; 2.6. 742b1ff.

liver that is generated from the nutriment is generated via the heart, the liver, and the other organs of digestion that are relevant[x] to this process. Now if this is the case, i.e., this [formative] power creates the limbs in their entirety without using any instrument, whereas the power in the organism makes only a part of the limb and does so only by means of an instrument, it is evident that the former is different from the latter (although the latter is similar to it), and that it is infinitely superior to the latter. Nor is it possible to say that this superior power in the seed derives from the seed-bearer,[y] for the seed-bearer has no such marvelous power; it [merely] has the power to generate something like itself.

It would also be false [to assert] that the organism endows the nutriment with this animate power. If this were so, then the nutriment would have the nutritive soul[21] and the formative power, and it would then be that which is nourished [by having the nutritive soul], and the organism would not be that which is nourished by the nutriment.[z] For things that have the same kind of nutritive soul are such that it is impossible for one of them to be nourished from another. If this were possible, one part of the flesh in the hand, for example, would be nourished from another part of it. But this is absurd. In general, the nutriment is[a1] worked upon by an animate power in the organism that is being nourished, and in this way the nutriment becomes part of the organism. The nutriment [itself] does not have this animate power by means of which it can work upon something different from it; rather it has merely the disposition to be worked upon by something different from it. Now if this is true of the nutriment, all the more so is it true of that which is a residue of the nutriment [the seed]; for the latter is even less similar to that which is nourished.[22] Therefore, it is not possible for the seed to have a power of this kind deriving from the seed-bearer; for the seed is merely the residue of the nutriment, as we have mentioned. What the seed does possess is a kind of heat that is similar to the natural heat of the seed-bearer. But it is clear that this heat is not a soul; rather it is in some sense an instrument for the soul, as has been explained in the sciences. Hence, it has been shown that in reproduction a divine power, i.e., an intellect, is required, since this power does not use an instrument in its operations, as do the corporeal powers of the soul [e.g., sensation].

One might object that this power is not an intellect, since the activity of an intellect, i.e., cognition, is self-contained, whereas this power works upon

---

21. The nutritive soul is the set of capacities and functions involved in growth and development. Cf. Aristotle, *On the Soul* 2.2–3.

22. Aristotle, *Generation of Animals* 1.18.

something other than itself, as Averroes says in his *Epitome of* On the Soul.[23] That is, this power operates via the elemental heat in the semen, and hence should not[b1] be an intellect. In reply let us distinguish two kinds of activities characteristic of an intellect: (1) self-knowledge and (2) an activity that terminates in a body. The heavenly bodies illustrate [both kinds]. Their movers [the separate intelligences] have an activity that is self-contained, i.e., self-knowledge, and a motive activity that involves the nature of the heavenly bodies that are moved by them. It is fitting that from the latter activity this motion be accomplished[c1] [i.e., the motion] that is caused by separate intelligences.[d1] And by virtue of this activity they [the separate intelligences] exert some influence upon the terrestrial domain via the heavenly bodies, as has been explained in the sciences. Now the former kind of activity, i.e., self-knowledge, does not involve an instrument at all, whereas the latter type that operates on a body requires an instrument that makes the body capable of receiving the influences [emanating from these intelligences]. The same is true with respect to the practical intellect. Its self-knowledge does not require an instrument; but those activities that result from it do require some instrument, as is self-evident. It has been, therefore, demonstrated that this power is an intellect, as Aristotle has said.

Moreover, even if we were to admit that this generation is the result of some kind of power in the semen, it still would be impossible to attribute this generation to the semen alone without another cause that apprehends all the various orders [in the world] in a unified way. For the various forms which the primary matter can receive are such that some of them exist for others, as Aristotle has explained; hence the receiving of these forms [by the primary matter] right up to the completion of the generation is one [unified] process of generation.[24] Since a unified generated system, in so far as it is unified, is necessarily attributed[e1] to a single cause, the agent of these forms in their entirety must be one and must apprehend the goal towards which these things are generated. Otherwise, the attainment of the goal intended by this generation would be merely accidental, which is impossible in this kind of generation that occurs regularly. All the more so is it impossible for it to occur [by accident] when the processes are observed to be the best possible that can be realized for the intended goal. It is clear that this agent is separate [i.e., incorporeal]; for if it were a corporeal agent it would be

23. Averroes, *Epitome of Parva Naturalia*, p. 16; Aristotle, *Metaphysics* 9.8. 1050a23–1050b1.

24. Husik suggests emending this passage to: ולזה יחוייב שיהיה קבולו אותם עד הגעתו אל תכלית ההתהוות התהוות אחד. Husik, "Studies in Gersonides [2]," p. 132. I follow his suggestion.

subject to generation and corruption, and it would be[f1] identical with one of those things for whose generation it is responsible. But this is absurd.

Finally, since this generation is continually being conceived by one conception, and such a conception insofar as it encompasses all of time [i.e., is not limited to a particular range of instances—it is universal], is necessarily an intellectual concept [i.e., an act of reason, as opposed to imagination], it follows that this agent [responsible for generation] is an intellect. That this agent is the Agent Intellect follows from the fact that the knowledge of the latter is the very same as that which has to be present in the former. In both cases the knowledge must be that of a unified system of cognitions. Now since the intellect and that which is known are numerically one, these intellects must be numerically identical, for that which is known in both is identical. Some of the modern philosophers have rightly described the Agent Intellect as the agent of the sublunar world and have called it "the giver of forms."[25] This point shall be more fully discussed in Book five, where it shall be demonstrated that there is an agent that is responsible for generation in the sublunar world and that it is identical with the Agent Intellect, whose existence was proven in *On the Soul*.[26]

The claim that according to Aristotle generation is brought about by a soul that emanates from the heavenly bodies clearly implies that this soul is identical with the Agent Intellect. For, since the knowledge in the Agent Intellect is identical with the knowledge in this soul that emanates from the heavenly bodies, as we have just shown, it is necessary that they be the same [intellect]; for separate substances that do not differ essentially cannot be numerically differentiated. Numerical differentiation accrues to essences as the result of matter; but when essences are construed as abstracted from matter they cannot be conceived as being enumerated at all.[27] For example, when a corporeal form is considered as embedded in[g1] matter, it can have many instances; but when it is abstracted from matter, plurality in no way can be attributed to it.[28] This is obvious to anyone who reads this book; unless we were to suppose that there is a difference between them with respect to this knowledge. That is, the knowledge of the Agent Intellect is the perfection and form of the knowledge of this soul that emanates from

---

25. Avicenna, who is mentioned by Thomas Aquinas in *Summa Theologiae* 1. q. 84, a 4.

26. Aristotle, *On the Soul* 3.5; infra, Bk. 5, pt. 3, chap. 13.

27. According to Aristotle, matter is the principle of individuation. Aristotle, *Metaphysics* 8.6; Maimonides, *Guide* 2. introduction, principle 16.

28. Although there are instances of the concept *dog*, e.g., Fido, Lassie, Rin Tin Tin, there is only one concept *dog*.

the heavenly bodies. For it is the Agent Intellect that imparts to man a certain kind of knowledge, whose existence cannot be accounted for by the soul that emanates from the heavenly spheres;[h] i.e., the knowledge [transmitted by the Agent Intellect is that] of the heavenly bodies and their movers, which constitute the perfection and form of the generated and corruptible things, whose existence can be attributed to this soul that emanates from the spheres. Moreover, according to Averroes's reading of Aristotle, the Agent Intellect is active in the generation of man, whereas the soul that emanates from the spheres is active in the generation of other kinds of substances.[29]

Now, in the generation of man the knowledge of all other things is comprehended, since man is the final end and perfection of all composite substances, and the perfection [of something] is not separable from that of which it is the perfection. Hence, the form of man contains in some sense all the other forms which matter can become,[i] for they are like matter in respect to the form of man. Furthermore, when we have claimed that the Agent Intellect knows the order of man by virtue of which man is an existent and that this order is the perfection of other orders, it is clear that this knowledge does not terminate [only] in the fact that man exists by virtue of this order, but in the knowledge of all the various orders of which the order [in man] is their perfection.[30] Hence, it evidently follows from this that the Agent Intellect is the agent of all sublunar phenomena. For I do not see what could prevent it from generating all phenomena besides man; for it knows all their[j] orders, and that which generates them does so in this sense [i.e., in having knowledge of their orders, or patterns].[31]

Moreover, the capacity of the prime matter to receive the form of man is actualized by one act of generation, for it is a process towards one definite end, as we have seen. And a particular act of generation, insofar as it is one, necessarily presupposes one agent, unless its occurrence is accidental, which

---

29. Gersonides has supposed for the sake of argument that the Agent Intellect differs from the soul emanating from the spheres in their respective cognitions. If such a difference could be established, then it would be possible to make a genuine distinction in kind between these supernal intellects on the basis of their diverse functions, or natures. This would then correspond to the rabbinic doctrine that each angel has only one function (Maimonides, *Guide*, 2, chap. 6; Genesis Rabbah, chap. 50). However, Gersonides will now proceed to show that this supposition is false.

30. The term *siddur* normally connotes 'order'. In this context it signifies the plan, or pattern, according to which something is made.

31. The hypothesis suggested in the previous paragraph has been rejected. There is no need to differentiate between the Agent Intellect and the intellect that emanates from the heavenly spheres. The principle of economy prevails: whatever can be performed by the latter can be done by the former.

is the case when there are various levels of skills, or crafts, some being subordinate to others. In truth, however, an activity completely derives from the master-craft that directs all the subordinate crafts in what they are supposed to do. Now it is impossible to claim that the soul that emanates from the spheres is subordinate to the Agent Intellect in this activity [of generation], since the Agent Intellect does not need any intermediary [i.e., subordinate] intellect in performing this activity. For just as this activity can be done by that intermediary [intellect], it can also be done by the Agent Intellect. The use [of subordinates] occurs in human activities, where in order to lighten the labor and trouble a man makes use of aids. But with respect to the separate intellects, whose action reaches everything that is ready to receive this action without effort or trouble, it cannot be conceived that they require an intermediary, unless it requires for this activity a particular instrument which it lacks[k1] but is possessed by the intermediary.[l1] In this manner, God performs many activities by means of the movers of the heavenly spheres, since the movers possess instruments, i.e., the heavenly bodies,[32] by virtue of which[m1] the activity is accomplished. In the case of the separate intellects now under discussion, however, it is clear that they do not have instruments through which they accomplish their work except the disposition for blending[33] inhering in the thing that receives its generation[n1] via the heavenly bodies. This instrument [the disposition] no more belongs to one of the movers of the heavenly bodies than to any other, since it is impossible[o1] to say that one of these intellects moves the heavenly bodies and the other[p1] does not. On this hypothesis it would be the case that this instrument would belong[q1] to one of these intellects but not to the other; for, since each one of them on this view bestows a form, each [one of them] is necessarily numerically one [i.e., distinct from the other]. And this is the case with the Agent Intellect

---

32. In the Aristotelian cosmology the term 'heavenly body' denotes planets, stars, the sun, and the moon. These bodies are carried by and located in spheres, each one of which has movers that are responsible for their motion. These movers were believed to be separate from the spheres. Hence, the doctrine of the unmoved movers was merged with the notion of the scale of intellectual principles, characteristic of later Platonism. Ultimately the biblical doctrine of angels entered the story, and the angels were identified with the unmoved movers and as separate intellects. Gersonides gives a detailed discussion of these matters in Bk. 5, pt. 3. Cf. Maimonides, *Guide* 2.3–12.

33. *Ha-hakhanah ha-mizgit; tahyi'a mizāj;* or *dispositio commixionis.* This term denotes the capacity of the body to receive the four elemental forms, or qualities, so as to result in a *blend,* or chemical combination (Maimonides, *Guide* 2.38). This kind of mixture differs from the combination wherein the elements are merely mechanically, or spatially, juxtaposed. The latter type of combination is called *harkabah shikhnit.* That which results from this former process is the *blend* itself: *ha-ẓurah ha-mizgit;* κρᾶσις; *mizāj.* Aristotle, *On Generation and Corruption* 1.10; Goichon, *Lexique,* pp. 380–81, pars. 665–66; infra, Bk. 5, pt. 3, chap. 2, n. 24.

insofar as it perfects the material intellect, as has been explained previously. On the other hand, the movers of the heavenly bodies are necessarily many, as has been demonstrated in the *Metaphysics* and shall be proven in Book five of this treatise.[34] Therefore, each one of these agent intellects [on the hypothesis that there are two such intellects: the agent intellect proper and the soul that emanates from the heavenly bodies] would have to be different from the movers of the heavenly bodies.[35] Accordingly, it is evident that this instrument no more belongs[r1] to one of these intellects than to the other. Therefore, neither intellect is an instrument for the other.

Finally, even if we were to grant that one of these intellects has an instrument, it would not follow from this[s1] that there must be two such intellects. For the intellect having the instrument could have sufficient power to bring about the generation of all sublunar phenomena and to effect the actualization of the material intellect from its potential condition. For this intellect would possess all the knowledge that the Agent Intellect imparts to the material intellect. There is no necessity to postulate an additional agent intellect.[36] In general, the agent that produces the end also produces that which precedes [i.e., the means to] the end.[t1] In this way the whole [process] of generation is directed toward one goal. Thus, that which generates man [i.e., the Agent Intellect] is also that which generates all other terrestrial beings.

Indeed, I believe that Aristotle really was referring to the Agent Intellect when he spoke of the soul that emanates from the heavenly spheres; for that which acts upon the sublunar world[u1] and generates sublunar phenomena must emanate from the spheres. That which bestows the form, which is the goal of the generation, is properly that which gives the mixture by virtue of which the matter is prepared to receive this form. For this entire process is really one act, and a unitary action necessarily proceeds from one agent. Accordingly, since it is evident that the heavenly spheres supervise the sublunary world in so far as they produce the mixture in the forces which simultaneously derive from the spheres, it is necessary that the giver of form, which is [itself] a form,[v1] also emanate from all of the spheres,[w1]

---

34. The movers of the heavenly spheres are differentiated by the differences in the movements of their respective spheres. Since these movements are diverse, the movers are numerically different. Aristotle, *Metaphysics* 12.8; infra, Bk. 5, pt. 3, chap. 6.

35. The agents of generation are not defined by or distinguished in terms of their relationships to a specific heavenly body, as are the intellects that serve as movers of the heavenly spheres.

36. Even if it is admitted that the Agent Intellect requires some instrument—an assumption that Gersonides rejects—there is no need to introduce a second agent.

so that all of them cooperate in giving the form as well as in creating the mixture.[x1] For it would be absurd to say that there are two agents for one act, unless these two agents are really one in some sense.[37] Thus, it has been shown that the Agent Intellect is identical with the soul that emanates from the spheres, i.e., from their *movers;* for it is impossible for an intellect to emanate from a body. Herein is also demonstrated that the Agent Intellect knows *all* the various orders obtaining in this world in so far as it comprehends them as a unitary system. This is the case either because it makes this order from the forms of terrestrial phenomena; or because it imparts to the material intellect the knowledge of these orders.

One might object to this latter point concerning the role of the Agent Intellect in effecting knowledge in the material intellect, saying that there is no need for an agent to actualize the material intellect. For the imaginative forms [images, or phantasms] are sufficient to accomplish this function, since the objects of knowledge, which the material intellect apprehends, are already embedded in some sense in these images. Even though they are therein associated with the corporeal accidents by virtue of which the images are particularized, there is no intellect required to abstract the objects of knowledge from these corporeal features with which they are associated. For it is possible for the material intellect, without another intellect abstracting these features, to apprehend these objects of knowledge in the imaginative forms, in which they are contained, without their being associated with the accidental features [of the image]. It could be argued that[y1] the proper object of cognition for the material intellect is the general nature [or universal]; hence, it is possible for [the material intellect] to apprehend the latter without the corporeal features [of the image]. This is similar to the way sight apprehends the color of a visible object abstracted from the heat or cold and the other accidents that are found together with the color in the object, but whose apprehension is not attributed to the faculty of vision when the object causes the color to be apprehended. Nothing else is needed to separate the color from the other properties.[38]

Upon close examination, however, it will be seen that this objection is groundless. The sense of vision, for example, perceives colors abstracted from some[z1] of the other qualities with which they are found in the visible object because it cannot in any way perceive those other properties. The material intellect, however, can by its very nature apprehend any object

---

37. Husik, "Studies in Gersonides [2]," pp. 139–40.
38. Aristotle, *On the Soul* 3.4. 429a15.

whatever.[39] But[a2] it is the case that most of its knowledge consists in accidental properties and in whatever exists in them from the general natures belonging to them. Therefore,[b2] it is clear that there is nothing in this world that does not in some sense fall within its cognitive range.[c2] Accordingly, it is impossible to suggest that the imaginative forms are sufficient to generate knowledge of the general concepts which are embedded in them without recourse to another cause that abstracts these concepts from the accidental properties with which they are associated in the imaginative forms. Moreover, if it were claimed that the material intellect can apprehend the general natures[d2] in the imaginative forms without the accidental properties since it is its character to apprehend only the general nature, then the material intellect would not be able to construe an accidental property as an essential property, just as the sense of sight cannot perceive tastes as colors. But this is absurd. For the material intellect frequently makes mistakes of this kind; indeed, most of its mistakes are of this type, as is quite evident to anyone who reads this book.[40] Furthermore, if the material intellect had this power [to know the general nature without the help of the Agent Intellect], it would not need many[e2] sense-data for the acquisition of a concept. On the contrary, as soon as it perceives one sensible object it would obtain the concept from it. But this too is absurd; for there are many[f2] things in this world that require repeated observations and great effort before we acquire the concepts of them. Hence, it is evident that we must postulate an Agent Intellect in order to account for the operation of the material intellect, i.e., its actualization from a state of potentiality, in the acquisition of knowledge.

It has, therefore, been demonstrated that there must be an Agent Intellect to account for the operations of the material intellect in the acquisition of knowledge, i.e., its actualization from the state of potentiality, and for the generation of[g2] sublunar phenomena. We have also been able to show as far as was possible in this context what some of its properties are, i.e., it knows the various orders of the sublunar world in such a way that they constitute one order.[h2] For a complete treatment of this subject, however, we must wait until we arrive at Book five of this treatise, where, with God's will, we shall convincingly demonstrate the absurdity of Averroes's position that the agent

---

39. This point was discussed earlier in this chapter (cf. nn. 8 and 9). Here Gersonides contrasts the limited range of a particular sense-faculty, e.g., vision, with the unrestricted capacity of our intellect to comprehend all kinds of concepts.

40. If the material intellect could exercise its powers without the Agent Intellect, it should not mistake accidental features for essential features; for if it can operate independently of another intellect, it should be competent to apprehend correctly all kinds of properties.

responsible for the sublunar world is not an intellect [which is contrary to what] has been thought by the commentators of Aristotle.

It should be noted that our proofs have dissipated all the doubts that some of the ancients have brought forth either against the possibility of knowledge or for the introduction of Forms that exist outside the mind. Both views are false, as has been shown in the *Metaphysics*.[41] These philosophers thought that that which exists outside the mind is unstable, since as individuals such things are subject to continual change and corruption. However, knowledge, if there is such a thing, must itself be stable and be of a stable entity, as has been demonstrated in the *Posterior Analytics*.[42] From these [facts] some ancient philosophers [the sceptics] inferred that there is no knowledge at all. The later philosophers, however, realized that there is knowledge, for we find it insofar as the world exhibits a uniform and regular order. As the result of this [order] they introduced self-subsistent universals outside the mind to account for this knowledge. But this hypothesis has led to many unavoidable absurdities, as has been indicated in the *Metaphysics*.[43] If, however, the Agent Intellect is understood according to our own theory, knowledge will be of a stable and subsistent object outside the mind, and this is the order in the mind of the Agent Intellect. However, universality accrues to [this order] by virtue of its grounding[i2] in perceived particulars existing outside the mind.[44] And just as the order [or plan] that is in the mind of the craftsman is embodied in some sense in every one of the tools that is made according to it [i.e., the plan], so too is the order [of the sublunar world] exhibited in every one of the things that is generated according to this plan. It is, therefore, evident that our theory avoids the difficulties inherent in the thesis that universals exist outside the mind.

---

41. Aristotle, *Metaphysics* 1.6, 9 and 4.5.
42. Aristotle, *Posterior Analytics* 1, chaps. 2, 6, and 31. Cf. Plato, *Timaeus*, 29b–c.
43. Aristotle, *Metaphysics* 1.9, 7.13–15, 13.4–5.
44. The error of those (e.g., Plato) who introduced universals as independently existing entities was their belief that since knowledge is stable and general, there must be permanent and universal *things* that ground this knowledge. Gersonides will discuss this point in detail in chapter 10 of this book. Here he is content to affirm that although universality is characteristic of knowledge—after all, physics consists in general laws of motion, not statements about particular bodies in motion—this universality can be explained without introducing universal entities. His explanation makes use of the analogy with art. The universe exhibits order and regularity because it has been created according to a plan, just as a house exemplifies the design inherent in the blueprint. Each aspect of the universe betrays its partial role in the overall scheme of things represented in the Agent Intellect by its orderly arrangement and behavior. That is, universality is to be understood as the order pervasive throughout the whole creation, not as a special class of entities. This universality is exemplified in particular things in so far as particulars are parts of the general plan and behave accordingly.

Herein lies the solution to the problem that has arisen concerning the function of definitions in giving the essence of each individual of the defined genus [or species] in[j2] so far as [they state] the essence of each such individual.[45] The definition is the very order that is in the mind of the Agent Intellect according to which the genus is generated. This order is exhibited in some sense in each and every individual instance of that genus, as we have seen. It does not follow from this, however, that all these individuals are numerically one, as would be the case for those who believe in [Platonic] universals.[46] In this manner knowledge of accidental properties also is established, not just of essential properties, whereas for those who believe in [Platonic] universals, only essential properties can be known. The latter philosophers thought that since accidental properties cannot subsist by themselves, the universals corresponding to these properties do not exist outside the mind; hence for them accidents cannot be known. But on our theory of the Agent Intellect, the orders[k2] concerning the accidental properties are also outside the intellect, i.e., they exist in the mind of the Agent Intellect. Indeed, upon investigation it turns out that our theory solves all these problems and is in addition the truth, as we have demonstrated.

Perhaps this is what Plato really meant; he therefore thought that these forms are paradigms for the objects of sensation and called them universals, since they are the nature common to many things. But his theory leads to absurdities, since it expresses this [point] ambiguously. Moreover, his theory is incomplete,[l2] since he restricted these universals to substances; hence, since he realized that mathematical knowledge is immutable, he had to maintain that mathematical entities are substances, i.e., numbers, the unit, lines, surfaces, and mathematical extension [in general]. The absurdities inherent in this view are demonstrated in the *Metaphysics*.[47]

Aristotle's theory of knowledge and definitions, however, is itself not free from difficulties, as will be apparent to anyone who studies his views in the *Metaphysics*. I shall explain[m2] these difficulties in a commentary on the *Metaphysics*, if God grants me leisure to write it; and I shall show (God be willing) how that which we have proven with respect to the Agent Intellect solves completely all the problems that arise concerning knowledge and definitions. It shall also be demonstrated that our theory avoids all the problems

---

45. Aristotle, *Metaphysics* 7.10–12, 15.
46. Ibid. 7.13. 1038b8–14, 7.14.
47. Aristotle, *Metaphysics* 13, passim.

CHAPTER VII

A RESOLUTION OF THE DIFFICULTIES CONCERNING THE INFLUENCE OF THE AGENT INTELLECT ON THE MATERIAL INTELLECT [BY VIRTUE OF WHICH] THE LATTER ACQUIRES ITS COGNITIONS

NOW that we have discussed the Agent Intellect, we must try to remove the various difficulties concerning the influence of the Agent Intellect upon the material intellect. First,[a] it is difficult to explain how we arrive at knowledge of the practical arts, of mathematics, of the heavenly bodies and their movers, and of the First Cause. For it would seem from what we have proved about the Agent Intellect that it makes known the order of the sublunar world because it makes this order. But with respect to those things that it does not make, i.e., the things just mentioned, how do we attain knowledge of them by means of it,[b] all the more so of those things that are superior to it in rank, such as the heavenly bodies and the First Cause? It has been thought that the Agent Intellect has no knowledge of the latter entities; for if it did know them it would be identical with them, since in separate substances the intellect, that which is known, and the act of knowledge are numerically identical. But this is utterly absurd.

Second, it is also puzzling how we obtain knowledge of some subjects more than of others from one agent that is indifferently capable of giving us knowledge on all subjects and the recipient is indifferently capable of receiving this knowledge.[1] That the Agent Intellect can impart to us all knowledge indifferently can be easily shown. It imparts to us knowledge because such knowledge is actually present in it, and since all the knowledge that the Agent Intellect imparts to us is equally present in it, it follows that its capacity to give[c] us one particular piece of knowledge is equal to its capacity to give us another piece of knowledge, no matter what such knowledge may be. That the recipient is indifferently capable of receiving knowledge is also evident. It would seem with respect to any of the objects of knowledge that

---

1. If the agent intellect can give me knowledge of both astronomy and logic and if my intellect is capable of knowing both, why do I know more of one than the other?

the mind can apprehend truly that such apprehension does not admit degrees. If this were not so, then the material intellect would be both capable and not capable of apprehending the same thing. For [with respect to] something that it cannot apprehend truly, it cannot apprehend [at all]; for whoever apprehends an object of knowledge not as it truly is, apprehends it neither perfectly or imperfectly.[2] But it has been assumed that the material intellect can have such cognitions. This is an intolerable contradiction. Hence, the material intellect is capable of apprehending them truly, which implies that its capacity for knowledge does not admit degrees.[3]

The first difficulty can easily be disposed of. Even if it be admitted that insofar as the Agent Intellect makes these things [in the terrestrial world, and hence has knowledge of them] it does not follow that it has knowledge of the practical arts, the mathematical sciences and of other things which it does not make, nevertheless insofar as it does give us cognitions of these [latter things] it would follow that it has in some way knowledge of them as well, as has been indicated. It can be shown in a different way that the Agent Intellect has knowledge of all[d] the things about which there has been some doubt. It seems that the Agent Intellect possesses knowledge of the practical arts; therefore it endows man with organs to perform these arts in the best way possible. In this respect the Agent Intellect makes man its subordinate in reference to that which it intends,[e] in the same way as the subordinate arts serve the principal arts. For the principal art directs the subordinate art and establishes what is to be made by that art. This is clearly seen[f] among some animals in which there is a natural disposition to do some act that is beneficial for them, as the web of the spider and the honeycomb of the bees, etc. Moreover, these practical arts are directed towards the end which is determined by the Agent Intellect in many of the things that it does. For the Agent Intellect looks out for the preservation of living beings insofar as it endows them with organs for the acquisition of food; and in some animals these organs are the senses, imagination, and the appetitive power. In others it endows them with such organs as limbs, as in the case of the carnivorous animals, which have the necessary limbs for killing their prey. It endows other animals with

---

2. Aristotle, *On the Soul* 3.6. 430b26–30.

3. If it is the case that the human intellect either apprehends a concept or piece of knowledge completely, or does not apprehend it at all, then there should not be any differences of degree in the various cognitions it has. It should be capable of apprehending the concepts and principles of astronomy as accurately as it does those of mathematics. But the facts show that we are more successful in one science than in another.

organs for mental powers, such as the skill that nature has provided the bees in making honey, its food. Another example of the concern of the Agent Intellect for the preservation of living organisms is the provision of protection against the environment: for example, the wool, feathers, scales, and poison of those animals possessing these features; or the organs that enable the animal to fight, such as horns and hoofs in domestic animals.

An examination of the practical arts reveals that [they exist] for these purposes.g For example, since man, because of his rarified matter, has no bodily material for protection, such as wool or feathers, he has been given the capacity to make clothing and houses. And since for the same reason man has no natural organs for self-defense or for conquest over those animals he desires to eat, he has been given the ability to make weapons of war and for hunting. And since he cannot find proper food without labor, he was given the capacity to work the earth and to prepare food. In short, when we look at all the practical arts, we see that they are all directed towards the end that has been set by the Agent Intellect in those things that it makes. Therefore, art serves nature, as Aristotle says in Book two of the *Physics*.[4]

The Agent Intellect also possesses mathematical knowledge. It has knowledge of figures, for nature provides the right shapes for the activities that are performed by the bearer of these shapes.[5] Similarly, it has knowledge of quantities, for it makes sure that the quantitiesh and proportions of the members of the body are appropriate. These proportions are measured by nature; some of them are rational, others are incommensurate [i.e., not a rational number]. Furthermore, it knows numbers, for we find in the most noble of natural phenomena numerically determinate compounds, e.g., in the number of limbs, muscles, veins, tendons, bones, etc. These parts are determinate in number in each species of animals. [For] it is a characteristic of one who has complete knowledge of some genus that he know completelyi the features of the subjects in that [genus].

It seems too that the Agent Intellect possesses some kind of knowledge of the heavenly bodies, i.e., of that which emanates from them [and influences] the terrestrial domain. Indeed, it is this knowledge that makes it possible for us to have knowledge of this influence. That it possesses the knowledge of this influence that emanates from the heavenly bodies is evident, since this order [in this influence] acts as an instrument by means of which

---

4. Aristotle, *Physics* 2.2.
5. Aristotle, *Parts of Animals* 1.5.

the Agent Intellect performs the operations it intends to do. For the heavenly bodies generate the mixture [of the sublunary substances] and give it to the various existents[j] of the sublunar world, as has been shown in the sciences. This [mixture], then, is the instrument by virtue of which the form [of a sublunar substance] derives from the Agent Intellect, as has been explained. Moreover, since the Agent Intellect emanates from the movers of the heavenly spheres, as has been explained before, and since this order [i.e., the mixture] also emanates from the spheres, the relation between the Agent Intellect and this order, which derives from the spheres, is necessarily comparable to the relation obtaining between the movers of the spheres and the spheres themselves. And since the latter relation is one between the form and its matter, so too the relation between the Agent Intellect and this order is one between form and its matter. Hence, it is evident that the order inherent in the Agent Intellect constitutes the perfection and form of the order emanating from the heavenly bodies; and it is also evident that anyone who knows completely the perfection knows also that of which he knows the perfection. For example, he who knows the essence of a house knows also the boards, bricks, and stones of which the essence of the house is the perfection.

The Agent Intellect also possesses some knowledge of the movers of the spheres as well as of the First Cause. This knowledge is the knowledge possessed by the effect of its cause. When an effect knows itself in a perfect manner, and since its very being as an existent is brought about by another,[k] it must know itself as an effect. And since cause and effect are relational terms, and since knowledge of relations is a single cognition, it is necessary that the effect have some knowledge of its cause.[6] Nevertheless, this knowledge is defective, since it is possessed by the Agent Intellect in a less than perfect form; hence, the knowledge *we* acquire of these things is defective. Thus, the first objection has been removed; a more complete proof will be given, with God's help, in Book five of this treatise.

The second objection can also be easily disposed of. That we have a more perfect knowledge of some things than of others is attributable to either or both of the following two reasons: either the Agent Intellect has this knowledge in an imperfect form, as in the case of its knowledge of the heavenly bodies and of the First Cause; or the material intellect requires sensation in the reception of the influence from the Agent Intellect, and hence our knowl-

---

6. To know that X is a father is at the same time to know that some Y is X's son. Accordingly, if I know that I am caused by some being, I must know something about this being.

edge cannot be perfect if the sense-data are not available for this knowledge, as is the case with the order that emanates from the heavenly bodies. Moreover, defective knowledge is also a result of the character of the subject matter; for if the subject matter is imperfect so will the knowledge of it be defective, as is the case in political philosophy and related subjects.[7]

---

7. Political philosophy and ethics, i.e., the practical sciences, were regarded by most medievals as of lower cognitive status than physics or mathematics, i.e., the theoretical sciences. This prejudice goes back to Aristotle, who in the *Metaphysics*, where he is concerned with wisdom or the first science, characterizes mathematics, the natural sciences, and theology (i.e., metaphysics) as theoretical science (*Metaphysics* 6.1). In the *Nicomachean Ethics* Aristotle characterizes the principles of political philosophy and ethics as being less precise than those of the theoretical sciences and as akin to δόξα, or 'opinion' (*Ethics* 1.3). Accordingly, the arguments used in ethics will be *dialectical*, as opposed to those in the theoretical sciences, which, if valid, are *demonstrative* (Aristotle, *Prior Analytics* 1.1; *Topics* 1.1; Maimonides, *Treatise on Logic*, chap. 8).

CHAPTER VIII

VIEWS OF OUR PREDECESSORS CONCERNING THE IMMORTALITY OF THE MATERIAL INTELLECT

HAVING determined the nature of the Agent Intellect, it is now proper to return to our original question, Is it possible for the material intellect to become immortal, and if possible how? We shall first cite[a] the views of our predecessors, (for the same reason as in our discussion of the views of our predecessors concerning the nature of the material intellect.) There are three main positions among the philosophers on the question of immortality [and we discuss them in turn].

There is first the view of Alexander, Themistius, and Averroes, which is presented in Averroes's *Epitome on Aristotle's* On the Soul and in some of his letters.[1] They maintain that the material intellect is capable of immortality and subsistence when it reaches that level of perfection where the objects of knowledge that it apprehends are themselves intellects, in particular the Agent Intellect. For it is believed that [only] the latter, of all the separate intellects, is capable of being known [by man]. These philosophers also claim that immortality is not possible insofar as the material intellect apprehends the objects of knowledge pertaining to the sublunar world, since such concepts are generated and originated in us after being in a state of potentiality; and whatever is generated is destroyed, according to their view. However, when it apprehends that which is itself an intellect, there is then nothing that is generated; rather that which is apprehended is the intellect itself. Hence, it is immortal when it is united with the Agent Intellect. This theory is based upon four premises, as follows Premise 1: The objects of knowledge pertaining to the sublunar world are generated and originated in the material intellect. Premise 2: Everything that is generated is corruptible. Premise 3: Apprehension of the Agent Intellect is possible for us. Premise 4: In apprehending the Agent Intellect, the material intellect becomes[b] immortal.

---

1. In this chapter, as well as in subsequent chapters, Gersonides uses several different Hebrew terms to connote immortality of the intellect: נצחי, השארות, and תמידי. The first literally means 'everlasting,' the second 'survival,' and the third 'continual.' Whatever nuances

The second view is that of Avicenna and his followers, which is recorded in Averroes's *Epitome on Aristotle's* On the Soul.[2] Avicenna maintains that the acquired intellect (*ha-sekhel ha-niqneh*) is immortal, and he bases his view on two principles: (1) the objects of knowledge pertaining to the sublunar world are neither generated nor corruptible; (2) the material intellect is neither generated nor corruptible. Accordingly, he did not deny that it was possible for the acquired intellect to be immortal, for [on his theory] there is nothing that is both generated and immortal, since the material intellect is immortal. Hence, it is not impossible for the acquired intellect to be immortal when it is perfected [by the apprehension of] the objects of knowledge pertaining to [the sublunar world]. Moreover, these objects of knowledge are not generated essentially, although they are generated in the material intellect.

The third position is that of Al-Farabi, who denies completely the possibility of immortality of the material intellect or[c] of its being everlasting. His view is based upon two principles: (1) the material intellect is generated; (2) it is impossible for a generated thing to become everlasting. Hence, he concluded[d] that the view that the material intellect can be united with the Agent Intellect is nothing more than a foolish vanity. However, in *The Letter Concerning the Intellect* in which Al-Farabi explains the word 'intellect,' we find another view according to which he ascribes immortality to the material intellect in a way similar to the view of Themistius and his followers. He calls our intellect "the acquired intellect" when it apprehends that which is itself an intellect and says of it[e] that it is everlasting life.[3]

---

these terms might severally have, they can be ignored, since Gersonides uses these words interchangeably. They shall therefore be treated as synonyms. However, all of these terms, both in Hebrew and in English, have to be distinguished from the term 'eternal,' קדום ; for this latter word signifies infinite duration both in the past and in the future, whereas the former terms signify infinite time in the future only. The issue here is not the infinite duration, or eternity, of the human soul—a thesis that all of the medieval philosophers discussed here would deny—but its survival after bodily death.

2. Averroes, *Drei Abhandlungen*, p. 28 ff.; Gersonides, *Supercommentary on Averroes's Epitome of* On the Soul, (Neubauer 1373),ff 245 ff.; Alexander Altmann, "Ibn Bājja on Man's Ultimate Felicity" in *Harry Austryn Wolfson Jubilee Volume* (Jerusalem, 1965), 1:47:48.

3. Gersonides, *Supercommentary on Averroes's Epitome of* On the Soul, ff. 243 ff.; Avicenna's views on immortality are expressed in his *The Deliverence: Psychology*, which has been translated by F. Rahman as *Avicenna's Psychology* (Oxford, 1952). The relevant part of this work has been reprinted in Hyman and Walsh, *Philosophy in the Middle Ages*, pp. 258–61.

4. Al-Farabi, *The Letter Concerning the Intellect*, reprinted in Hyman and Walsh, *Philosophy in the Middle Ages*, pp. 215–21. For useful discussions of and relevant literature on Al-Farabi's views on this topic, see Altmann, "Ibn Bājja," p. 49, n. 4, and Herbert Davidson, "Al-Farabi and Avicenna on the Active Intellect," *Viator* 3 (1972): 109–78.

CHAPTER IX

ARGUMENTS IN FAVOR OF THESE VIEWS

NOW that we have cited these various opinions concerning immortality of the intellect, it is necessary, as in our previous discussions, to examine the arguments that have been adduced in favor of these views in so far as we have found these arguments in the writings of our predecessors, explicitly or implicitly. This [kind of] examination will be of help in our pursuit of truth on this topic, as it has in the past.

The view of Alexander and his followers on this topic is plausible and is based upon four premises, as we have seen. The first of these premises—that the objects of knowledge apprehended by the material intellect are generated and originated in it—seems to be[a] correct from several points of view. First, it would seem that these cognitions do originate in the material intellect after having been there only potentially; they do not exist there always in actuality, as Plato thought. For if this were the case, why doesn't an individual apprehend them immediately upon birth? Is there something that prevents their appearance in him[b] when young, even though they are in him potentially as Plato believed? For [on his view] these objects of knowledge are submerged in the bodily humors during youth.[c] [1] If this opinion were true there would be no point to learning in the acquisition of these objects of knowledge. For if the bodily humor disappears, i.e., the obstacle preventing the appearance of these cognitions, then they will be apprehended without any learning, and the act of learning then would be otiose. If the humor does not disappear, then it will not be possible for this knowledge to be realized, and the act of learning then will again be futile. Indeed,[d] there would be no real learning at all; learning would be merely recollection, as Plato claimed.[2] In a similar manner it can be shown that on this hypothesis there would also[e] be no need for sensation in the apprehension of these cognitions. But this whole theory is utterly absurd.

Second, it would seem that these objects of knowledge are generated essentially and exist sometimes potentially and sometimes actually; for that

---

1. Averroes, *Commentary on Plato's* Republic, p. 196 (English).
2. Plato, *Meno*, 85–86, and *Phaedo*, 13.

which is apprehended of them is not identical with that which corresponds to them outside the mind, since that which exists outside the mind is not actually one of these objects of knowledge but[f] only potentially. Insofar as these objects of knowledge are believed to be universals, it is evident that they do not exist in sensible objects except potentially; for the universal as such is infinite, and whatever is infinite does not exist outside the mind except potentially. The individual instances of the universal, however, are necessarily finite. Moreover, the general nature is not found in the individual instance except potentially, since that which actually exists corresponding to it [i.e., the general nature] is something with [all] the corporeal properties by virtue of which the individual is particularized. Furthermore, that which exists outside the mind corresponding to these [universal natures] is not itself an intellect [or a cognition]; but that which is apprehended of these [natures] is[g] an intellect [or cognition] when we apprehend it.[3]

One might say, however, that these objects of knowledge are not essentially generated, although they are potentially in the material intellect at one time and actually at another, if it is also claimed that what is apprehended is identical with that which exists outside the mind, and that this existent thing[h] is not generated. For example, if the color that is perceived in the faculty of the perceiver is [numerically] identical with the color that is actually in the visible object outside the mind, then there is no essential generation with respect to the color when it is perceived by the perceiver, as is self-evident. The color, however, has an essential generation in so far as it has been generated in the visible object. Now if this color had not been generated in the visible object, the color would not be essentially generated at all, although it is generated in the faculty of the perceiver. But since it has been proven that these objects of knowledge are generated in the material intellect and that they are not identical with that which exists outside the mind, they are essentially generated when they appear in the material intellect.[4]

Third, it seems that these objects of knowledge exhibit features of material forms in so far as they are material[i]; hence, they are themselves corporeal

---

3. In the act of cognition the intellect, the intellectual act, and the object of knowledge are all identical. Thus, when I see a tree, I sensibly perceive all its particular idiosyncratic properties; but I also intellectually apprehend the general nature of this tree. In grasping the nature or form of the tree, my mind virtually becomes identical with this form, and conversely. (Aristotle, Metaphysics XII: 9, 1075a 1–4; *On The Soul*, III: 4, 430a 4–5, III: 5, 430a 20, III: 7, 431b 17–18.)

4. That is, since the objects of knowledge are not identical with that which corresponds to them outside the mind, whether the latter is generated or not is irrelevant to the question of the generation of the former. Cf. Husik, "Studies in Gersonides [2]," pp. 148–49.

and cannot always exist in actuality. For if they could, they would be separate forms not corporeal forms. That they do exhibit the characteristics of material forms insofar as they are material can be proven as follows. As Averroes has pointed out[j] in his *Epitome on Aristotle's* On the Soul, material forms as such exist in something as the result of some essential change.[5] For example, the material form [e.g., color] that reaches the faculty of vision when it sees a visible object is consequent upon a change occurring in this faculty resulting from the impression of this form on it. For if this sense were not affected in this particular manner, this form would not be generated in it. The same holds for these objects of knowledge: their generation in man is consequent upon an essential[k] change in the senses. Such objects of knowledge are necessarily either primary principles, i.e., principles that are nondemonstrable, or secondary principles, i.e., the conclusions of proofs. The latter presupposes the former; the former, however, are acquired[l] only by means of sensation, as is evident from their very nature. Principles that are acquired by means of repeated sensations obviously require the senses, but they also presuppose imagination and memory, as has been explained in the *Posterior Analytics*.[6]

That first principles whose temporal origins in us we do not know—as for example, the proposition that the whole is greater than any of its parts, and others of this type—are acquired only by means of sensation can be proven as follows. It has been proven that the material intellect is bereft of any particular form; hence, it does not possess any concept a priori; rather, all concepts are acquired. Now, since all acquired knowledge implies some previous knowledge, as has been proven in the *Posterior Analytics*, that which is acquired presupposes some other cognition.[7] The latter is necessarily either an intellectual cognition or derived from some other of our faculties, such as sensation, imagination, estimation, or memory. It cannot be from the former, since a first principle would then presuppose some prior knowledge, which is self-contradictory. Consequently, a first principle must be acquired by means of a cognition that derives from one of the other faculties. Since these other cognitions are either sensations or presuppose sensations—the common sense, the imagination, the estimative faculty, and memory all derive from sensation, as has been shown in *On the Soul* and *On Sense and Sensible Objects*[8]—it is clear that these [primary] principles presuppose sensation.

---

5. Gersonides, *Supercommentary on Averroes's Epitome of* On the Soul, Bk. 1.

6. Aristotle, *Posterior Analytics* 2.19.

7. Ibid. 1.1.

8. Aristotle, *On the Soul* 3.5; *On Sense and Sensible Objects* 7; Wolfson, "The Internal Senses In Latin, Arabic and Hebrew Philosophic Texts."

Nevertheless, we do not know when we have acquired them, for the acquisition of such principles does not require repeated[m] sensory experience; but as soon as we perceive, for example, a quantity, it is evident to us that the whole is greater than any of its parts, and similarly with other things of this sort. It is, therefore, evident that all knowledge ultimately derives from sensation, which is what we suggested at the outset.

Corporeal forms, insofar as they are corporeal forms, are also multiple [i.e., individuated] by virtue of the multiplication of their subjects. This is quite obvious. And this is true in some sense of these objects of knowledge as well, as can be seen from several points of view. First,[n] these objects of knowledge are based upon the individual images of sensible objects existing outside the mind. Consequently, a concept that I have, for example, differs from the concept of someone preceding me, for my concept is based upon individuals that exist now, whereas the concepts of my predecessors were based upon individuals that existed in the past.

That these objects of knowledge are based upon images of individual sensible objects existing outside the mind can be shown as follows. A concept is true if there corresponds to it an individual thing outside the mind upon whose imagined form [i.e., the image] the universal concept[o] is based. And whatever has no such thing outside the mind upon which the universal could be based is false, as in the examples of fabulous animals and the phoenix. Accordingly, it would seem that the reality possessed by these concepts is based upon the images of their individual things.

It can be shown in a different way that there obtains between these universal objects of knowledge and the particular images of individual things a basis in terms of which the universals [can be said to] exist. A universal has existence, insofar as it is a universal, only because of the particular, for these are correlatives; and all correlatives are such that they acquire their existence as a correlative from the existence of the other correlative. That the universal is a correlative to the particular is evident, for it is impossible for a universal to exist by itself, as Plato believed. Aristotle refuted this idea in his *Metaphysics*.[9] The universal is a correlative, however, of a particular insofar as it is a universal, for it comprehends and encompasses it. Hence, the universal is never found without a particular, since correlatives must exist together.[10]

Second, if these objects of knowledge were not individuated by the individuation of their [individual] subjects, several ineluctable absurdities would

---

9. Aristotle, *Metaphysics* 8.8, 13–14, and 13.4–5.
10. Aristotle, *Categories* 7. Cf. Husik, "Studies in Gersonides [2]," pp. 150–53.

result. In the first place, on this hypothesis it would follow that a concept apprehended by one man could exist in other men; accordingly, the knowledge attained by Aristotle could be present in somebody who never learned it. But this is utterly absurd. That this absurdity follows from this hypothesis can be shown as follows. [On this hypothesis] the object of knowledge is the same for all men, since it is not ex hypothesi individuated according to the number [of subjects]. Now it is clear from the nature of numerical unity that it exists either potentially or actually, but not both at the same time. But it is evident that it is impossible for one and the same concept, on this hypothesis, to be apprehended by one man but not apprehended by another; for if this were possible, one and the same concept would be simultaneously actual and potential—which is false.[11]

It has been objected that this absurdity does not follow if it is maintained that one and the same thing can exist [simultaneously] potentially in some respect and exist actually in another respect. Accordingly, it would not be impossible [for the same concept] to be possessed by one man potentially and at the same time be possessed by another actually. For with respect to the latter the concept is related to the capacity possessed by him; whereas with respect to the former the concept is related to the capacity he has for potential knowledge, which differs from the capacity possessed by the man who actually knows.

Our reply is as follows. It is quite obvious that capacities that are capacities for one particular activity are numerically identical; for capacities are defined[p] with respect to the activity for which they are capacities. Therefore, if the activities are many in kind, the corresponding capacities are many in kind. If the activities are numerically many, the corresponding capacities are numerically many. And if the activity is numerically one, its corresponding capacity is numerically one. Hence, it is evident that if the activity of the material intellect is numerically one—and this is the object of knowledge— the corresponding capacity must be numerically one. And since the capacity is numerically one, it is evident that if the object of knowledge is apprehended by one man but not apprehended by another, one and the same thing is simultaneously in potentiality and actuality in the same respect [i.e., apprehension]. And this is absurd.

In the second place, it would follow from this hypothesis [the hypothesis that objects of knowledge are *not* individuated according to individual knowers] by the very same argument that when one man forgets some piece of

---

11. Averroes, *Long Commentary on De Anima*, in Hyman and Walsh, *Philosophy in the Middle Ages*, p. 323.

knowledge, other men will forget it [too], both those who know it as well as those who do not know it. But this is absolute nonsense.

In the third place, on this hypothesis it would follow that there would be no learning or forgetting. For if these objects of knowledge are not individuated according to the number of subjects, they are separate forms, since a material thing insofar as it is material is individuated according to its subjects. But if they are separate forms, they would not be subject to generation or corruption, since the latter features accrue to a form only insofar as it is material, as has been explained in the sciences.[12] If they are not subject to generation or corruption, they exist continually in actuality; and then no learning or forgetting would be possible.[13] This is completely absurd.

The second of these premises mentioned originally upon which [Alexander] has established his theory is the principle[q] that whatever is generated is corrupted. The truth of this principle has been thought to have been demonstrated in *On the Heavens*.[14]

The third premise, which is that it is possible for the material intellect to apprehend the Agent Intellect, has several arguments in its behalf. First, according to Aristotle the relation between the intellect and the object of knowledge is analogous to the relation between the senses and the objects of sense. With respect to the latter it is clear that there are three factors: (1) a recipient (i.e., the sense organ), (2) that which is received (i.e., the form that reaches the sense faculty as the result of the sensation), and (3) the cause (i.e., the sensible object actually existing outside the mind). Analogously, with the intellect the three factors present are: (1) a receiving intellect (i.e., the material intellect), (2) that which is received (i.e., the acquired intellect), and (3) the agent [or cause] (i.e., the Agent Intellect). Now when it is assumed that this analogy is identical [in both cases], and since it is evident from the nature of the sense faculty that it can receive the sensible object that exists in actuality outside the mind, it follows that the material intellect can apprehend the Agent Intellect.

Second, since our intellect can apprehend that which is not essentially an intellect, it is evident that the intellect should be more able to apprehend what is essentially an intellect.

Third, the Agent Intellect is responsible for making the imaginative forms

---

12. Aristotle, *On Generation and Corruption* 1.3.

13. Learning and forgetting involve processes, or transitions, from potential to actual knowledge.

14. Aristotle, *On the Heavens* 1.9–12.

actually known whereas previously they were only potentially knowable. Now it is evident that that which is responsible for another thing having a certain property is itself more fitting to have that property than the latter thing. For example, fire makes something hot; but it is more appropriate for the fire to be hot than the thing that was made hot by the fire. Accordingly, it is more fitting for the Agent Intellect, which is responsible for making the imaginative forms intelligible, to be an object of our knowledge.

Fourth, the objects of knowledge in the sublunar world are potential cognitions, for they are cognitions of a potentially infinite set of existent objects. That is, they are cognitions of an infinite set of individuals that are comprehended by these universal concepts[r] and that exist only potentially; for whatever is infinite[s] exists only potentially, as Aristotle has explained in the *Physics*.[15] Since that which exists outside the mind corresponding to these cognitions exists only potentially [because it is infinite] and since the definition of truth is the correspondence between what is conceived by the mind and what exists outside the mind, it is evident that these objects of knowledge are potential cognitions. Now, since it is evident that in any species, that which is potentially true of that species will necessarily become actually true of that species, and that the material intellect moves from a state of potentiality to actuality in the acquisition of the objects of knowledge, the object of knowledge to which it aspires is necessarily actual. And since the object of knowledge that is actual is a separate intellect—for the objects of knowledge in the sublunar world are only potential cognitions—the material intellect is capable of apprehending the separate intellect. At first, however, the material intellect moves toward cognition of that which is potentially knowable, as happens to many natural phenomena which receive the perfections, which they are capable of receiving, by means of the perfections of other things. For example, bread, which[t] is potentially a part of the organism that is fed, becomes an actual part of the organism when it is first changed into something that is potentially a part of the organism, the blood.[16]

The fourth of these aforementioned premises, upon which their doctrine is based, asserts that when the material intellect knows the Agent Intellect it becomes immortal. There is one argument in behalf of this claim. Since the object of knowledge [of the material intellect], when the latter knows the Agent Intellect, is identical with that which it receives, there is nothing here that is generated as the result of this cognition such that it would be subject

---

15. Aristotle, *Physics* 3.5.
16. Aristotle, *On Parts of Animals* 2.1. 647b5–8; *On Sleep and Waking* 3.

to corruption because it has been generated. Rather [the object of knowledge] is the Agent Intellect itself, which is everlasting.[17]

Avicenna's position on this question too has several arguments in its favor. For the first of the premises on which he bases his view—the claim that the objects of knowledge of the sublunar world are neither generated nor corruptible—seems to be true on several grounds. First, it would appear from the nature of the forms of the objects of knowledge [e.g., the essence or definition of the concept of a triangle] that they exist in man in a way different from the manner in which material forms exist in that in which they inhere. By 'material forms' I mean either forms themselves, such as heat or cold among the elements, the mixture in homogeneous parts, the nutritive soul in plants, the perceptual soul in animals, or the cognitions that are perfections of some material forms (e.g., the form that is received by the sense faculty in perception or [the form received] by the imagination in the imaginative faculty). For when we examine these material forms we find that their existence in their individual subjects,[u] i.e. their material existence, differs from their existence [as] apprehended. This is obvious. For they are numerically one insofar as they are apprehended; they are [in this sense] not multiplied [i.e., individuated] in terms of the multiplication of the subjects in which they inhere. But they are multiplied insofar as they are particular and [embodied] in matter. This latter follows[v] from their being material forms. With respect to the forms of the objects of knowledge, however, it seems that their existence as apprehended is the very same thing as their particular existence in the material intellect.[18] Now if this is the case, i.e., that which is apprehended of them is identical with their very existence, and since this is the

---

17. This argument claims that in apprehending the Agent Intellect the material intellect would not receive any sense-data or imaginative forms; it would grasp the Agent Intellect directly, and hence receive what it apprehends. Averroes, *Drei Abhandlungen*, Hebrew text, pp. 13–14; Ludwig Hannes, *Die Möglichkeit der Konjunktion* (Halle 1892), Hebrew text, p. 8; Gersonides, *Supercommentary on the Three Short Essays of Averroes*, Bodleian MS. 1337.

18. This difficult philosophical point makes use of equally difficult technical terminology, for which recognizable and uniform English equivalents are not readily available. The general philosophical point Avicenna wants to establish is this. There are certain kinds of entities, i.e., the forms of material objects, whose existence in particular bodies differs from their existence as objects of thought. The form of a house is different from the plan of this house as it is conceived by the architect. As the Latin Scholastics would have said: their *esse intentionale* (*esse obiectivum*) differs from their *esse reale*; or, in Descartes's scholastic usage, their *realitas formalis* or *actualis* differs from their *realitas obiectiva* (*Meditations* 3). On the other hand, there are other kinds of entities, i.e., the forms of the objects of knowledge, whose *esse intentionale* = *esse reale*. Since by definition an object of knowledge is a cognitive entity, its very being is to be conceived. Such entities, Avicenna claims, are ontologically distinct from the forms of material objects; they are 'separate', i.e., independent of matter, incorporeal.

nature of a separate form—for if it were a material form its existence as apprehended would differ from its[w] existence outside the mind, as we have seen—it is evident that these objects of knowledge are separate [forms]. Hence, they are subject neither to generation nor corruption, for the latter features are characteristic of substances that are composed of matter and form insofar as they are so composed, as has been explained in the *Metaphysics* and in the first Book of the *Physics*.[19]

Second, these objects of knowledge differ from other cognitions of the soul, for the latter are finite in so far as they are corporeal, i.e., they make judgments only about a definite individual,[x] whereas the former cognitions are infinite, i.e., the judgment covers all individuals of the class that exist at any time. From this it seems that these objects of knowledge do not exist in us in a corporeal way, and hence, as we have seen, they are neither generated nor corruptible.[20]

Third, this intellectual cognition differs also from the other cognitions of the soul insofar as [here] the act of knowledge, the object of knowledge, and the knower are all identical. That the act of knowledge is[y] identical with the object of knowledge is evident from the fact that the former is the general nature inhering in a substance, and this is the case also for the object of knowledge. And since the general nature is neither many nor subject to numeration, it is clear that the act of knowledge is identical with the object of knowledge. That the act of knowledge is identical with the knower is evident from the following considerations. The acquired intellect is nothing different from the knowledge it acquires of these forms, since the material intellect has been shown to be no more than a disposition. None of this is true for the other cognitions. For example, the form that is perceived by the visual faculty in seeing a color is not the visual faculty itself; nor is it itself the color of the body existing outside the mind. From this it would seem to follow that these objects of knowledge [the intelligible forms] are not material; for if they were, it would not be possible for the act of knowing them, the object of knowledge, and the knower to be numerically identical. This feature

---

19. Aristotle, *Metaphysics* 7.10; *Physics* 1.7. Avicenna's point is that the objects of knowledge are not subject to genesis and corruption because their ontological status is relatively simple: in their case, to exist is to be known. Entities that have a more complicated ontological status, however, are subject to generation and corruption. Such is the case with all composites of form and matter. But since the objects of knowledge are incorporeal, they are not subject to generation and corruption.

20. Perceptual judgments are finite in scope; e.g., 'I see *this* dog'. Intellectual judgments can range over an infinite class; e.g., 'All men are mortal'. The latter kind of proposition is infinite in its extension by virtue of the fact that it has as its constituent elements *general* terms, or predicates, that can be infinite in their scope.

is one of the properties uniquely characteristic of separate intellects insofar as they are separate. And since it has been shown that these objects of knowledge are not material, they are neither generated nor corruptible, as has been explained.

Fourth, this knowledge differs from other kinds of cognitions in that it involves no affections [or passions], whereas the latter do. The senses, for example, suffer some kind of passion when they perceive the sensible object. Thus, when we see a brilliant object and then turn from it, we cannot immediately see something that is less bright. This is a necessary characteristic of these cognitions, since they are corporeal. For this reason they require a corporeal organ by virtue of which it receives its perceptions; and since the form that derives from this cognition makes an impression on this corporeal organ, a change occurs. But the former kind of cognition is free from this; when we understand a difficult topic and then turn to an easier problem, we understand the latter more quickly. From this it would appear that this kind of cognition is not corporeal. It follows from this that the objects of knowledge apprehended in this type of cognition are neither generated nor corruptible, as has been explained.

Fifth, a further differentiating characteristic of this type of knowledge is that it increases[z] with old age, whereas the other [corporeal] cognitions suffer just the opposite. This is true for the latter because they are corporeal, and hence these cognitive powers make use of corporeal organs by virtue of which they receive their data. But since these corporeal organs weaken with age it follows that the cognitive powers also weaken at this time, but not because of the form which is proper to these organs, as we have said earlier; for the form as such never weakens. This shows that this intellectual cognition is not corporeal; for if it were, it would diminish in old age, as is the case with the other kinds of cognition. But when it is proven that they are not corporeal, it is evident that they are neither generated nor corruptible, as has been pointed out.

The arguments in behalf of Avicenna's second premise—the material intellect is neither generated nor corruptible—have been mentioned previously. They are the very same arguments that we cited in favor of Themistius's view concerning the material intellect. We have shown, however, that these arguments do not prove that the material intellect is not generated.

Al-Farabi's view on this topic also has several arguments in its favor. The first of his premises—the material intellect is generated—can be proven without any doubt from the second of the arguments adduced in favor of Alexander's doctrine. Al-Farabi's second premise—the impossibility of union between the material and Agent Intellect—might be defended as follows. First, if this union were possible, the effect would be transformed into its own cause, which is impossible; for cause and effect are contrary[a1] types of existents, since they are correlatives. Second, if this union were possible, that which cannot be eternal would be immortal. For, insofar as it is generated, the material intellect must be corruptible,[21] but if it is [alleged] to apprehend the Agent Intellect, then it would become identical with the latter, which means that it would be incorruptible. But this is impossible.

---

21. Aristotle, *On the Heavens* 1.12.

CHAPTER X

A DEMONSTRATION SHOWING THAT NONE OF THESE ARGUMENTS IS EITHER VALID OR REFUTES THE CONTRARY VIEW

NOW that we have stated the various positions on this issue and have presented the arguments in their behalf, it is proper that we examine whether these arguments are sufficient to establish the respective conclusions. And since the arguments that have been adduced in favor of these views allegedly refute the conclusions of the contrary views, it is necessary that we determine whether these [alleged] refutations are valid.

It is clear that the first argument for the thesis that the objects of knowledge acquired by the material intellect are generated in it does establish that these cognitions are generated in the material intellect; but it doesn't imply that they are generated essentially. This can be seen from our presentation of that argument.[1] It is also evident that it doesn't follow that they are generated essentially simply because it has been demonstrated by that argument that these cognitions are generated and found in the material intellect in actuality after having being in it previously only potentially. For it is not the case that every new relation acquired by a thing to some other thing implies an essential generation. The sun, for example, is closer to us in the summer, but this newly acquired relation doesn't entail that the sun was essentially generated. Accordingly, it is possible for someone to maintain that these objects of knowledge exist continuously in actuality, but also that the material intellect apprehends them at a definite moment, although not in a way such that these objects would exist differently in the material intellect than they exist in themselves. In the case of corporeal cognition, e.g., sensation and its like, however, the perception differs from that which is perceived outside the intellect.[2] It is clear, therefore, that this argument does not refute any of the other three views previously cited on this topic; however,

---

1. Supra, chap. 9.
2. If the object of knowledge had different kinds of existence, then essential generation would take place. Cf. Husik, "Studies in Gersonides [2]," pp. 155–56.

it does refute the Platonic thesis that those objects of knowledge continuously exist in actuality in the material intellect.[3]

The second of these arguments purporting to establish the essential generation of these objects of knowledge—since that which is apprehended is not identical with that which exists outside the mind [hence it is essentially generated]—is not valid. They adduce three arguments in behalf of the principle that the object of knowledge does not exist outside the mind. First, the object of knowledge is a universal, and universals exist outside the mind only potentially.[4] Second, these objects of knowledge pertain to the essence and the general nature of a substance; but the general nature is found in particulars existing outside the mind only potentially. Third, that which exists extramentally is not an intellect, whereas the objects of knowledge are intellects [in so far as the objects of knowledge, the act of knowledge, and the intellect are identical].

Now the first of these arguments appears to be invalid on several grounds. Firstly, it has already been demonstrated that these objects of knowledge exist extramentally in actuality in the Agent Intellect. Accordingly, they possess existence outside the [human] mind as thought-objects,[5] although they do not exist as objects of sense. And if they have extramental existence as thought-objects [in the Agent Intellect], it doesn't follow that they are essentially generated when they are arise in the material intellect, unless it has been established beforehand that they possess a kind of being in the material intellect different from the being they have in the Agent Intellect. But this latter point doesn't follow from this argument or from any of these other arguments. Hence, all of these three arguments are refuted in this manner. The third of these arguments, however, is especially vulnerable, since it is incompatible with the point we have just established; namely, these

---

3. In Plato's *Phaedo* and *Meno*, it is suggested that the knowledge of the Forms is preexistent in the mind of the individual but requires certain kinds of stimuli for their recollection. The stimulation of this knowledge, however, differs from the kind of change involved in Aristotle's analysis of the cognitive process. In the latter the concepts are at first not in the mind; rather they have to be acquired through sensation. For Aristotle, sensation is not a mere stimulus or cue; it is the very source of knowledge. Cf. Aristotle, *On the Soul* 3.4–6.

4. Averroes, *Tahafut al-Tahafut*, trans. S. von der Bergh, 2 vols. (London, 1954), vol. 1, first discussion, par. 3, p. 65.

5. *Bi-meẓi'ut ha-muskal*. The problem here is to find a suitable English equivalent for this technical phrase that captures Gersonides' philosophical point and that is free from ambiguity. Gersonides claims that the objects of knowledge exist in actuality outside the *human* mind but *in* the mind of the Agent Intellect. Thus, they do not exist as objects of sense, i.e., as possible objects of perception, but as the objects of knowledge of the Agent Intellect. Accordingly, they exist for the Agent Intellect as objects of thought.

objects of knowledge are themselves intellects existing outside the [human] intellect [but] in the Agent Intellect.[6]

Second, it is not necessary for the objects of knowledge to be universals and encompass an infinite number of individuals, as is assumed in this argument. This is especially evident in objects of knowledge of things that are unique, e.g., the heavenly bodies, etc.[7] If it is claimed that the object of knowledge in these cases is the existent thing, it would follow that some of these objects of knowledge, i.e., the universal objects of knowledge, would be generated essentially, whereas others would not be generated, i.e., the objects of knowledge of unique things. But this is contrary to their initial assumption that *all* objects of knowledge are essentially generated, and hence corruptible.

Third, it can be demonstrated that these objects of knowledge are not universals. If they were universals, the knowledge of them by the material intellect would entail the following dilemma: Either this knowledge would be of the universal construed as a unit, i.e., the aspect in terms of which the universal encompasses and ranges over all the individuals that fall under it; or this knowledge would be of the universal construed as a plurality, i.e., the material intellect apprehends the infinite number of individuals [that fall under this universal].[8] The material intellect cannot, however, have knowledge of the universal construed as a plurality, for the intellect has no concept of the individual as an individual. Hence, it cannot apprehend a plurality of individuals,[a] all the more so an infinite number of individuals; for what is infinite cannot be reached by knowledge precisely because it is infinite, as is obvious.[9] It won't do to say that the intellect does know infinite magnitudes since it does understand the divisibility of magnitudes, which[b] is infinite. The intellect does not know the magnitude as it is divided into infinite parts; rather, it knows the magnitude in so far as it *can* be divided indefinitely.[10]

---

6. Again it must be remembered that for the Agent Intellect, its act of cognition and that which is known are always identical. In this sense, then, that which the Agent Intellect apprehends is itself an intellect.

7. For example, there is only *one* planet Mars.

8. Two interpretations can be given to the claim that in knowledge we know universals. That which we know is a universal either in the sense that it is *one species* that encompasses many individuals, or in the sense that this universal consists in *these individuals themselves*, and these may be infinite in number.

9. Aristotle, *Physics* 1.4. 187b6–14, 1.5; *Posterior Analytics* 1.18, 31.

10. Gersonides is alluding here to his distinction between a magnitude that actually has infinite parts and a magnitude that can be divided indefinitely, i.e., a magnitude that can always be divided further. This point is discussed in detail in Bk. 6, pt. 1, chap. 11. Cf. Aristotle, *Physics* 3.6–8.

Thus, the intellect can apprehend that the generation of sensible objects is potentially continuable, and thus generation does not terminate. But it is impossible for it to apprehend an infinite number of *individuals*.

Similarly, I say that it is clearly impossible for the material intellect to apprehend the universal construed as a unit, i.e., as a species or genus.[c] Since the universal is a correlative of the individuals which it comprehends and encompasses, and since it has just been demonstrated that the intellect cannot know the individuals as particulars, i.e., as the correlatives to the universal, it is clear that it cannot know the universal as universal [i.e., as a genus or species]. If one cannot know one of the correlatives, he cannot know in any way the other; for correlatives are defined in terms of one another. Hence, one [correlative] cannot be conceived by someone who has not conceived of the other. For example, one who has no idea of what a double is has no idea of what a half of something is. Now, if it be assumed that these objects of knowledge are universals in either of the two senses distinguished above (there is no third sense), and since it has been shown that it is impossible for the intellect to know universals in any of these ways, it is evident that the objects of knowledge apprehended by the intellect are not universals—which is contrary to the original hypothesis. Rather, the object of knowledge of the material intellect is the individual, not as a definite individual, but as any individual whatsoever, and this thing exists actually outside the [human] mind, i.e., it is the individual thing. This point shall be explained more completely later on.

Fourth, it can be shown by induction that these objects of knowledge are not universals. An object of knowledge is either a concept or a judgment.[11] Now the concept, i.e., the definition, cannot be a concept of a universal. If it were the concept of a universal in any of the two senses distinguished above, the definition would inform us of the essence of the individual; for the individual is different both from the universal that encompasses it and from a plurality of individuals. Therefore, it is impossible for the definition of a universal to be attached to the individual;

---

11. 'Concept': *Ziyyur*; *tasawwur*; νόημα. True judgment': *'immut*; *tasdiq*; κατάφασις. Cf. Husik, "Studies in Gersonides [2]," pp. 232–34, Goichon, *Lexique*, par. 374 and 361; Harry A. Wolfson, "The Terms *Tasawwur* and *Tasdiq* in Arabic Philosophy and Their Greek, Latin and Hebrew Equivalents," *Moslem World* 33, no. 2 (1943): 1–15; Altmann, "Ibn Bājja," p. 82, n. 31.

In *On the Soul* Aristotle distinguishes between the apprehension of essences of things and the affirmation or negation of predicates to subjects, i.e., judgment or assertion. Aristotle, *On the Soul* 3.6. 430a25–28, 430b26–30. In the Latin tradition this distinction was expressed by the terms *incomplexum* and *complexum* respectively. William Ockham, *Philosophical Writings*, trans. and ed. P. Boehner (Edinburgh, 1957), p. 18 ff.

for things that are different have different definitions.[12] In general, just as the definition of a house is not true of a brick [in the house] and the definition of the number *ten* not true of the number *two* [which is included in the number *ten*], so too is it impossible on this hypothesis for the definition [of the universal] to be true of the individual, as is self-evident. A definition, however, by its nature informs us of the essence of each one of the *individuals* that are comprehended by this definition. Hence, it is evident that the definition is not a definition of a universal. Moreover, if the definition were the definition of a universal, it would be so in so far as the universal is a unit; for there is no plurality in a definition. For example, in the definition of man it is not stated, 'Men are rational animals', but, 'Man is a rational animal'. Hence, it would appear that the definition defines a single thing. Now when it shall be proved that it is impossible for a definition to be a definition of a universal as a unit, it will be thereby shown that the definition cannot be a definition of a universal at all.

We claim that it is impossible for a definition to define a universal insofar as the universal is regarded as comprehending and encompassing [all of its instances], i.e., insofar as it is a genus or species [i.e., its unitary aspect].[13] If the definition did define the universal, i.e., the genus or the species, since it would thereby be a relation it would necessarily incorporate this relational aspect, i.e., the comprehension of its instances, just as in the case of the definition of a slave a reference to the master is included. But this is impossible in definitions.[14] Moreover, it is evident that every part of a definition is affirmatively predicated of that which is defined. But if the definition denotes a universal, the species would be identical with its genus—which is absurd. For example, since 'man' is defined as a 'rational animal', it would follow [on this hypothesis] that 'man' is 'animal', and then the species would be identical

---

12. Since the individual and the universal are different ontologically, they must have different definitions. Cf. Aristotle, *Metaphysics* 8.4–8, 10.

13. To appreciate the metaphysical and logical dimensions of this whole argument against universals, one should read J. Guttmann's essay "Levi ben Gerson's Theorie des Begriffs," which has been translated into Hebrew and included in the collection of his essays entitled *Dat u-Mada* (Jerusalem, 1955), pp. 136–48; see also Touati, *Gersonide*, pp. 413–23.

14. Since the concept of a universal is a correlative, reference to its correlation—the individual—would have to be part of its definition. Accordingly, on the hypothesis that definitions are of universals, the definition would always include a reference to its instances. For example, on this view 'man' should be defined as 'rational animal such as Socrates, Plato, Aristotle, *ad infinitum*'. But, according to Gersonides, this is not the nature of a definition. Husik, "Studies in Gersonides [2]," p. 236.

with its genus.[15] Furthermore, it would follow that the last species [i.e., the lowest species] would be identical with the highest genus. Since, for example, a 'man' is defined as 'animal' and since the definition of 'animal' is 'organism capable of both nutritive and sensory functions', it would follow then that man [qua species] is the nutritive function [or power]. But since the definition of the nutritive power is also applicable to a growing body, it would follow that man [qua species] is [the genus] body. By parity of reasoning, man, the infima species, would ultimately become identical with the most general of the genera [i.e., being]. But this is utterly absurd.

Nor does the judgment refer to a universal. A judgment is a proposition about something that has been conceptualized; hence the concept is prior to the judgment.[d] Now, since it has been demonstrated that the concept [or definition] is not a concept of a universal, it is evident that the proposition does not refer to a universal. Moreover, by its very nature a universal proposition [e.g., All S is P] does not refer to a universal insofar as the universal is construed in its comprehensive and encompassing [i.e., its unitary] role. For the subject of such a proposition refers in no way to a universal in its comprehensive[e] and encompassing role. Indeed, if the subject in this proposition did refer to a universal in this capacity, that which is not many would become multipliable. For example, in the proposition 'Every man is rational', there is a reference to the plurality of men, and therefore the term 'every' is employed in this proposition. But if the subject of this judgment were *the species man*, then the proposition [by using the term 'every'] would imply that the species is multipliable. But it is obvious that the species is not multipliable nor even two in number. Hence, it is evident that the subject of a universal proposition is not something that comprehends and encompasses [all individuals as a unit, i.e., the genus or species]. The same thing is true for the indefinite proposition, for the quantitative particle doesn't change the denotation of the subject. This is obvious.[16]

---

15. This argument presupposes Aristotle's discussion and criticism of the Platonic theory of Forms. One argument against this theory is the following. If we define 'man' as 'rational animal' and if in a definition the constituent terms denote universals, then the species *man* would be identical with the genus *animal*. For, a thing is identical with its essence (Aristotle, *Metaphysics* 7.6.), and if the genus is alleged to be a universal defining the essence of the species, then the species would be identical with the genus (ibid., 7.14. 1039b9–15).

16. Indefinite proposition': *ha-gezerah ha-stamit;* e.g., 'Man is rational'. In indefinite propositions there is no quantitative particle, or operator (*homah*), that indicates the range of denotation of the proposition. In ordinary English these logical operators are expressed by such words as *all, every, no, some.* Husik, "Studies in Gersonides [2]," pp. 238–41; Joseph, *Introduction to Logic,* p. 176.

Indeed, if we maintain that the universal proposition refers to the universal in its comprehensive and encompassing aspect, several absurdities would ensue. First, from this hypothesis it would follow that a universal proposition would not be falsified when it is not true of any of its instances; for the universal is different from the individual, and it would not be necessary when the proposition is false of the individual that it be false also of the universal. For it is possible that a judgment can be true of the whole and yet be false of any one of its parts. For example, Reuben is a man although no one of his parts is a man. But [all of this] is utterly absurd; for it is obvious that a universal proposition is falsified if it is false of any *one* of its instances, all the more so if it is false of *every* one of its instances.[17]

Second, this hypothesis implies that the universal proposition would never be true. If such a proposition is true, there must be a correspondence between what exists extramentally and what is thought [or asserted], for this is the definition of a true proposition.[18] But on this hypothesis it is evident that it is impossible for a universal proposition to correspond with that which exists extramentally; for it [ex hypothesi] refers to a universal, and a universal in its comprehensive and encompassing aspect does not exist outside the mind. What does exist extramentally, however, are individuals. [But] on this hypothesis the proposition does not refer to them at all, just as a proposition about the number *ten* does not [on this hypothesis] refer to the number *two* nor a proposition about a house refer to a brick. Again, all of this is absurd. A true universal proposition, from its very nature, is always true;[f] e.g., the sentence 'All animals have sensation' is always true for any living creature.

Third, from this hypothesis it would follow that every mathematical theorem[19] demonstrating that one thing is either equal to, greater, or smaller than another thing is false. Consider, for example, the theorem 'The interior

---

17. The example addressed by this objection trades on the ambiguity used in the term *ḥeleq*. This word can mean 'individual' or 'instance', as well as 'part'. Similarly, the term *Kollel* means 'whole' as well as 'universal' (Aristotle, *Metaphysics* 5.26. 1023b29 ff). The objector rightly claims that what is true of the whole need not be true of any of its parts. From this he infers that what is true of a universal need not be true of any one of its instances. It is odd that Gersonides does not reply to this objection by pointing out the aforementioned ambiguity. Instead he appeals to the very concept of a *universal* proposition: it is true of *all* the individuals that fall under its scope. Hence, it is falsified merely if it is false of one of these individuals.

18. This is a version of the so-called correspondence theory of truth: "To say of what is that it is not, or of what is not that it is, is false, while to say of what is that it is, and of what is not that it is not, is true." Aristotle, *Metaphysics* 4.7. 1011b26–28.

19. *Temunah limudit; śakl handasī.* Although the more common use of *temunah* in mathematical contexts is to connote 'figure', it can also connote 'theorem'. G. Sarfati, *Mathematical Terminology*, pp. 193, n. 80, 220; Maimonides, *Treatise on Logic*, chap. 8.

angles of a triangle equal the sum of two right angles'. Now if we mean by 'triangle' the universal that encompasses an infinite number of triangles, this statement would be false, for its angles would be infinite, and it would be impossible for them to be equal to *two* right angles.[20] If it is objected that by 'right angles' is meant *all* the individual right angles, these too are infinite in number, and it would turn out that what is infinite is *equal* to what is infinite, and this is absurd; for equality results from finiteness. Moreover, since its angles are equal to two right angles, they are double the universal right angle[g] which is infinite [i.e., which encompasses an infinite number of right angles]; and therefore what is infinite is double what is infinite. This is obviously absurd. Similarly, it can be shown that mathematical theorems proving that one thing is greater or smaller than another would be false. For it is impossible to say that one thing is smaller or greater than another unless one or both of them are finite. But when the subject is universal and encompassing, it is necessary that the predicate be universal and encompassing; for if the predicate were individual, the universal would be the individual. This is evident in propositions that affirm a predicate of a subject.[h] But if the subject and the predicate are universal and encompassing, each one of them would be infinite, and [thus] no one of them could be smaller or greater than the other. [But this is absurd.][21]

Fourth, it would follow from this view that there are capacities and dispositions that would never be realized. Many of the predicates in universal propositions are the differentiating properties[22] of the subjects, and some of these differentiating properties are powers and dispositions. For example, in the sentences, 'Man is rational' and, 'An animal has sensation' [the terms

---

20. In this and in the subsequent examples Gersonides makes use of the Aristotelian principle that quantitative relationships such as 'equal to', 'greater than', and 'less than' obtain only between *finite* magnitudes (Aristotle, *On the Heavens* 1.6. 274a7–8). Moreover, these examples also trade on the previously mentioned ambiguity with respect to the terms *Kollel* and *ḥeleq*. Indeed, as Guttmann has pointed out, it is difficult to make sense out of these arguments if we don't remember that Gersonides conceives of the *Kollel*, or 'universal', as a *whole* having *parts*, just as he conceives it as a species having members. Thus, given this conception of universals, if a universal is said to encompass an infinite number of individuals, it can be regarded as an infinite totality. Gersonides will then argue that one cannot ascribe to infinite totalities properties like *equality* or *being larger than*. Guttmann, "Levi ben Gerson", pp. 144–45.

21. Here Guttmann's analysis is especially pertinent. The argument makes sense only if it is assumed, as Gersonides does assume, that a universal contains its instances as a whole contains its parts. If the universal so construed is alleged to encompass, i.e., contain, an infinite number of individuals, it is an infinite totality, and one infinite totality cannot be larger or smaller than another such totality.

22. A differentiating property (*hevdel;* διαφορά) defines the species. Cf. Aristotle, *Categories* 3 and 5; *Topica* 1.4–5.

'rational' and 'has sensation' denote] differentiating properties. Now if the judgment in these propositions is concerned with the universal in its comprehensive and encompassing role, these dispositions would never be realized; for the *universal* animal, for example, never has the property of sensation.[23] But this is quite absurd, since in *On the Heavens*, it has been shown that every capacity must be realized at some time.[24]

Fifth, if the subjects and predicates of these propositions were comprehensive and encompassing, as is entailed by this hypothesis, the predication of the genus of the species would be false, for the species is not its genus. Therefore, the proposition, 'Man is an animal', for example, would be false—but this is absolutely absurd.[25] In conclusion, then, a universal proposition does not refer to a universal in its comprehensive and encompassing role, i.e., its unitary aspect [as a genus or species].

Nor does the universal proposition refer to the universal qua plurality [of individuals] insofar as it makes one judgment about this plurality taken all together. This is evident from what we have demonstrated with respect to the impossibility of a universal proposition referring to the universal in its comprehensive and encompassing aspect; for all the absurdities that followed in the latter case also ensue in the former case, except the first. The first objection—it will be recalled—maintained that if the subject of a universal proposition were a universal, then that which is not multipliable could become multipliable. In this case, however, this absurdity does not follow; for here the subject allegedly refers to the individual and the quantitative particle encompasses all the individuals together. All the other absurdities (which we have enumerated) that follow from the original assumption are, however, entailed by the present hypothesis. This can be easily seen with a bit of reflection. But we shall examine one of them in order that the reader see how these absurdities do in fact follow from this hypothesis.

We claim[i] that from this hypothesis it is implied that a universal judgment would not be falsified because it is false of each of its instances; for [on this hypothesis] it judges them collectively, and it is not necessary that what is

---

23. Individual living animals have sensation, not abstract entities such as universals. The specific difference, then, is true of individuals, not of a universal.

24. Aristotle, *On the Heavens* 1.12.

25. If in the proposition, 'All men are animals', the terms 'men' and 'animals' denote universals, the proposition would be false. For the species *man* as such is not the genus *animal*, neither in the sense of being identical with the genus *animal* nor in the sense of having the property of being an animal. That is, in universal propositions we are not predicating one universal of another universal.

true of each of the individuals taken together be true of one of them.[26] Similarly, it can be shown that all the other absurdities follow from this hypothesis.

It is, therefore, evident that a universal proposition does not refer to a universal, neither in the sense of a unit [i.e., a species or genus], nor in the sense of a plurality to which the proposition refers collectively as a single judgment. Thus, if the universal proposition refers to a universal, it would do so insofar as it refers to the universal as a plurality referring to each one of them individually [i.e., not collectively]. For if the universal proposition does refer to a universal, it would necessarily do so in either of two ways: either as a unit or as a plurality. If the latter, it does so either collectively or distributively. Since it has been proven that it cannot refer to the universal, neither as a unit, nor as a plurality construed as a collection, it can refer to [a plurality] only distributively. But since there is no determinate part [i.e., subset] of this plurality besides the individual to which the proposition might refer, it follows that it refers [distributively] to each and every one of the individuals [of the plurality].[27] That there is no determinate part of the plurality besides the individual to which the proposition refers can be easily seen in propositions whose subjects are the last species. For example, in the proposition, 'All men are rational', there are no determinate groups[j] of individual men distinguished from one another such that the judgment would refer [distributively] to any one of these [groups] taken collectively. Whereas it is obvious that in 'All men are rational', it is intended that *each* individual man is rational. Now, if this is the case in propositions whose subjects are the last species, it is also true for other propositions. For in the case of propositions whose subjects are the genera, if it is assumed that the proposition refers to different parts of the genus, i.e., one of the determinate groups into which the genus can be divided (e.g., one of the species that are comprised by that genus), all the absurdities previously adduced concerning the universal judgment in its collective interpretation would ensue. This is self-evident.

---

26. If the universal be construed as an aggregate of individuals to which the universal proposition refers collectively, then it need not be the case that whatever is true of the aggregate, or whole, is true of each and every one of the individuals in the group. I. Copi, *Introduction to Logic*, 2d. ed. (New York, 1961), p. 79.

27. One last argument remains to Gersonides' opponent: to construe universal propositions in such a way that their constituent terms refer distributively to groups, or subsets, within the extension of the term. For example, the term 'dog' in 'All dogs are warm-blooded' denotes distributively the *subclasses* of dogs such as Dobermans, collies, dachshunds, etc., which are taken collectively, i.e., as groups. Gersonides then proceeds to reject this suggestion. Husik, "Studies in Gersonides [2]," pp. 244–46.

After having shown that the universal proposition refers distributively *to each individual* that falls within the range of this proposition, we shall now show that true universal objects of knowledge exist always extramentally in the way that they are conceived, which is contrary to what has been claimed in the argument that we have been considering.[28] For a [true universal] proposition does not imply the existence of the subject; rather it asserts that the predicate is true of the subject, if the latter exists, or it negates this predicate of the subject, as is obvious.[29] It is, therefore, evident that the proposition as conceived corresponds to what exists extramentally; for each individual that does exist extramentally and is included[k] in the scope of this proposition exhibits the property that is asserted by the predicate in that proposition. In this way the proposition always corresponds to what exists outside the mind. Indeed, that which it asserts corresponds exactly to that which exists extramentally. For if the proposition is true of that which exists outside the mind, it can also be true of other individuals ad infinitum.[30] Similarly, with the individuals existing outside the mind: if there are individuals of a certain [kind], there can be other individuals [of that kind] ad infinitum.[31]

It has been objected that the object of knowledge in a universal proposition differs from that which exists extramentally since it refers collectively to all the infinite individuals existing outside the mind, whereas these extramental individuals are [in fact] finite in number. We maintain, however, that the object of knowledge as such does not refer to an individual plurality at all, for the object of knowledge cannot represent the individual in such a way[l]

---

28. The original objection to the claim that the acquired intellect is immortal was that its objects of knowledge are essentially generated and that whatever is generated essentially is subject to corruption. It was also claimed that if the acquired intellect were immortal, there would be a disparity between thought and reality. (This is the second argument referred to in the beginning of this chapter.) One argument in behalf of the latter thesis was that the object of knowledge is a universal and universals exist only potentially outside the mind. Gersonides has just completed his discussion of the first part of the latter argument; he now proceeds to analyze the second part of this argument.

29. Here Gersonides makes a significant and perhaps original contribution to the logical analysis of universal propositions. In Aristotelian logic such propositions were regarded as having *existential import*, i.e., it was presupposed that the constituent terms in these propositions do denote individuals. (Joseph, *Introduction to Logic*, p. 242, n. 1; W. and M. Kneale, *The Development of Logic* (Oxford, 1962), p. 58. According to Kneale, no medieval logician recognized the non-existential interpretation of universal propositions (ibid., p. 265). This assertion needs to be qualified in the light of Gersonides' present claim.

30. If a universal proposition is true, it is always true and ranges over an infinite number of individuals.

31. If there are three dogs in the world, there is no logical reason why there can't be five or any other number of dogs.

that a plurality is possible. Rather it represents an individual as any individual whatever, not as a particular individual.[32] A universal proposition,[m] however, does indicate some kind of plurality in so far as it is a composite of the intellect and of sensation, as Aristotle mentions[n] in *On The Soul*.[33] Accordingly, it is evident that the object of knowledge as such does not refer to each and every one of an infinite number of individuals; rather it denotes an individual only as *any* individual whatever, and this is a thing that could exist outside the mind. Moreover, this objection would have some force if the [universal] proposition were to judge that this infinite number of individuals exists collectively. But it doesn't have any existential import at all, as has been explained; all the more so it doesn't refer to these individuals collectively. It asserts, however, that if the proposition is affirmative, the predicate is true of whatever individuals [which are denoted by the subject] that may exist, or if the proposition is negative, it denies [that the predicate is true of any individual denoted by the subject]; and this is something[o] that is always true outside the mind [if the proposition is true]. It is, therefore, evident that the aspect in which the proposition has infinite scope is in agreement with that which exists outside the mind, which [may] be infinite.[34]

It has been further objected that the object of knowledge in a universal

---

32. A concept-term denotes its instances not as definite particulars but as any particular of that kind. E.g., the term 'dog' is true of any number of dogs, but it doesn't pick out the dog Lassie any more than Fido.

33. I have not been able to discover in *On The Soul* a passage that exactly corresponds to Gersonides' point. However, there are several places in this treatise where Aristotle does say that judging involves the use of sense-images, and in this sense the judgment involves both intellect and sensation. Aristotle, *On The Soul* 3.7. 431b2–3, 3.11. 434a15–17, 3.3. 427b28–30.

34. The objection alleged that there is a discrepancy between the infinite scope of the universal proposition construed collectively and the finite collection of individuals that constitute the actual range of this judgment. Gersonides dissipates the force of this objection first by denying that universal propositions have any existential import at all. He proposes a hypothetical analysis of the traditional categorical universal proposition: instead of, 'All S is P', he suggests, 'If anything is S, it is P'. This proposal is the method used in modern logic. Second, universal propositions do not refer to collections. The domain of such propositions is the world of individuals, construed as *any* individual of a specific type. Thus, the proposition, 'If anything is an S, it is P', asserts that if there is some X that has the property S, it has also the property P. If this universal proposition is true, then all individuals that fall under the subject-concept are always characterizable by the predicate-concept. Finally, if one were to require that the infinite range of the universal proposition must correspond to an equally large collection of individuals in the world in order for the proposition to be true, this demand is satisfied, Gersonides suggests, by the notion of any arbitrary individual of the specified type referred to in the proposition. That is, *any individual whatever* that falls under the concept S, and they may be infinite, is also P. Thus, universal propositions, Gersonides claims, are true no matter whether the domain over which they range is infinite or finite. They are true so long as *any* individual of which the subject-concept is true is also characterizable by the predicate-concept 'ad infinitum'.

proposition differs from that which exists outside the mind, since it represents all these individuals collectively, whereas the individuals do not exist in reality as a collection. This objection, however, is invalid. As we have said before, the object of knowledge as such cannot represent[p] an individual plurality at all.

Now that we have demonstrated that the object of knowledge is either a concept or a proposition and that neither is a universal but represents any individual whatever [of a certain kind], it is evident that the claim[q] that the objects of knowledge are universals is false. We have also shown that the universality which is inherent in some sense in the universal proposition does not imply that the object of knowledge is different from what exists. Indeed, this is the exact opposite of what this argument tried to establish. Since the object of knowledge refers to any individual whatever [of a certain kind], it is acquired from repeated perceptions; i.e., when the intellect abstracts from the sensible individual the material accidents by virtue of which plurality accrues to the individual.[r,35]

The second major argument claims that since the objects of knowledge refer to general natures, and that the general nature exists extramentally only potentially, the object of knowledge differs from that which exists extramentally. This objection fails. It is necessary that the general[s] nature exist actually in every one of the individuals of which it is the common nature; for this general nature is the definition or part of the definition, and the definition informs us of the essence, or substance, of the individual. And the substance is present in the individual in actuality,[t] not potentially; otherwise, the thing would be only potentially itself, which means that it would be contradictory to itself, since potentiality and actuality are contradictions. But this is utterly absurd. It is clear, therefore, that the general nature is found actually in every one of the individuals of which it is common nature. In short, just as the color is actually present in the colored object even though it is associated with other things (i.e.,[u] other accidental qualities and the essence), so too the essence is actually present in the individual even though it is associated with other things; i.e., in every individual the essence is associated with accidental qualities.

Moreover, the general nature is the essence,[v] and the essence is that which makes the individual actual, i.e., we can say that the individual exists because of its essence. Now[w] with respect to that which possesses a property by virtue of some other thing, that from which this property is derived is more

---

35. Aristotle, *Metaphysics* 1.1. 980b29–981a5; *Posterior Analytics* 2.19; Husik, "Studies in Gersonides [2]," p. 248.

fitting to possess this property than that which received the property from it.[36] For example, if it is the eye that makes it possible for Socrates to see, the eye itself is more fitting to be described as seeing than Socrates. Accordingly, the essence [itself] is more appropriately described as actually existing than the essence that exists along with the accidental features by virtue of which the object is particularized. But this is contrary to what is maintained by this argument. Finally, all the accidental and particular features of a thing exist in actuality [only] because they inhere in its[x] essence. Therefore, the essence is more appropriately described as actually existing than those accidental features. Aristotle already explained this point, saying that 'exists' is said of a substance primarily, and[y] if it is said of the accident, it is predicated secondarily, or derivatively, because of its inherence in the substance.[37] And so it is evident that the essence of a thing exists in actuality in that thing.

The third objection—which maintains that since that which outside the mind corresponds to the objects of knowledge is itself not an intellect, whereas these objects of knowledge exist as intellect in the material intellect, thus that which exists outside the mind is different from the object of knowledge— is not valid, as has been shown previously. For it has been demonstrated that that which exists extramentally[z] corresponding to the objects of knowledge is in some sense an intellect in so far as it exists in the Agent Intellect. Accordingly, it does not follow from these arguments concerning the objects of knowledge that the objects of knowledge are essentially generated [simply] because they are generated in the material intellect.

Nor is the further claim of this third objection—that the objects of knowledge are corporeal and not separate—valid [at least not] in the manner in which it has been argued. They [the defenders of the objection] present two arguments here: first, that the generation of the objects of knowledge in the material intellect results from some essential change, as is the case in material forms; second, these objects of knowledge are multiplied according to the plurality of subjects [having them]. Now the first of these points can be seen to be false quite easily. Corporeal forms are generated as the result of some kind of essential change, and they are generated immediately as a result of the change. For example, the form of a color which reaches the visual faculty is generated immediately after the eye is affected by the color, i.e., after the color is impressed upon the eye. Analogously, with the other corporeal forms. These objects of knowledge, however, are not generated in the material

---

36. Aristotle, *Metaphysics* 2.1. 993b24–26.
37. Aristotle, *Metaphysics* 4.2.

intellect except[a1] accidentally; that is, insofar as they require for their existence in the intellect something that is itself an effect of some [essential] change,
i.e., a sensory perception. We observe, therefore, that sometimes the object
of knowledge is generated in the intellect *considerably after* the sense organ is
changed by the sense object. Moreover, if they admit that whatever[b1] exists
as the result of some accidental change is corporeal, it would follow according
to them that that which is cognized by the material intellect in apprehending
the Agent Intellect is also corporeal. For they believe that this cognition[c1]
requires for its existence objects of knowledge of the sublunar world whose
existence in turn requires something that is itself the effect of some essential
change. Hence, the original object of knowledge requires for its own existence
something that is the effect of essential change. If this were[d1] the case,
according to their own position, this object of knowledge would be corruptible, which is contrary to their hypothesis.[38]

The second of these arguments—the claim that these objects of knowledge
are made many by the plurality of their subjects, as in the case of material
forms, and hence are themselves material—is also invalid in the form presented, as we shall now show. In behalf of this thesis they advance three
arguments: (1) these objects of knowledge depend upon individuals existing
outside the mind; (2) if this thesis were not correct, it would follow that
when a man learns or forgets some piece of knowledge that other men learn
or forget it as well; and (3) if this thesis were not true, there would not be
any learning or forgetting.

We maintain that the first of these points is false. They attempt to establish
it in two ways: first, that the truth of a piece of knowledge depends upon
that which exists outside the mind; second, that these objects of knowledge
are universals, and universals exist only in so far as particulars exist extramentally.

We shall now show that the first of these two methods is erroneous; i.e.,
the claim that since the existence of these objects of knowledge derives from
the individuals upon which they depend, and since the individuals upon
which the object of knowledge possessed by Reuben, say, depends differ
from the individuals upon which depends the object of knowledge possessed
by Simon, the object of knowledge is necessarily multiple, and hence corporeal. For the following are the possible alternatives in this matter:[e1] (1)
either the existence of the object of knowledge is based upon images of
individuals that have been generated from the sense perception of these

---

38. If something is corporeal it results from or admits accidental change, all the more so if
it admits essential change. Husik, "Studies in Gersonides [2]," pp. 250–51.

individuals; (2) or it is based upon the images of individuals which [actually] exist at that moment; (3) or it is based upon any individual whatever.

Now, if we assume that the object of knowledge is based upon images of individuals [and that] it has been generated in the material intellect from the sense perception of these individuals, and that in this way it is multiplied, several absurdities ensue. First, it would follow that the object of knowledge would perish as soon as the particulars from which it is generated perish. For if the existence of the object of knowledge necessarily implies the existence of individuals, from the perception of which this object of knowledge has been generated by means of the senses in the material intellect, it would follow that when those individuals perish the object of knowledge perishes, and that the knower would have to perceive other[f] particulars from which he would again acquire that object of knowledge which he formerly possessed. But this is absurd. Second, it would follow from this hypothesis that a true object of knowledge would at one time be true and at another false. For if it is assumed that the truth of such objects of knowledge is based upon individuals existing outside the mind, as is assumed in this argument, it would follow that when these individuals perish, the object of knowledge would be false, since there is [now] no subject outside the mind to which it refers. But this is contrary to what it said about these objects of knowledge; namely, that they are true all of the time.[g] Third, it would follow that these objects of knowledge are both corporeal and incorporeal, which is impossible. For if multiplication in the object of knowledge results from the difference in the particulars from which the object of knowledge is generated in the perceiving of such particulars, it would turn out that the object of knowledge possessed by many men would be one and the same if it was generated in them by the perception of the very same[h] particulars. But what is numerically one in many objects is incorporeal; for it is impossible for a corporeal thing to be numerically one and yet be present in many objects. But [it was assumed] to be corporeal! Hence [this hypothesis] is absurd.[39] Fourth, on this hypothesis some objects of knowledge would be corporeal whereas others would be incorporeal, which is contrary to the original hypothesis. For, the objects of knowledge that are generated as the result of the perception of objects that are generated and corruptible are multipliable and corporeal insofar as they arise in different men as the basis of the perceptions of different particulars. But the objects of knowledge that derive from the perception of eternal particulars, as occurs in astronomy, would not be multipliable or

---

39. Ibid., pp. 252–53.

corporeal, since these objects of knowledge correspond to only one particular outside the mind.

However, if we assume that the objects of knowledge are grounded in images of particulars, which [in turn] exist extramentally at that time, several absurdities would also be entailed. First, since on this assumption the object of knowledge in one man differs from that of another man (for one is grounded on images of particulars at that time, whereas the other is grounded in other images of particulars at a different time), an analogous difference would follow, i.e., the object of knowledge apprehended by one [and the same] man on the basis of a certain set of particulars at one time will differ from the object of knowledge apprehended on the basis of a different set of particulars. It is evident from this assumption that a man who has acquired some piece of knowledge would have to relearn it when the particulars on which it was grounded have vanished; for when these particulars perish so too does the object of knowledge upon which it was based. And if he acquires an object of knowledge[i] from another set of generated particulars, it would be a different object of knowledge, not the previous one.

Second, it would also follow from this assumption that an object of knowledge could be false even if there is a corresponding subject outside the mind. The object of knowledge that is grounded on a certain set of particulars outside the mind would be necessarily false when they disappear and a different set of particulars appears. For the object of knowledge which is true on the basis of the latter set of particulars is, on this hypothesis, different from the one that is based upon the earlier set of particulars. Accordingly, the first object of knowledge would be false when the second set of particulars is present; for, if it were true, one and the same object of knowledge would be many. But this is impossible.

Third, this assumption entails that the objects of knowledge in mathematics would be falsified [despite] the strong verification that accrues to it. It is apparent that many mathematical entities cannot have [exactly corresponding] particulars existing outside the mind. For example, there is no straight line outside the mind which is exactly like the line that the geometer postulates; for the line that is a limit of a body is such that its points do not all fall evenly on itself;[ii,40] nor is it always divisible and augmentable indef-

---

40. The technical term *nekhoḥi* usually has the meaning 'parallel', although Wolfson has distinguished several other connotations (Wolfson, *Crescas' Critique of Aristotle*, p. 387). In this context, however, the term has a different meaning. The passage is concerned with the notion of the straight line in plane geometry. Euclid defined a straight line as follows: "A straight line is a line which *lies evenly* with the points on itself" (Euclid, *Elements*, trans. T. L. Heath, 3 vols. [Cambridge, 1908], 1: 153). In the Hebrew translations of Euclid or in the medieval Hebrew

initely, as the geometer assumes. The reasons for this are all attributable to the matter [of the body]. Nevertheless, the nature of the straight line does allow [for infinite divisibility and augmentability].[41] Similarly, a circle outside the mind never is tangent to a straight line at a point, nor is a sphere tangent to a straight surface at a point. For this reason some of the ancients said that the proofs of the geometers were[k1] false, as Aristotle reported.[42] In short, on this theory there could be no object of knowledge with respect to a thing that is impossible from one aspect but possible from another aspect and [knowable] from this possible aspect.[l1, 43] But this is false.[m1] For there are many true objects of knowledge concerning entities that are impossible [from one point of view] but possible from another point of view. The sciences have demonstrated many such objects of knowledge, as is evident to anyone familiar with natural science and mathematics.[44]

Fourth, from this assumption it would follow that the objects of knowledge would be both corporeal and incorporeal. The object of knowledge with respect to something would be numerically one when all the knowers exist simultaneously, since it is grounded upon the same[n1] particulars. But this means that it is incorporeal, for it is impossible for one and the same corporeal thing to be present in many subjects. It was assumed by this hypothesis, however, that the objects of knowledge were corporeal; but now they are both. This is absurd.

Fifth, it also follows from this assumption that some of the objects of knowledge are incorporeal, i.e., those of the eternal substances, e.g., the heavenly bodies; for that which exists of these entities outside the mind is continually one and the same. Hence, the object of knowledge corresponding to these substances is not multiplied according to the multiplication of subjects. But whatever is of this sort is incorporeal, whereas it was assumed that all of them are corporeal. This is an intolerable inconsistency.

However, if we assume that the objects of knowledge are grounded in

---

texts on geometry the key term ἐξ ἴσου in Euclid's phrase ἐξἴσου τοῖς ἐφ' ἑαυτῆς σημείοις κεῖται was rendered by the Hebrew phrases 'al nekhoḥut, al nokhaḥ eḥad (G. Sarfati, *Mathematical Terminology*, pp. 74–75). I adopt Heath's translation: "evenly on itself."

41. Gersonides is distinguishing between the mathematical concept of a line in pure geometry and its exemplification in bodies. The latter never exemplifies the former completely or perfectly.

42. Aristotle, *Metaphysics* 3.2. 997b35–998a6.

43. Husik, "Studies in Gersonides [2]," p. 254.

44. Gersonides is alluding to ideal entities, or theoretical constructs, such as the point, the straight line, etc. His point here is that the hypothesis under discussion is too empiricistic and would render mathematics false. Such entities are not realizable in the world of sense perception, but they are needed in the theories that are used to explain this world.

some one or another of the particulars outside the mind and not in one definite particular, they would not be multipliable according to the multiplication of subjects because of their foundation in particulars; for in this case there is no difference in the particulars in this respect. It is, therefore, evident that from this assumption it does not follow that the objects of knowledge are corporeal; rather it does follow that they are incorporeal, since they are not[o1] multipliable according to the multiplication of subjects, which is the sign of an incorporeal object. It can also be demonstrated that the being of an object of knowledge does not accrue to it [by] virtue of its being grounded in some definite particular[p1]; rather it is grounded in some one or another particular. For if this [i.e., the former] were necessary, it would be impossible to have knowledge of many mathematical entities, as we have seen, since they do not have any corresponding particulars outside the mind. In short, it would be impossible for us to have any knowledge of that which is impossible from one aspect yet possible from another aspect,[q1] insofar [as it is knowable] from its possible aspect. But all of this is absurd. Moreover, if the existence of knowledge were dependent upon the existence of sensible objects outside the mind, the existence of the latter would then be prior to that of the former. But this is absurd; for it has been shown that the existence of the object of knowledge is the cause of the existence of the sensible object, which is indeed derived from the object of knowledge as existing in the soul of the Agent Intellect. The existence of the sensible object is, however, responsible for the occurrence of the object of knowledge *in us*, but not for its existence as such. Hence, it is evident that once we are in possession of an object of knowledge, it is not necessary that a corresponding sensible object also exist.

The second method of demonstrating that the objects of knowledge are grounded in particulars—that is, since such objects are universals and universals exist because of the existence of their correlatives, the particulars—has already been shown to be absurd. For it is utterly false to say that these objects of knowledge are universals. Moreover, even if we were to admit that they are universals, it would not follow that because they are grounded in particulars they are thereby multipliable. For it is obvious that they are grounded in particulars insofar as the latter are construed as any individuals whatever,[r1] but not insofar as they are construed as definite individuals; and from this aspect there is no multiplication of particulars. Therefore, it doesn't follow that the objects of knowledge are multipliable from this aspect; for one term of a relation can be accidentally related to many things without thereby being itself many. For example, one species of number, e.g., the number *three*, is accidentally related to many numbers larger than it when it is described as 'small'. But it doesn't follow from this that it is multipliable according[s1] to the number of things to which it is related. For the relation that it essentially has because of this attribute is a relation to the number that is larger than it in so far as this number is larger than it, not in so far as that number is the number *four* or *five*.[45] Finally, it has already been proven that it is absurd to maintain that the being of the objects of knowledge is [completely] founded upon the existence of particulars outside the mind, as is claimed by this hypothesis.

The second of these objections—which maintains that if the objects of knowledge are not multipliable according to the multiplication of their subjects, it would follow that if a man had learned or forgotten a piece of knowledge, other men would learn or forget it as well—is also false.[46] It is not impossible for one and the same thing to have many different relations to many different things. The sun, for example, is near one man yet distant from another; it sets in one horizon and shines in another horizon—but it is one and the same sun. It is, therefore, evident that it is not impossible for a piece of knowledge to arise in one man but not in another, although it is one and the same piece of knowledge for both men. Nor is it necessary if the activity is one and the same that the capacities for this activity be one and the same, as is maintained by this objection. This would be true if the activity were material; but if it is assumed to be separate [i.e., incorporeal], this is not the case. This is evident to the reader of this treatise. Avicenna, however, is open to this absurdity; for he maintains both that the capacity here is numerically one and that the material intellect is separate, ungenerated, and incorruptible.

The third of these objections—which maintains that if the objects of knowledge are not multipliable according to the multiplication of subjects, there would be no learning or forgetting—is also false. Even if we were to concede to them that a separate substance is neither generated nor corruptible, it is thereby still not impossible for the objects of knowledge to be generated and perishable in the material intellect. What would be impossible, however, is that they should be *essentially* generated or corruptible.

The second of the premises on which this theory is based, which asserts that everything generated is destroyed, and Aristotle's proof of this principle, will be shown later to be invalid.[47]

[Now let us consider the arguments] in behalf of the claim that the material

---

45. The fact that there are an infinite number of natural numbers larger than the number *three* doesn't mean that the latter is thereby multipliable since each one of these numbers is correlative to it. Every number greater than *three* bears *the same* relation to *three*.

46. Averroes, *Long Commentary on De Anima* in Hyman and Walsh, *Philosophy in the Middle Ages*, p. 322.

47. Infra, bk. 6, pt. 1, chap. 27.

intellect can apprehend the Agent Intellect.[48] The first of these arguments maintains that since, according to Aristotle, the relation between the intellect and that which is known is analogous to the relation between the senses and that which is sensed, and since the senses can actually receive the sense-object, it follows that the intellect can receive[t1] actually its objects of knowledge, i.e., the Agent Intellect, as has been maintained by this view. I shall argue that this argument does not establish the conclusion that the material intellect can comprehend the Agent Intellect. This argument in its behalf is merely an analogical syllogism,[49] and analogical syllogisms are not absolutely true. Indeed, from this very argument the opposite conclusion follows! For, we can say that just as the sense does not have the capacity to receive the sense-object itself but receives something related and[u1] similar to it—e.g., the eye does not receive the color that is in the object but receives something like it in some sense [i.e., the color impression]—so too the material intellect does not have the capacity to receive the Agent[v1] Intellect itself but receives something in some sense similar to it.

The second argument in behalf of this thesis maintains that if the material intellect can apprehend something that is essentially not an intellect, all the more so should it be able to apprehend that which is essentially an intellect. In truth, I do not see why it should be so capable! For if they were[w1] to maintain that if that which is not essentially an intellect [i.e., material form] in the material intellect becomes an intellect when it is known by the material intellect, then it is obviously more fitting that that which is essentially an intellect should be an intellect when it is known—this would indeed[x1] be correct. Nevertheless, it does not follow from *this* argument that the material intellect can apprehend the Agent Intellect. Indeed, one who[y1] has the capacity to apprehend lower-level forms need not have the capacity to know more superior forms; for the knowledge of the latter is more difficult. It is evident that the more superior in rank the form the more difficult is the knowledge of it. This is clear in the case of the material forms themselves. For it is evident that if one has the capacity to do something, it does not follow that he can do something that is more difficult. For example, if someone can lift a weight of three talents, it doesn't follow that he can lift something much heavier than it. This is obvious. It is, therefore, evident that just

---

48. Supra, chap. 9.

49. *Heqesh ha-hemshel;* συλλογισμὸς διὰ παραδειγμάτων. Aristotle classifies arguments by examples as a species of *rhetorical syllogisms* (Aristotle, *Posterior Analytics* 1.1. 71a9–10). Rhetorical syllogisms are low in the scale of logical rigor and persuade only through their oratorical and poetical devices. Actually they are *inductive* inferences rather than deductive syllogisms (Aristotle, *Rhetoric* 1.1–2).

because the material intellect can apprehend material forms it need not have the capacity to apprehend forms of a superior rank, i.e., those forms that are intellects; for the apprehension of these forms is more difficult. And whatever has the capacity for some act need not have the capacity for an act that is superior to it.[z1] Indeed, they [the defenders of this argument] themselves admit that the apprehension of the Agent Intellect by the material intellect is more difficult than its apprehension of the forms which it is naturally capable of apprehending. Therefore, they say, this apprehension, if it is attainable by man, can only be attained after the material intellect has been perfected by the apprehension of all the material forms. Thus, this argument is obviously absurd: it is contrary to their own statements and contrary to the real nature of the subject.

The third argument maintains that since the Agent Intellect makes the imaginative forms actually intelligible[a2] in the material intellect after being only potentially intelligible, it is more fitting that the Agent Intellect itself be known by the material intellect. For anything that is responsible for something else being in a certain condition is itself more fitting to be in that[b2] condition than the thing whose condition is derived from the former. I claim that this argument is invalid. It is sometimes possible for a thing to bring about a condition in something else such that this condition is the consequence of both the nature of the recipient and of that which it receives from the agent[c2] of this condition. Then,[d2] it is not necessary that the cause of this condition itself exhibit this condition. For example, a particular craft makes a piece of iron capable of cutting; it is evident, however, that the craft itself is not describable as 'cutting', for this condition is a feature of the iron as the result of its nature and the shape it receives from the craft. Similarly, the art of medicine makes a sick man healthy; but the art itself is not because of this describable as 'healthy'. Accordingly, one could argue that the imaginative forms may be actually intelligible because of their own nature and of what they have been endowed with by the Agent Intellect. Hence, there is no need to describe the Agent Intellect as an object of knowledge of the material intellect.

That it is possible for the imaginative forms to be intelligible because of their own nature and of what they[e2] have been endowed with by the Agent Intellect is evident; for[f2] it is not the case that anything is affected[g2] by anything else. Indeed,[h2] the material intellect cannot apprehend any form[i2] except those of the sublunar world and can apprehend them only after the Agent Intellect makes them intelligible. Moreover, it is evident that the Agent Intellect does not work upon the imaginative form at all; i.e., the latter is not affected by it in such a way that it is [substantially] transformed and becomes an object of knowledge after having been a mere image; the image remains an image. Rather, the Agent Intellect works upon the material intellect and enables it to become cognitive[j2] in actuality after having been cognitive only potentially. Accordingly, the Agent Intellect renders the image intelligible in actuality after having been intelligible potentially merely[k2] in an accidental sense; i.e., in so far as it enables the material intellect to apprehend the image in actuality, whereas previously it was only potentially capable of apprehending the image. But it is evident that it does not follow from the fact that something responsible accidentally for another thing having a certain condition that it too exhibits this condition. Fire, for example, makes some things black and bitter; but this does not entail that fire is both black and bitter. This is so because the fire is only accidentally responsible for these conditions; for the condition that these things acquire essentially from fire is either heat or dryness, and it is by the condition that it gives[l2] them essentially that the fire is more correctly describable. Indeed, sometimes fire accidentally makes some things cold, i.e., when it separates from them the hot portion; but it is not possible to describe fire as cold. And so it is evident that it is not necessary to say that the Agent Intellect is known by the material intellect simply because it accidentally is responsible for the actual intelligibility of the image after the latter was only potentially intelligible. Nevertheless, what does follow from this proposition [i.e., that whatever is responsible for a condition in another thing is more fitting to possess that condition], if we concede its truth, is that since the Agent Intellect is responsible, if only accidentally, for the cognition of the image by the material intellect whereas the image was previously only knowable potentially, the Agent Intellect is more capable than the material intellect of knowing the image. This is evident from what has been previously established, for it has been demonstrated that the Agent Intellect knows all these objects of knowledge.

Indeed, it would follow from this premise[m2] in behalf of their [main] thesis—the premise[n2] that whatever is responsible for a condition in another object is more fitting to possess that condition—that the intelligible [order][50]

---

50. In this discussion Gersonides introduces and makes use of a technical notion that is extremely important in his philosophy and recurs throughout the treatise. It is the notion of the *siddur muskal*. This is a difficult term to render into English; Husik suggests 'intelligible prototype' (Husik, "Studies in Gersonides [2]," p. 259). In Bk. 3, chap. 2, where Gersonides also makes use of this phrase, it is translated by Wolfson as 'conceptual order' and 'the order . . . as conceived . . .' (Wolfson, *The Philosophy of Spinoza*, 2:28). Touati renders it as 'l'ordre intelligible' (Touati, *Les Guerres du Seigneur*, p. 84.) However it is translated the term connotes the plan or pattern of intelligibility of sublunar phenomena as an object of thought for God or the Agent Intellect. In the present passage Gersonides compares this pattern to the plan of an artifact as it is conceived in the mind of the artisan.

The phrases 'intelligible prototype', 'l'ordre intelligible', 'conceptual order', all connote the

of the image possessed by the Agent Intellect is more appropriately an object of knowledge for us than the image itself. For, since the image becomes intelligible to the material intellect because of the conceived order pertaining to it[o2] in the Agent Intellect, that conceived order ought to be the object of knowledge of the material intellect rather than the image. This is without doubt true. For the image in no way becomes intelligible, since the particular is, as particular, not knowable; rather, what is known is the order corresponding to the image as present in the Agent Intellect. That the image is knowable only because of the intelligible [order] corresponding to it in the Agent Intellect is evident. For if it were not the case that the sensible object derives its existence from the intelligible order, it would not be knowable; just as it would not be possible to know the causes of an artifact if it did not derive from the intelligible order in the mind of the craftsman. This point is explained by Themistius in his commentary on book twelve of Aristotle's *Metaphysics*.[51] But it doesn't follow from the fact that this order in the Agent Intellect is known by the material intellect that the Agent Intellect itself is known by us, so long as we do not know all these forms and know them as a unified system. Indeed, this is something whose possibility has not yet been proven. Therefore, it is clear that from this principle it does not follow that the Agent Intellect is known by the material intellect.

One might object that on this principle the Agent Intellect is knowable by us, since it makes the image a mover of the material intellect and hence is itself more appropriately the mover of the material intellect. Nevertheless, even if we were to admit that the image is a mover of the material intellect, we maintain that the image could have this feature as the result of both its own nature and from what it acquires from the Agent Intellect; hence, it is not necessary to say that the Agent Intellect has this feature, as we have shown before. Moreover, the Agent Intellect does not make the image a mover except accidentally; for the Agent Intellect, as we have seen, really does not work upon the image. Hence, there is no need to ascribe to the Agent Intellect this feature. Furthermore, the image does not move the

---

plan itself as an object of thought; whereas Wolfson's second rendition 'the order . . . as conceived' connotes the act of thinking of this plan. In some contexts the former fits better; in others, the latter. But the difference is slight.

51. Themistius, in Aristotle's *Metaphysicorum Librum Lamda Paraphrasis*, ed. Samuel Landauer, included in *Commentaria in Aristotelem Graeca* (Berlin, 1903), vol. 5, pt. 5, p. 29 (Hebrew), pp. 31–32 (Latin).

In this passage Themistius refers to this intelligible order as *ha-'olam ha-muskal* or *mundum intelligibilem* (ibid., p. 33). This whole notion has Philonic overtones; for the Philonic *Logos* is characterized by Philo as an *intelligible world*, κόσμος νοητός (Philo, *On Creation of the Universe* 4; Wolfson, *Philo* 1: 226–30).

material intellect, as we have seen; the Agent Intellect moves it by means of the image. Now it does not follow that if something moves another by means of some instrument that it can move it without the instrument. For example, the vital heat [of the body] moves the stone that is thrown by the hand by means of the hand. It does not follow from this[p2] that it can move the stone by itself, without an instrument; indeed, this is impossible. What is implied by this objection is that the Agent Intellect is more entitled to be considered the mover of the material intellect than the instrument by means of which it does move the material intellect. It does not follow, however, that the Agent Intellect moves the material intellect without the use of images. Accordingly, it has not been demonstrated that the material intellect can apprehend anything besides these objects of knowledge of material things.[q2]

Let us now consider the fourth argument. It maintains that since the material intellect moves from potentiality to actuality in order to acquire knowledge, and since it is evident that whatever moves from potentiality to actuality moves to that which is actual in that genus, the material intellect necessarily moves toward the acquisition of an actual object of knowledge. But whatever is of this type is an[r2] object of knowledge that is itself an intellect. For[s2] the objects of knowledge which were acquired first by means of images[t2] are knowable potentially, since they are universals, and the universal is found outside the mind only potentially.[52] Indeed, the fact that the material intellect first moves toward that which is knowable potentially is similar to what happens[u2] in many natural phenomena: they move toward perfections that they are capable of acquiring by means of other perfections. I aver that this argument is invalid. It has been proven that these objects of knowledge are not universals and that they are not grounded in particulars outside the mind in the way assumed by this view. It does not follow therefore that, because those individuals comprehended by the universal exist potentially, the object of knowledge of them is only potential. On the contrary, the object of knowledge of them is actual, since it exists in the Agent Intellect and as such is itself an intellect, as has been explained.[53]

---

52. It is assumed by this argument that the universal encompasses an *infinite* number of particulars, and thus as infinite these particulars are only *potentially* knowable (supra, chap. 9). Thus, for knowledge to occur there must be something actual that terminates or completes the act of cognition, i.e., the Agent Intellect.

53. There is no need to say that the object of knowledge is the Agent Intellect because otherwise knowledge would only be potential. Rather, the act of cognition is terminated or completed by an actual object, i.e., the pattern in the Agent Intellect. Thus, for Gersonides the Agent Intellect is itself not known, although the patterns in the Agent Intellect can be known.

Moreover, one could object that the [premise] that asserts that everything which moves from potentiality to actuality moves towards that which is *completely* actual in that genus is not true. What is true is that whatever moves from potentiality to actuality moves toward that which is completely actual relative to the potentiality [or capacity] it has, i.e., the goal of the whole motion. For if the [whole] motion[v2] has no goal[54] in this sense, then it has no end at all. If a thing moves toward a goal for the sake of another goal and there is no end in this motion that is not an end for the sake of another end, then this motion has no goal at all. But it is not necessary that the final goal in this motion be a goal that is essentially not for something else. This is quite obvious. But it is necessary that this goal of this motion not be for *this* motion a goal for something else.[55] It is therefore evident that a thing can move toward perfection that is the complete actualization of this movement, and [yet] at the same time this actualization is also from one aspect potential as well as from another actual. For this reason many of those things that move from a state of potentiality to actuality remain in an intermediary state. For many generated substances move to acquire some form, which from one aspect is actual yet from another aspect potential. This includes all generated things except man. For the form of man is a form that is completely actual; whereas all other forms are intermediate between complete potentiality and complete actuality, since they are all for the sake of the form of man. Accordingly, it does not follow because the material intellect moves toward objects of knowledge that are from one aspect potential and yet actual in another aspect, that they move to an object of knowledge that is completely actual [i.e., the Agent Intellect]. That on their assumption these objects of knowledge are in one respect potential and in another, actual, is evident from the fact that the material intellect moves essentially from potentiality to actuality by virtue of them, and hence they are actual in some sense. And so none of[w2] these arguments establishes the claim that the material intellect can apprehend the Agent Intellect. Hence, Al-Farabi's position is unaffected by these arguments.

Indeed, the argument by means of which they attempt to establish the immortality of the material intellect when it apprehends the Agent Intellect— i.e., the argument which asserts that since this object of knowledge [i.e., the Agent Intellect] is not essentially generated, the material intellect is not

---

54. The term *shlemut*; ἐντελέχεια; *kamāl* here expresses Aristotle's notion of the terminus ad quem of a motion or change. The end, or goal, of such a process represents its completion or actuality. Wolfson, *Crescas' Critique of Aristotle*, p. 526, n. 6.

55. The end of a process may very well be an intermediate stage for *another* process; but it must be the end-state of *its own* process.

perishable when it apprehends it but becomes immortal, since the Agent Intellect with which the material intellect has become identical,[x2] is itself everlasting—contradicts[y2] their principle that whatever is generated is corruptible. For, even if it is true that the object of knowledge is not *essentially* generated when it is apprehended by the material intellect, it is generated *in* the material intellect. Accordingly, on their premise it must follow that the object of knowledge is corruptible insofar as it is generated, i.e., this form will disappear from the material intellect even though it is not corruptible essentially. This is obvious. Therefore, Al-Farabi is more consistent than they are. Unless, of course, they are prepared to say that the material intellect is identical with the Agent Intellect but that it does not know itself because of its conjunction with us. Averroes maintains this latter view in his *Three Letters*, his *Commentary on* On the Soul, and his *Commentary on the* Metaphysics. We have already demonstrated the absurdities inherent in this view.

Let us now consider Avicenna's first argument in behalf of the claim that the objects of knowledge are neither generated nor corruptible. This argument asserts that since that which is apprehended of these objects of knowledge is identical with that which exists of them[z2] in the material intellect, it is necessary that they be separate [i.e., incorporeal]; for if they were material, that which is apprehended of them would not be identical with that which exists [of them outside of the mind].[56] And since they are separate, they are necessarily neither generated nor corruptible. I maintain, however, that this argument implies only that these objects of knowledge are separate [i.e., incorporeal] but not that they are generated, so long as it has not been demonstrated that it is impossible for a separate thing to be generated in the way that these objects of knowledge are generated in the material intellect [i.e., accidentally]. This kind of generation is only homonymous with [the kind of] generation that Aristotle showed is impossible with respect to the form itself [i.e., essential generation].[57] A fully adequate proof of this [latter] point has not yet been given; however, perhaps a compelling proof may be forthcoming[a3] afterwards. In general, it is necessary that true beliefs agree with reality; we should not deny reality in order to preserve our own beliefs. Accordingly, if[b3] it were necessary that these objects of knowledge be separate and that they be generated in some sense, it would clearly not be impossible that a separate substance be generated in some sense, as shall be proven shortly.

---

56. Supra, chap. 9, nn. 18–19.
57. Aristotle, *Metaphysics* 7.9.

Indeed, Avicenna's position that the objects of knowledge are not generated entails the following disjunction: Either he means that they are not generated in the material intellect but are always present there in actuality; or he means that they are not essentially generated but only generated [accidentally] in the material intellect. The former alternative is subject to the refutation previously mentioned. The latter alternative implies that the acquired intellect is corruptible, which is contrary to his theory. For Avicenna would admit that everything that is generated is corruptible; hence,[c3] these objects of knowledge are corruptible in so far as they are generated in the intellect. Thus, the acquired intellect would itself be corruptible. Similarly, I maintain that the other arguments of Avicenna in behalf of the thesis that the objects of knowledge are neither generable nor corruptible establish only that the objects of knowledge are separable [i.e., not corporeal]. This is clear from our original presentation of these arguments. It does not follow, however, from these arguments that the objects of knowledge are not generated at all in any sense of[d3] generation, as we have mentioned before. This is quite evident from our discussion of these arguments and further discussion would be superfluous.

Indeed, Al-Farabi's claim that the material intellect is generated is necessarily true, as can be seen from the preceding. But the first of his arguments in behalf of the thesis that the material intellect cannot apprehend the Agent Intellect is invalid. It maintains that if this were possible the effect would become identical with its cause, which is impossible since cause and effect are contrary states. Now when a cause performs some kind of complete operation on its effect, it makes the latter like itself. When fire, for example, heats something[e3] it makes the latter like itself, unless the matter of the recipient prevents it from doing so. But if it were possible for a corporeal form to make a form on its own level of perfection, it would be all the more fitting for a separate form to do so unless the nature of the recipient frustrates its activity, since its action is stronger and superior [to that of a corporeal form]. Now when a separate form makes a form on its own level of perfection, it becomes numerically identical with that form—for separate substances that are the same in essence cannot be numerically individuated. It would therefore be possible for the cause and the effect to become[f3] numerically identical in separate substances, unless the effect frustrates this activity, i.e., it cannot receive perfectly the activity of the cause. But this [latter] point has not been demonstrated by Al-Farabi's argument. Moreover, it would indeed be impossible for the effect to become numerically identical with its cause, since these [states of] existences are in some sense contraries, if we assumed that the effect is in these two [states of] existence *simultaneously*.[g3] But it would not be impossible for the effect to be in the [state] of existence possessed by a cause *after having been* in the state of existence possessed by an effect, just as it is not impossible for a body to be hot after having been cold. This is obvious.

The second of his objections—that it is impossible for the material intellect to apprehend the Agent Intellect; for if it were possible, that which is generated would become everlasting—is also invalid. For it does not follow from this assumption that the generated does become everlasting. The object of knowledge acquired by the material intellect in apprehending the Agent Intellect is generated in the material intellect, although it is not generated essentially. Thus, it would follow, if we were to accept the principle that everything generated is corruptible, that this object of knowledge is perishable in the material intellect, although in itself it is not perishable. This is not absurd; for it is clear that its perishability in the material intellect is not impossible [merely] because it is imperishable in itself. In conclusion, then, none of Al-Farabi's arguments refutes the claim of those who maintain that the material intellect can apprehend the Agent Intellect.

CHAPTER XI

AN EXPOSITION SHOWING THAT THE ACQUIRED INTELLECT IS EVERLASTING

HAVING discussed the views of our predecessors concerning the topic of immortality and having demonstrated that none of these views has been proved by the arguments adduced in its behalf, and that the contrary views are not entirely refuted by these arguments, it is now proper for us to examine this problem directly to determine which of these opinions is the true one. It is necessary that we not forget that it has been demonstrated in our previous discussions of these arguments that the objects of knowledge are generated in the material intellect and that the acquired intellect is separable. Now, if it is necessary that every generated thing be corruptible, as it has been believed on the basis of the proof in *On The Heavens*,[1] it is evident that there is no individual immortality, as Al-Farabi maintained. It is therefore necessary to determine the truth of this principle, i.e., whether or not everything generated is corruptible. And if it is not necessarily true, then we must determine if *this* particular generated thing, i.e., the object of knowledge which the material intellect apprehends, is necessarily corruptible; or if it is impossible for it to be corruptible; or if one aspect of it is corruptible, yet another incorruptible.

We shall demonstrate[a] in our investigation of the problem of the creation of the universe that Aristotle's arguments in *On The Heavens* with respect to the principle that everything generated is corruptible are not demonstrative.[2] Hence, it does not follow from this [principle] that there is no personal immortality. Accordingly, we must examine whether this generated entity, i.e., the acquired intellect belonging to the material intellect, is corruptible or incorruptible; or if there is some part of it that is corruptible, i.e., the knowledge of sublunar phenomena, and some part of it that is incorruptible, i.e., the knowledge of those substances that are incorporeal and are themselves intellects, as has been maintained by our predecessors.

It is clear that the acquired intellect is the perfection of the material

---

1. Aristotle, *On The Heavens* 1.12.
2. Infra, Bk. 6, pt. 1, chap. 27.

intellect brought about by the Agent Intellect. Now this perfection is of two types: (1) conception [i.e., the apprehension of essences]; and (2) the act of making judgments [or propositions]. Now conception is clearly independent of particulars outside the mind; rather, it is the cognition of the very order inherent in the Agent Intellect. The judgment, however, does refer to in-dividuals outside the mind; e.g., the judgment,[b] 'All animals have sensation' [is based upon particulars] accidentally insofar as it is a compound of both perceptual and intellectual activities. Hence, the perfection that the material intellect derives from[c] the Agent Intellect is conceptual only and does not depend upon particulars existing outside the mind. This is the case too with the forms that are perceived by sight when we judge accidentally[d] that a thing is sweet on the basis of our visual perception of the yellow color of that object; this visual form is yellow not sweetness.[3] Accordingly, it is evident that the acquired intellect is itself the order obtaining in the sublunar world that is inherent in the Agent Intellect. We have already demonstrated this point, i.e., that the object of knowledge pertaining to the sublunar world that is present in the Agent Intellect is known by us (i.e., in the material intellect); the object of knowledge is not the imaginative form, for the latter is not intelligible, although it is helpful in the acquisition of knowledge.[4] From this it follows that the acquired intellect is immortal; for what it ap-prehends of these objects of knowledge is itself an intellect in the Agent Intellect.[5]

The immortality of the acquired intellect can be shown in a more satis-factory way as follows. The acquired intellect is immaterial, and an imma-terial substance does not have the conditions requisite for corruption; and whatever lacks these conditions is incorruptible. This compound syllogism[6]

---

3. Gersonides is alluding to Aristotle's doctrine of the proper sensibles, according to which each sense organ has a special and proper range of perception within which its perceptions are nonerroneous. E.g., a normal eye is always or most usually correct in its perception of color. On the other hand, we are liable to make errors in perceptual judgments when on the basis of past empirical associations we judge that a particular visual sensation that we have had is also characterized by a nonvisual property that we are not now perceiving. Aristotle, *On The Soul*, 2.6.

4. This is a criticism of Averroes, who maintains that the imaginative forms play a more than auxiliary role in cognition. Averroes, *Long Commentary on Aristotle's* On The Soul 3, text 5, in Hyman and Walsh, pp. 316–24.

5. That which the acquired intellect apprehends is the order obtaining in the sublunar world, which order is an object of knowledge for the Agent Intellect as well and is inherent in its mind. Now since the intellect and its object are identical in the act of knowing, the acquired intellect obtains its immortality by means of its apprehension of this plan.

6. *Ha-heqesh ha-murkab; qiyās murakkab.* This is the sorites, or polysyllogism, of classical logic: a series of syllogisms, the conclusion of one being the premise of the other. Goichon, *Lexique*, p. 343, para. 611:8; Joseph, *Introduction to Logic*, p. 354.

entails the immortality of the acquired intellect. The first of these premises is evident from what has been previously demonstrated. The third is self-evident, since the relation between a thing and its causes is a necessary relation; hence a thing cannot exist without its causes.

The second of these premises—that which asserts that an immaterial substance lacks the conditions for corruption—requires proof. It has been shown in Aristotle's scientific works and the *Metaphysics* that corruption is the result of matter not form; for the form is the source of being and good and it keeps[e] the possessor of the form in existence in every way possible.[7] Matter, however, is the source of corruption and evil because of its resistance to the form, as is explained in *Meteorology* 4; for corruption occurs when the passive powers predominate over the active powers.[8] Since, then, matter is the cause of decay, and since an incorporeal substance has no matter, it is obvious that an incorporeal substance lacks the causes of decay. It has been thought [however], that the acquired intellect is corruptible, and for two reasons that have been mentioned by the earlier philosophers. First, since the existence of the acquired intellect in the material intellect results from corporeal cognitions,[f] [i.e., those deriving from the sensory faculties], as has been explained earlier, and since all perceptual knowledge is perishable, it follows that the acquired intellect too is perishable. For if that upon which the acquired intellect is dependent perishes, the acquired intellect [too] must perish. Second, this intellect is said to be the perfection of the human soul; but in the dissolution of the latter so too its acquisitions and perfections perish.

Now the first of these objections is easy to dispose of. It is indeed true that when[g] the cause departs the effect also disappears if the effect depends upon the cause, which is the case when the cause is an essential cause.[h,9] Corporeal cognitions, however, are only accidental causes of the existence of the acquired intellect, not essential causes. The essential cause of the existence of the acquired intellect is the intelligible order in the Agent Intellect, as has been explained. Moreover, even if we were to admit that the corporeal cognitions are the causes of the existence of these objects of knowledge in the material intellect, they are the causes of knowledge [only], not of the existence of the intelligible order[i] [in the Agent Intellect] pertaining to them. Indeed, the reverse is true: the existence of the intelligible order pertaining to them is the cause of their very existence. For the existence of

---

7. Aristotle, *Physics* 1.9; *Metaphysics* 7.15, 8.3, 5.
8. Aristotle, *Meteorology* 4.1.
9. Maimonides, *Guide* 1.73, 11th proposition.

this intelligible order in the Agent Intellect is the cause of the existence of all sublunar phenomena. Hence, the intelligible order obtaining in the things of the sublunar world does not perish when these things disappear, for its existence does not depend upon them. What does in fact perish along with these things is the acquisition of knowledge, since it is impossible for the material intellect to obtain knowledge after the corporeal cognitions have perished. This is obvious. This can be more easily seen from the following. Let us assume that a man invents some utensil by himself; then another man sees this object and from the mere observation of it he recognizes the plan in the craftman's mind, and later on the utensil disappears. It is obvious that the knowledge of the utensil acquired by the second man does not vanish even if the utensil vanishes; for the utensil is the cause of the *acquisition* of this knowledge but not of the intelligible order of it.[10]

It might be objected that the imaginative forms have some kind of effect in the establishment of the objects of knowledge; for we observe that in men whose imagination has been impaired the objects of knowledge disappear from them. Moreover, they recollect[i] the object of knowledge when they first remember the image which[k] gives rise to this object of knowledge in them. It is therefore evident that, since images do bring about the objects of knowledge, when the images disappear the objects of knowledge also vanish.

Nevertheless, even if we were to admit that men whose imagination has been impaired no longer know what they formerly knew and[l] that they remember the object of knowledge when they first remember[m] the image, which gives rise to this knowledge, it is not necessary to admit that the object of knowledge disappears when the image vanishes. There are[n] three types of objects of knowledge: (1) the object of knowledge that is completely potential, i.e., the object of knowledge that a man is capable of learning but has not yet learned; (2) the object of knowledge that is completely actual, i.e., the object of knowledge that a wise man has when he actually uses it;[o] and (3) the object of knowledge that is in a manner[p] intermediate between these two, i.e., the knowledge possessed by a wise man when he doesn't use it.[11] [The third] is like forgetting in an accidental sense; since the soul is a unity, a wise man is not conscious that he has a particular piece of knowledge while he is engaged in something else; but when something stimulates this piece of knowledge so that it is used, then the man realizes that he[q] does

---

10. In this example the utensil corresponds to the sense-image. From this sense-image the mind can abstract the plan according to which the table was made. This plan is the real object of knowledge and is independent of the sense-image.

11. Aristotle, *On the Soul* 2.1; *Metaphysics* 9.6.

know it. The same is true in the present case. For when the image disappears, then there is no longer a stimulus for the exercise of that particular piece of knowledge; but when the man recalls the image[r] he then knows it, and therefore no further learning or inquiry is required. And so with someone whose imagination is impaired: when he has been cured, he puts into play his previous knowledge without new inquiry and learning. If this knowledge had disappeared from him, he would obviously have to relearn afterwards [what he formerly knew]. Moreover, we see that some men whose imaginations have been impaired can correctly reply to questions that are asked of them on certain topics. This shows that their knowledge has not disappeared with the impairment of their imagination.

In general, with respect to the object of knowledge there is no disappearance and forgetting, as has been previously explained; for these objects of knowledge are not subject to decay. It was for this reason that some of the ancients maintained that forgetting is impossible with respect to knowledge.[12] (It is as if the truth forced itself upon them.) On the other hand, the term 'knowledge' may be used homonymously, connoting the case where there is no true knowledge of causes; then of course [there is forgetting]. This happens with some people who are learning geometry, especially where many theorems are required for the proof of a [particular] theorem. [In such a case] these people do not try to understand intellectually the thing in question in terms of its causes [i.e., the theorems from which the desiderated theorem is derived]; rather they look in the book with respect to a particular theorem and [focus upon] the language there [i.e., in the proof of that theorem only to see] if something has been explained by it[s] that they need for the proof[t] of this theorem.[13] Therefore, they forget this knowledge, since it really is not *known* by them; they know only that the author of that[u] book has proved those theorems.

---

12. Gersonides may be referring here to Plato. In the *Meno* Plato argues that although some kind of stimulation may be required for the exercise of knowledge, knowledge is preexistent and never destroyed. Once we know something we do not have to relearn it, even if we may need some prodding to revive it in our consciousness. Thus, the kind of forgetting that Gersonides is here ruling out involves complete loss of the piece of knowledge. Plato, *Meno*, 81 ff.

13. This example is not perspicuous, and not only because of the textual variants. The term *temunah* has several geometrical connotations, as I have already indicated (supra, chapter 10, n. 19). In this context the term again seems to have the meaning of theorem, although it is possible to render this passage with sense by translating it as 'figure' or 'construction'. I have preferred the former because of the term *sibbotav*. Gersonides draws a contrast between those who understand a proof or theorem, since they understand the theorems on the basis of which this theorem is demonstrated, and those who look at the proof of this theorem only. The term *sibba* is frequently used to connote 'reason', 'principle', 'premise', all of which are logical terms. Hence, the rendering 'theorem' seems more appropriate.

The second of these objections claiming that the acquired intellect is corruptible is sophistical. There are two kinds of perfections: (1) the kind that is intertwined with that of which it is the perfection, as is the case with the other perfections of all the other material forms; and (2) the kind that is not so intertwined, which is the case, as has been explained, with the material intellect. Corruption is indeed inevitable in the former type when the bearer of the perfection perishes; but if the perfection is not intertwined with the bearer but exists independently, it is not perishable. This is quite evident. In conclusion, then, it does not follow from these considerations that the acquired intellect is perishable; rather it is immortal, as has been shown.

CHAPTER XII

THE IMPOSSIBILITY OF MATERIAL INTELLECT APPREHENDING THE AGENT INTELLECT SUCH THAT THEY BECOME NUMERICALLY IDENTICAL

HAVING demonstrated these[a] [features of] the acquired intellect, it is now proper to ask if there is a more perfect form of human happiness; [e.g.,] some of [our] predecessors believed that it is possible to apprehend the Agent Intellect. We believe that if this were possible, it would occur only after we have acquired all the objects of knowledge; for all of them obtain in the Agent Intellect in a unitary manner, as has been explained previously. It is necessary that we have this complete knowledge before we know them as a unit, just as it is necessary that we know the essences of the boards, of the bricks, and of the stones from which the house is made before we know the essence of the house. Therefore, Averroes has said that the apprehension [of the Agent Intellect] is posterior to the apprehension of all the [sublunar] objects of knowledge. It is as if the truth forced itself upon him. He said also that even if this is very difficult, it may be achieved[b] in a perfect society where people cooperate with each other.[1] Now if it is impossible for a man to acquire all this knowledge, it is evident that he cannot apprehend the Agent Intellect. Similarly, if he can acquire all this knowledge but cannot apprehend it in a unitary manner [he cannot apprehend the Agent Intellect].[2]

These points having been understood, we shall now prove that it is *impossible* for man to apprehend the Agent Intellect; for it is impossible for him to acquire all the requisite knowledge. There are many animals, plants, and minerals in this world of which man has no knowledge. And in some of the species it is impossible to know the order of their parts and the wisdom of their particular structure; for their small size prevents our perception of these parts and their relations. Even in species whose individuals are large it is impossible to know the order of their parts in their entirety. Concerning man, for example, there has been continuous investigation ever since antiquity on the limbs, veins, sinews, nerves,[c] and muscles; yet there is no complete

---

1. Averroes, *Drei Abhandlungen*, Hebrew text, p. 9.
2. Husik, "Studies in Gersonides [2]," p. 262.

knowledge of them such that we know their exact number, or their difference in size, quality, and shape. This is evident to anyone who reads this book. Moreover,[d] the Agent Intellect possesses complete knowledge of the necessary influences of the heavenly bodies upon the sublunar world, as shall be proven later in this book;[3] but this knowledge is unattainable by man because of the small[e] number of principles he has abstracted from sense perception. In general, it is impossible for man to know the [complete] truth of the order of the sublunar world. This is nicely illustrated in astrology, where frequently false predictions are made. All the more so is it impossible for man[f] to know the general order of the sublunar world by means of its causes so that his knowledge would be perfect.[4]

Moreover, even if we were to concede the possibility of obtaining all the knowledge present in the Agent Intellect, it would still be impossible for man to apprehend the Agent Intellect, since it is impossible for him to apprehend this knowledge in its hierarchical relations and in a unified manner. There seems to be in the sublunar world a definite order in the receptivity by the primary matter of all the forms, such that this process ultimately terminates in the production of the form of man. But it is not possible to know this order as it develops species by species. For example, the primary elements serve as matter for the minerals, and among themselves one element functions as matter [in the generation of another element from it].[5] For earth serves as matter for water, and water is matter for air, which in turn is matter for fire. The minerals serve as matter for the plants, which are in turn matter for the animals. It seems to be true that the forms of the minerals serve as matter for each other, until something is reached that is intermediary between a mineral and a plant, e.g., corals. Similarly, with respect to plants: they serve as matter for each other until something emerges that is intermediary between a plant and an animal, e.g., the water-sponge[g] and snail. It is analogously with animals, which eventually terminate in the species man.

That this hypothesis is true will be apparent from what I shall now say. The primary matter undergoes with respect to these forms a transition from privation to existence. Accordingly, all forms are from one aspect privation and from another aspect existence; i.e., they have existence with respect to that form prior to them; they are privations with respect to the forms subsequent to them. This is analogous to motion: the parts of motion are actual

---

3. Infra, Bk. 5, pt. 3.
4. According to Aristotle, perfect knowledge is knowledge of causes. See *Posterior Analytics* 1.2; *Metaphysics* 1.1.
5. Aristotle, *On Generation and Corruption*, passim.

with respect to the preceding phases of the movement and potential with respect to the succeeding phases. Thus, each form necessarily serves as matter for another form superior to it, so that the whole scheme terminates in the form of man.[6]

Moreover,[h] it is impossible for two forms to be on the same level [or coordinate]. For if this were possible, either both of them[i] would be the end-states [or termini ad quem] for the forms which the primary matter receives, or both would be the intermediate forms, or one would be the end-state and the other the intermediate. That both of them[i] are the end-states is false. For if this were possible, they would either be end-states for one and the same motion or end-states for different motions. The former alternative is false, since a motion obviously has only one end-state. And if we say that they are end-states for different movements, i.e., the forms which the primary matter[j] receives until one of its end-states[k] is reached are not identical with the forms received by it in arriving at the other end-state, it would follow from this that there is nothing having a form resulting from one of these processes that would be capable of receiving[l] any form of the other process. This hypothesis implies that there are *two* primary matters: one receiving the forms of one process; the other[m] receiving the forms of the other process. If this is the case,[n] each one of these primary matters would possess some form by virtue of which the nature of one receives certain forms, whereas the nature of the other receives other forms. But this is impossible, as has been shown in book one of the *Physics*.[7] Moreover, if this were true, there would be no form that every generated and destructible phenomenon could become; for it is necessarily[o] one of the forms of one of these motions, and it would be impossible for the things in the other motions to assume this form. But this is false. For all phenomena [subject to generation and destruction] can become one of the elemental forms, as has been explained in the sciences; for the elemental forms can become any of these phenomena and any compound substance is analyzable into these elemental forms. In short, it has been proven in Book one of the *Physics* that there is only one primary matter.[8]

But if it is assumed that both these forms are intermediate terms, it is evident from the preceding that we cannot maintain that they are intermediate terms in two different processes. Hence, they must be intermediates in one process, assuming this is possible. Therefore, the primary matter would

---

6. Aristotle, *Physics* 1.7–9.
7. According to Aristotle, the primary matter has no definite, or natural form. Aristotle, *Physics* 1.7–9.
8. Aristotle, *Physics* 1.3–4, 6.

receive one of them before the other. But, I say, if this is the case, the posterior of them would be superior to the prior, for in one motion each part is for the sake of the subsequent part until[p] the final[q] end is ultimately reached. For example, drinking a boiled medicine is for [the purpose] of drinking a laxative, whose purpose is to purge the noxious[r] fluid, and the purgation of the unhealthy fluid[s] is for the purpose of health. Accordingly, each one of the parts of these intermediate stages is in a sense[t] the end-state of the preceding part. And since the end is superior to that which precedes the end, the form that is posterior in the generation is superior to the other [i.e., prior] forms. Hence, it is impossible to maintain that one form is the end-state and the other the intermediate; for if this were possible, this would be necessarily true of one and the same process, and the form that is the end-state would be superior to the form that is the intermediate.[9]

It can be demonstrated in a different way that these forms are[u] hierarchically ordered from the extremes of deficient existence to that of perfect existence. In nature all the possible mixtures of the elements have a corresponding form; hence, the number of forms of sublunar phenomena corresponds[v] to the number of possible mixtures [of elements]. Since these combinations are hierarchically ordered according to the degrees of thickness and thinness such that the mixture which most approximates[w] thinness serves as form to that mixture which is thicker, their forms are arranged similarly; for the relation of one matter to another matter is the relation of one form to another form. Therefore, just as the various mixtures are hierarchically ordered from the most deficient existence to the most perfect existence, so too these forms are ordered from the most defective to the most perfect.[10]

Now, it is evident that man cannot understand completely the order obtaining in these various mixtures; all the more so is he incapable of understanding the order obtaining among the forms.[x] [At best] he understands the remote relations [among them]; e.g., that minerals serve as matter for the most primitive kind of plant, that the latter serves as matter for the more perfect plant, that the latter serves as matter for a primitive animal, that the latter serves as matter for aquatic life, that the latter is matter for the birds, and that the latter is matter for terrestrial animals. Hence, it is impossible for us to know completely the way in which all this knowledge constitutes a unified system; for, if we do not know their various relations, we cannot know the way in which they constitute a unitary system. Thus, it is im-

---

9. Thus, two forms cannot be coordinate.

10. Averroes, *The Epitome of the* Metaphysics, printed in *Die Metaphysik des Averroes*, ed. and trans. Max Horten (Halle, 1912), pp. 200–201.

possible for us to apprehend the Agent Intellect—unless someone were to say that we apprehend the Agent Intellect to the degree that we understand these sublunar phenomena; for they are comprised in the knowledge possessed by the Agent Intellect, and in this way there is a union between us and the Agent Intellect. It was this way of thinking that misled our predecessors[y] into believing that it is possible for man to apprehend the Agent Intellect.

Do not think that this controversy was discussed only by the philosophers; you find some of the rabbis of blessed memory also [discussing the problem]. In the Midrash,[11] Rabbi Judah bar Simon says concerning the passage in *Genesis* 1, "God saw that the light was good": "God separated the light for Himself [and] said, 'no creature can[z] use it except Me.' This agrees with the statement, 'The light dwelleth[a1] with Him.' (Dan. 2:22). This would be like a king who sees something nice and says, 'This is for me'." [On the other hand], some of the rabbis maintained that God caused the light to shine for him, i.e., to give it to the righteous in the World-to-Come. This agrees with the passage, "Light is sown for the righteous" (Ps. 97:11). It is clear that they are referring to the light of the separate intelligences, since the light that can be seen is used by an organism having sight. Accordingly, Rabbi Judah bar Simon maintains that man cannot[b1] apprehend the separate intelligences; whereas those who differ from him say that man has at first[c1] a feeble apprehension of them, which comes intermittently upon him. It is as if that light[d1] which is apprehended by him is like lightning. For this reason it is said, God *caused* the light to shine for him. They maintain that this emanation is given to the righteous in the World-to-Come. What they mean is that the feeble knowledge that we initially possess of the separate intelligences prepares us so that we can attain a more perfect knowledge of them and thus [be able to] cleave to them.

---

11. Midrash Rabbah Genesis 3.6.

CHAPTER XIII

A RESOLUTION OF THE DIFFICULTIES THAT ARISE CONCERNING OUR THEORY OF HUMAN HAPPINESS

S INCE we have determined that human perfection lies[a] in the acquisition of knowledge of the sublunar world, let us now consider the various difficulties that this doctrine may occasion. First, it has been thought that this perfection is empty and worthless. For, since this knowledge which is acquired by the material intellect is the very same knowledge in the Agent Intellect, nothing really novel occurs in our acquisition of this knowledge. But an activity that produces nothing new is otiose. Second, it would seem this doctrine implies that one object would have many ends. The intended end of man is to acquire knowledge; but since there are many objects of knowledge, there would seem to be many ends for one man. This is, however, impossible. For the purpose of[b] one thing is itself necessarily one, since the purpose is the form and perfection [of the thing], and it is impossible for one thing to have more than one perfection, as is obvious. Third, it would seem that the attempt to know many things is futile. For, since our purpose is immortality of the intellect, which can be attained by the acquisition of merely one piece of knowledge, there would be no point in acquiring more knowledge. And so the level of perfection of someone who has acquired the knowledge of only some trivial piece of knowledge would be equal to the level of perfection of someone who continuously pursues knowledge until he knows the secrets of the universe, if this is possible. But this is absurd; for those who pursue knowledge always have the desire to increase their knowledge, and natural desires[c] cannot be in vain.

The first objection can be easily disposed of. It does not follow from the admission that the knowledge we have acquired is the same as the knowledge in the Agent Intellect that the acquisition of this knowledge is otiose. For, although these objects of knowledge are not essentially generated, they are generated in the material intellect. Moreover, the knowledge acquired by us is [really] not identical with the knowledge in the Agent Intellect; for knowledge in the Agent Intellect exists in a unified manner. But it is impossible for knowledge in the material intellect to exist in this way, as[d] has been explained.

The second objection can be removed when it is demonstrated that the acquired intellect is numerically one, and this can be done quite easily.

Human knowledge is such that some cognitions are the perfections and forms of other cognitions, no matter what kind of cognitions they are. In the [knowledge of] one science, it is evident that some of its parts are related[e] as the perfection and form of the other parts. In the [knowledge of] many sciences some are also related as the perfection and form of the other sciences. Accordingly, it is evident that the acquired intellect is numerically one.[1] And in this way it follows that the various objects of knowledge are multipliable together with the multiplication of [their] subjects. For one piece of knowledge can be common to Reuben and Simon yet differ in them insofar as the kind of unity[f] differs in them; so that, for example, the unity in the acquired intellect of Reuben differs from the unity in the acquired intellect of Simon. These differences are attributable to the differences in the acquisition of this knowledge with respect to quality and quantity. For when someone[g] acquires more knowledge within a particular science, the unity of his knowledge in [his acquired intellect] differs from the unity of knowledge of someone who has acquired less knowledge in that science. Similarly, he who has acquired knowledge in a science different from the science in which another has acquired knowledge, his[h] acquired intellect differs from the acquired intellect of the other. In this way the levels of intellectual perfection are considerably differentiated. If the unity of knowledge approximates[i] the unity of knowledge in the Agent Intellect, then the possessor of that knowledge has attained a greater level of perfection, and the joy and pleasure[j] in his knowledge is greater. Differences are found such that the pleasure enjoyed by one man in his knowledge is[k] not the same as the pleasure enjoyed by another in his knowledge. And[l] thus the third difficulty has been resolved. It is also important to realize that each man who has attained this perfection enjoys the happiness resulting from his knowledge after death. We have some idea of this pleasure from the pleasure that we derive from the[m] little knowledge we now possess which subdues the animal part of our soul [so that] the intellect is isolated in its activity. This pleasure is not comparable to the other pleasures and has no relation to them at all. All the more so will this pleasure be greater after death; for then all the knowledge that we have acquired in life will be continuously contemplated and all the things in our minds will be apprehended simultaneously, since after death the obstacle that prevents this [kind of cognition], i.e., matter, will have disappeared.[2] For, since the soul is[n] a unit, the intellect is prevented from apprehending [simultaneously] when it

---

1. Although there are many pieces of knowledge and many types of knowledge, they are hierarchically arranged such that a unity results. Thus, the acquired intellect is a unity.

2. Thomas Aquinas, *Summa Contra Gentiles* 3. pt. 1, chap. 60.

[the soul] employs another of its faculties. Even when the intellect is operating alone it cannot apprehend its objects simultaneously except those to which it attends, as has been explained before. After death, however, it will apprehend all the knowledge it has acquired during life simultaneously. But it should be realized that after death the intellect will acquire no new knowledge, since it does not have the organs by means of which it can acquire such knowledge, such as the senses, the imagination, memory, and the other faculties making use of the senses.

From this it can be shown that there is no comparison between the pleasure obtained from a piece of trivial knowledge and the pleasure received from a knowledge of a superior kind. For the pleasure that we experience in the latter type of knowledge [even] in this life is quite different [from the pleasure experienced in the former type]. And our desire for the apprehension [of the superior knowledge] is greater so that we prefer a little knowledge of this higher knowledge to much knowledge of the inferior type of knowledge. Accordingly, our rabbis of blessed memory have maintained that there are different levels of righteous men in Paradise. In the Midrash[3] they say that there are seven classes of righteous men. (They chose the number seven to indicate plurality, not for any particular reason. For example, the prophets and other of our sages, may they be blessed, have said: "For a righteous man falleth seven times, and riseth up again";[4] and, "There° are seven abominations in his heart.")[5] They also agreed that human perfection is attained by the acquisition of knowledge, be it great or little. Hence, they said "All Israel has a portion in the World-to-Come."[6] They mean that since the Torah has directed Israel toward the acquisition of this knowledge in the marvelous way that is found in it, it is impossible that many should not acquire some knowledge, much or little.[7] The phrase 'all Israel' is [actually] equivalent to 'the majority of Israel'; for the general principles of the Talmud have this connotation.[8] Indeed, it has been explicitly pointed out [in the Talmud] that from general statements one cannot derive [a particular] even when the context specifies the exceptions.[9]

---

3. Yalkut Shimoni 20.
4. Prov. 24:16.
5. Ibid. 26:25.
6. Mishnah Abot 1. Prologue.
7. That is, people will differ in the amount of wisdom they attain, even though the Torah was given to all Israel.
8. I.e., phrases beginning with 'all' mean 'most'.
9. Erubin 27a.

SOME HINTS TO OUR READERS SO THAT THEY DO NOT ABANDON WHAT RELIGION AFFIRMS BECAUSE OF WHAT PHILOSOPHY SEEMS TO TEACH

IF anyone thinks that religious faith requires a conception of human perfection different from the one we have mentioned because[a] of certain passages about the Garden of Eden and Gehenna in various Midrashim, Aggadot, and statements of the prophets, let him surely know that we have not assented to the view that our reason has suggested without determining its compatibility with our Torah. For adherence to reason is not permitted if it contradicts religious faith; indeed, if there is such [a contradiction], it is necessary to attribute this lack of agreement to our own inadequacy. Hence, it is clear that someone who believes this [i.e., the view of the Torah] should follow his religious convictions. We, too, behave accordingly if we see that religion requires a different view from the one that our reason has affirmed. This is incumbent upon all the faithful; for if the door were open to any philosophical doubt with respect to religion, the religion would disappear and its benefits for its adherents would vanish. Moreover [all kinds] of controversies[b] and confusion would arise among the believers unless there is faith, and as the result of this, definite harm will come about. This fact should not be overlooked. This point that we have made here should be understood as applying to every other part of our book; so that if there appears to be a problem concerning which our view differs from the accepted view of religion, philosophy should be abandoned and religion followed. The incompatibility is to be attributed to our shortcomings.[1]

---

1. Gersonides claims here that if there is an apparent incompatibility between religion and philosophy on a given point or issue religion should be followed. Moreover, the incompatibility is only apparent, since there is only one truth, even if we are unable to recognize this fact. In the Preface Gersonides gives a somewhat different emphasis, stressing the competency of philosophy and the latitude given for scriptural interpretation.

· CRITICAL APPARATUS ·

Legend: The extreme left column lists the letter in the text that signals a faulty reading. The next column indicates the page in the translation in which this faulty reading occurs. The next column lists the page number of the Leipzig edition of 1866, followed by the Leipzig version and the corrected reading. The extreme right column records the specific manuscripts that were used to determine the correct reading. Where the manuscripts were unanimous, no specific one is mentioned. The manuscripts are abbreviated as follows:

V: Vatican
B: Bodleian, Pococke 376 (Neubauer 1286)
P: Paris 723

Super-script	Page in trans-lation	Page in Leipzig Edition	Faulty Reading	Correct Reading	MS.
			Invocation		
a	87	1	omits	פעלו	
b	89	1	בקרוב	בקרב	VP
c	89	1	תתהלל	תהלל	VB
			Introductory Remarks		
a	91	2	מדרגת האנשית	מדרגת האנשים	
b	91	2	נודעו	יודעו	P
c	91	2	תשלח	ישלם	
d	91	2	omits	ואיך מדרגתם קצתם עם קצת ואיך מדרגת השם ית׳ מהם	

Super-script	Page in trans-lation	Page in Leipzig Edition	Faulty Reading	Correct Reading	MS.
e	91	2	omits	מאחד	
f	92	2	במה שקדם מזאת הזמן	במה שקדם מהזמן	
g	92	2	קדומים	קודמים	
h	92	2	הסבה	מהסבה	
i	92	3	לזאת הראיה	לזאת ההויה	
j	93	3	מהחכמה האלהות	מהחכמה האלהית	
k	93	3	אם הוא או קדום או מחודש	אם הוא קדום או מחודש	
l	93	3	או	אם	
m	93	3	שיהיה דברינו	שיהיו דברינו	
n	93	3	התבאר	שהיה	
o	93	3	מטרדת הזמן	מטרדות הזמן	
p	94	3	דברים	דברינו	
q	94	4	שיצוייר לנפש	שיצוייר בנפש	
r	94	4	אם	הם	
s	94	4	בחכמות מהחכמות	בחכמה מהחכמות	
t	94	4	במה שלמדם מזולתו	במה שלמדהו זולתו	VP
u	94	4	omits	לנו	
v	96	5	אם לא נתבאר בטול מה שנתחייב ממנו אחד מחלקי הסותר בזאת החקירה כמו שקדם	אם לא יתבאר בטול מה שנחייב ממנו אחד מחלקי הסותר בזאת החקירה כמו שקדם	VB
w	96	5	לכל	לכלל	
x	96	0	omits	נכבדת	VB
y	97	5	omits	יותר	
z	97	6	בסבות	לאהבת	
a_1	97	6	omits	אפשר	
b_1	97	6	לו	לנו	
c_1	97	6	תוברר	ותוברר	
d_1	98	7	מלפני	מפני	
e_1	99	7	ההכפל	הכפל	
f_1	99	7	הוקדמנו	הקדמנו	VB
g_1	99	7	בכל ענין	בכל ענין מעניניו	VB
h_1	99	7	ידיעתם	הידיעה בהם	
i_1	99	7	בגשם מוחלט	בגשם במוחלט	
j_1	100	8	היה יותר מחוייב	היה היותו מחוייב	
k_1	101	8	להמון מזיקים	מזיקים אל ההמול	
l_1	101	8	omits	בענינים	
m_1	101	8	שנשים	שתשים	VP
n_1	101	8	במציאותם	במציאות	VP

Super-script	Page in trans-lation	Page in Leipzig Edition	Faulty Reading	Correct Reading	MS.
o_1	101	8	שלא ישמיט מהם דבר מן המחבר	שלא ישמט מהם דבר מן המחבר	
p_1	101	8	המספר	הספר	VP
q_1	102	9	מעט	מעט מעט	
r_1	102	9	omits	השתבש	VP
s_1	103	9	למה שיקיימהו או ירצה לקיימהו יהיה אז יותר	למה שירצה לקיימו יהיה אז יותר טוב	
t_1	103	9	חזוקו	חזוקו	
u_1	104	10	ספר	ספק	
v_1	104	10	וקיומו	וקיימו	VB
w_1	104	11	בהשגת	בהשגחת	VB
x_1	104	11	ומופתים	ובמופתים	

Table of Contents

a	107	12	ממהות	מהות	
b	107	12	The Leipzig edition interchanges the titles of chapters 7 and 13.		
c	107	12	דעת	דעות	

Chapter I

a	109	12	בכלי גופיים	בכלי גופיי	
b	109	12	ושנחקור	שנחקור	
c	109	12	ההשארה	ההשארות	
d	109	12	בזה	במהותו	

Chapter II

a	111	13	לבאר	לברור	
b	111	13	מדרגה היולי	מדרגת היולי	
c	111	13	שמה שיהיה כחיי	מה שהוא כחיי	
d	112	13	ההיולאני	השכל ההיולאני	
e	112	14	omits	הוא הווה ונפסד	
f	112	14	בהיות	בהיות	VB
g	112	14	omits	מחוץ	
h	112	14	באת	ובאה	
i	112	14	יתהוה	התהוה	
j	113	15	מהם	ממנה	

Super-script	Page in trans-lation	Page in Leipzig Edition	Faulty Reading	Correct Reading	MS.
k	114	15	התבאר באופן מה	יתבאר באופן אחר	
l	114	15	omits	שישיגה	
m	115	16	יותר	יותר חזק	
n	115	16	מקבל	מוגבל	
o	115	16	שתקרא לו	שתרקה לו	
p	116	17	לזאת ההכנה	בזאת ההכנה	
q	117	17	omits	או הנפש בכללה או איזה מהם שהונח נושא לה לפי דעת אלכסנדר	P
r	117	17	omits	אלכסנדר	
s	118	18	באיש	בהתחדש איש	
t	118	18	באופן	באופן מה	
u	118	18	omits	הכנה	
v	118	18	שיתכן בעצמה	שתהיה בעצמה	
w	119	18	שלא ימצאו	שלא מצאנום	
x	119	18	omits	בתכלית מה שאפשר	

Chapter III

a	120	19	omits	ולפי שלא יוכלל באלו הדעות כל חלקי הסותר אשר אפשר שיפלו בזאת החקירה	VP
b	120	19	omits	יחוייב	VP
c	120	19	הטענה	טענה	VP
d	120	19	omits	בזה התאר	
e	121	20	omits	אמנם	VP
f	121	20	המטעמים	הטעמים	
g	121	20	הוטבע	הטבע	
h	121	20	שתמשש	שנמשש	VP
i	122	20	omits	בהיולי	VP
j	122	20	הראות	הראות המראים	VP
k	122	21	רצונו	רצוננו	
l	123	21	והמאחרים	והמתאחרים	
m	123	21	omits	זאת	VP
n	123	21	בה	בו	
o	123	22	שתרבה	שתתרבה	VP
p	124	22	התחזק	התחזק יותר	BP
q	124	22	omits	זה	VP
r	125	22	בזה הבטול	כמו זה הבטול	VP

Super-script	Page in trans-lation	Page in Leipzig Edition	Faulty Reading	Correct Reading	MS.
s	125	22	מפני זה שנמצא	מפני מה שנמצא	VP
t	125	23	עד שנאמר	שנאמר	
u	125	23	omits	מה	
v	125	23	ולא	ולו	VP
w	126	23	ההשגה	ההכנה	V
x	127	23	ומהם מי	ומהם מה	VP
y	127	24	omits	הוא	
z	128	24	omits	מה שיצדק על השאר	VP
a_1	128	24	omits	או שכל	
b_1	128	24	הנחה	הכנה	
c_1	128	24	omits	כמו שההכנה מצטרפת לחמר	
d_1	129	25	הוא	הוה	VP
e_1	129	25	omits	שיתחייב	
f_1	129	25	omits	כי	

Chapter IV

Super-script	Page in trans-lation	Page in Leipzig Edition	Faulty Reading	Correct Reading	MS.
a	130	25	עד המעשה	לצד המעשה	
b	130	25	האנשית	הנפשית	VP
c	130	26	omits	אלו	VP
d	131	26	אשר השכל	אשר לזה השכל	VP
e	132	26	העיוניים	הענינים העיוניים	VB
f	132	26	למציאותו	למציאותנו	VB
g	132	27	מה שהתבאר	ממה שהתבאר	VP
h	132	27	דומה	מה	B
i	132	27	המושכלות האחרות	המושכלות האחדות	V
j	133	27	אל	אלו	
k	133	27	omits	בנבואה	
l	133	27	omits	שני	VP
m	135	29	omits	עושר	VB
n	136	29	omits	מהשגת השכל	V
o	136	29	חלק מחלקיו	חלק חלק מחלקיו	
p	136	29	omits	הפרטיים	VP
q	136	29	omits	כמו הענין בהשגתנו האמותית שהיא סמוכה אל האישים הנמצאים	VP
r	136	29	omits	שהוא משיג	
s	137	30	omits	מנהגה	
t	137	30	תחדש	יתחדש	VP

Super-script	Page in trans-lation	Page in Leipzig Edition	Faulty Reading	Correct Reading	MS.
u	137	30	הטבע אשר יתחדש	זה הטבע אשר התחדש	
v	137	30	משתנה הוא בעצמות	משתנה בעצמות	
w	137	30	omits	צד	
x	138	31	מושכלי	מושכל	
y	139	31	שתסתר נפשם	שתסתר נפשה	
z	139	31	נבדלת והנה לפי שהיא	נבדלת והוה ולפי שהיא	VP
a_1	139	31	ההויה	הוויה	VP
b_1	139	32	יהיו	יהיה	V
c_1	139	32	הבטול	זה הבטול	
d_1	139	32	omits	ישובו בו אחד	V
e_1	139	32	שיתרבו	שיתרכבו	
f_1	140	32	omits	אם	
g_1	140	32	omits	שישכילם	
h_1	140	32	omits	אני	VP
i_1	140	32	omits	בעצמו	
j_1	140	32	פעלתו	פעולתי	VB
k_1	140	33	יוצא	יוציא	VP
l_1	141	33	omits	ונמצאת	
m_1	141	33	שהוא	שיהיה	
n_1	141	33	omits	הוא	
o_1	142	34	שכל נבדל בעצמו	שכל נבדל נמצא בעצמו	
p_1	142	34	היה השכל ההוא הנושא	היה השכל הוא הנושא	
q_1	142	34	כח על המושכלות	כח על ההשכל	
r_1	142	34	ההכנה הנמצאות	ההכנה הנמצאת	
s_1	143	35	ויהיו אלו הציוריות כמו שכל מושכל מהם	ויהיה אצלו הציור במושכל מושכל מהם	V

Chapter V

a	144	35	מה הנושא לה	מה הוא הנושא לה	
b	144	35	omits	נושאת	
c	145	35	שבהם	שהם	
d	145	35	היבוש	היובש	
e	145	35	שתקבלם	יקבלם	
f	145	36	אשר מדרכם שיסודרו ממנה	אשר מדרכה שיסודרו ממנה	
g	145	36	omits	הוא	VP

Super-script	Page in trans-lation	Page in Leipzig Edition	Faulty Reading	Correct Reading	MS.

Chapter VI

Super-script	Page in trans-lation	Page in Leipzig Edition	Faulty Reading	Correct Reading	MS.
a	146	36	השלימו	השלמו	VP
b	146	36	אם לא	מה שלא	
c	146	37	omits	ואולם אמרנו באופן מה	VP
d	146	37	omits	מספר מהשכלים הפועלים כמספר המושכלות אשר הוא כחיי על השגתם ואולם שיהיה	VP
e	148	37	omits	שהוא מחוייב	
f	148	38	הנקנות	הנקנית	
g	148	38	omits	אם ... או	
h	148	38	מדע	טבע	
i	148	38	הטבע הטבעי הכולל	הטבע הכולל	
j	149	38	omits	כי	
k	149	38	שיברור ממנו הטבע הכולל וזה כי אין שם דבר ולא יתכן בה שיהיה מושכל	שיברור ממנה הטבע הכולל וזה כי אין שם דבר לא יתכן בו שיהיה מושכל	V
l	149	39	צבע	טבע	
m	149	39	יוכל	שיוכל	
n	149	39	מושכל	מושכל מושכל	
o	149	39	להשיג	להשגת	
p	150	39	omits	הפך	
q	150	39	בם	בה	V
r	150	39	omits	הלקוח	VP
s	150	39	omits	מבין שאר הדברים הנמצאים בו מזולת שישיג שאר הדברים אשר	VP
t	151	40	omits	ולזה יחוייב שתהיה לו ידיעה באלו הסדורים	
u	152	40	omits	היולי	
v	152	40	omits	הוא	VP
w	153	41	omits	יצייר	
x	154	41	מבואר	מבוא	VP
y	154	41	מבעל זרע	מבעל הזרע	
z	154	41	במזון	מהמזון	
a_1	154	41	omits	הוא	VP
b_1	155	42	שיהיה זה הכח גשם	שלא יהיה זה הכח שכל	VP
c_1	155	42	שישלם	שתשלם	VP
d_1	155	42	השפלים הנפרדים	השכלים הנפרדים	VB
e_1	155	42	שייחס	שייוחס	

Super-script	Page in trans-lation	Page in Leipzig Edition	Faulty Reading	Correct Reading	MS.
f_1	156	42	שהיה	שיהיה	
g_1	156	43	על החומר	עם החומר	
h_1	157	43	מהנפר הנאצלת מהגלגלים בהם	מהנפש הנאצלת מהגלגלים	
i_1	157	43	כחיי עליהן על קבולם	כחיי על קבולם	
j_1	157	44	בסדורים	בסדוריהם	
k_1	158	44	ואינו ראשון	ואינו לראשון	VP
l_1	158	44	לאמצע	לאמצעי	VP
m_1	158	44	omits	בו	VP
n_1	158	44	ההויות	ההויה	V
o_1	158	44	אפשר	אי אפשר	VP
p_1	158	44	ואין האחרון	ואין האחר כן	
q_1	158	44	omits	דבק לאחד מאלו השכלים זה הכלי ולא ידבק לאחר וזה כי כל אחד מהם לפי שהוא לפי זאת ההנחה	
r_1	159	44	דבקות	דבקותו	VP
s_1	159	44	omits	מזה	
t_1	159	45	אשר לפני התכלית	יתן מה שלפני התכלית	
u_1	159	45	אל הנמצאות השפלות	אלו הנמצאות השפלות	
v_1	159	45	omits	הוא צורה	VP
w_1	159	45	omits	בכללם	
x_1	160	45	בנתינת גשם המזג	בנתינת המזג	
y_1	160	45	omits	כי	
z_1	160	46	מצד	מקצת	VP
a_2	161	46	ובהיות הענין כן	omits	
b_2	161	46	omits	ולזה	
c_2	161	46	omits	שאין בכאן דבר שלא תיוחס אליו השגתו באופן מה	
d_2	161	46	מהצורה הדמיונית	מהצורות הדמיוניות	VP
e_2	161	46	אל השגות בחוש	אל השנות בחוש	
f_2	161	46	omits	רבים	
g_2	161	46	מאלו	באלו	V
h_2	161	46	אשר הם בו אחד	בצד אשר הם בו סדור אחד	
i_2	162	47	סמיכותינו	סמיכותו	V
j_2	163	47	על שם	על שהם	
k_2	163	47	לסדורים	הסדורים	
l_2	163	47	omits	לא השלים מאמרו בזה לפי שהוא	PB
m_2	163	47	נתבאר	נבאר	VB

Super-script	Page in trans-lation	Page in Leipzig Edition	Faulty Reading	Correct Reading	MS.
			Chapter VII		
a	165	48	omits	שהוא	BP
b	165	48	omits	ממנו	
c	165	49	יקנם	יקנה	
d	166	49	omits	כלם	VP
e	166	49	יתן	יכוין	
f	166	49	הראותו נגלה	הראות נגלה	
g	167	50	התכלית	התכליות	VB
h	167	50	בתמונות	בכמיות	VP
i	167	50	omits	ההוא בשלמות	
j	168	50	דברים	נמצאים	VP
k	168	51	omits	אחר	
			Chapter VIII		
a	170	51	ונזכור	ונזכיר	
b	170	52	שיהיה	שישוב	
c	171	52	ההשארות הנצחיות	ההשארות והנצחיות	PB
d	171	52	יחלוט	יחליט	VP
e	171	52	ואמר בן רשד	ואמר בו	V
			Chapter IX		
a	172	53	היותם	היותה	VP
b	172	53	או	בו	
c	172	53	שהם נוסעות בלחות בעת הנערות	שהם טבועות בלחות הנערות	
d	172	53	אבל כי לא יהיה	אבל לא יהיה	
e	172	53	omits	גם כן	
f	173	53	או	אבל	VP
g	173	54	omits	הוא	
h	173	54	omits	הנמצא	VP
i	173	54	omits	במה שהם היולאניות	VP
j	174	54	שזכר	שבאר	VP
k	174	54	נמשך בעצמו	נמשך בעצמותו	
l	174	54	שיקנם בו	שיקנם	
m	175	55	ההשגות בחוש	ההשגות בחוש	V
n	175	55	omits	מהם	

Super-script	Page in trans-lation	Page in Leipzig Edition	Faulty Reading	Correct Reading	MS.
o	175	55	יסמך המושכל	יסמך כלל המושכל	
p	176	56	נגדריים	נגדרים	
q	177	57	omits	ההקדמה	
r	178	57	omits	אשר יקיפו בהם אלו המושכלות הכלליות	VP
s	178	57	שיש לו תכלית	שאין לו תכלית	
t	178	58	הוא	שהוא	VP
u	179	58	שמציאותם בנושאם הוא זולת המציאותם הרמוז אליו והוא שמציאותם ההיולאני הוא זולת	שמציאותם בנושאם הרמוז אליו והוא המציאותם ההיולאני	
v	179	59	מהוייה	מחוייב	
w	180	59	omits	ממנה	
x	180	59	האיש הרמוז	האיש הרמוז אליו	
y	180	59	omits	הוא	PB
z	181	60	התוסף	תתוסף	
a₁	182	60	מקבלים	מקבילים	

Chapter X

a	185	62	omits	באישים	VP
b	185	62	שהם	שהיא	V
c	186	63	סגלה	סוג	V
d	188	64	קודם האמות	קודם לאמות	V
e	188	64	נושא	כולל	VP
f	189	65	בו	omits	
g	190	65	הזוייה	הזוית	
h	190	65	המחייבות לנשוא בנושא	המחייבות הנשוא לנושא	VP
i	191	66	omits	ונאמר	
j	192	67	כלים	כללים	
k	193	67	הכוללים	הנכללים	V
l	193	67	מצד	בצד	VP
m	194	68	קרה זה בגזרה הכוללת	קרה בגזרה הכוללת	
n	194	68	שבאר	שזכר	
o	194	68	omits	דבר	
p	195	68	ברבויי האישיי ציור כלל	ציור ברבוי אישיי כלל	
q	195	68	שמה שאמרנו	שמה שאמרו	V
r	195	68	אשר השיג אותם בעבורם ההתרבות	אשר השיג אותו בעבורם ההתרבות	V
s	195	68	omits	הכולל	VP

Super-script	Page in trans-lation	Page in Leipzig Edition	Faulty Reading	Correct Reading	MS.
t	195	68	בכל העצמות	בבעל העצמות	VP
u	195	69	omits	ממקרים ועצם כן המהות הוא בבעל המהות בפועל ואעפ"י שהוא מעורב עם דברים אחרים	
v	195	69	הוא המהות אשר לו	הוא המהות	
w	195	69	והוא מבואר שמשים זולתו בתואר מה מפני דבר מה הנה הדבר ההוא יותר ראוי בתואר ההוא	ומה שהוא בתואר מה מפני דבר מה הנה הדבר ההוא יותר ראוי בתואר ההוא	
x	196	69	במהות	במהותו	
y	196	69	וכבר יאמר	וכאשר יאמר	
z	196	69	omits	חוץ לנפש הוא שכל מצד מה שנמצא מהם בנפש השכל הפועל ובהיות הענין כן הוא מבואר שלא יחויב מאלו הטענות באלו המושכלות	
a₁	197	70	omits	אלא	
b₁	197	70	שמה	שמה שהוא	VP
c₁	197	70	ההרגשה	ההשגה	
d₁	197	70	omits	היה	
e₁	197	70	The Leipzig reverses the order of the first two alternatives; the sequence of the manuscripts has been followed.		
f₁	198	71	omits	אחרים	
g₁	198	71	בעת מן העתים	בכל עת מהעתים	VP
h₁	198	71	אישים אחרים	אישים אחדים	VP
i₁	199	71	omits	מושכל	
j₁	199	72	על הכחות	על נכוחתו	
k₁	200	72	היה	היו	
l₁	200	72	מה שהוא אפשר	מצד שהוא אפשר	
m₁	200	72	omits	והוא שקר כי בכאן מושכלות רבות אמתיות בנמנע מצד מה שהוא אפשר	
n₁	200	72	אחרים	אחדים	
o₁	201	73	omits	בלתי	
p₁	201	73	omits	זה האיש אלא מצד מה שהוא איזה איש הזדמן	VP
q₁	201	73	מושכל במה שהוא נמנע מצד אפשר מצד מה שהוא אפשר	מושכל במה שהוא נמנע מצד אפשר מצד מהצד שהוא אפשר	V

Super-script	Page in trans-lation	Page in Leipzig Edition	Faulty Reading	Correct Reading	MS.
r_1	201	73	omits	איזה איש הזדמן לא במה שהוא	
s_1	201	73	במספר	כמספר	B
t_1	203	74	לקנות	לקבל	
u_1	203	74	מתיחס דומה	מתיחס ודומה	V
v_1	203	75	השכל	השכל המניע	VP
w_1	203	75	omits	היו	
x_1	203	75	כחיי	בחיי	VP
y_1	203	75	כמו	במי	V
z_1	204	75	מהם	ממנו	
a_2	204	75	מושכל	מושכלות	
b_2	204	75	omits	ההוא	
c_2	204	75	מה שהקנהו ומי ששמהו	מה שהקנהו מי ששמהו	
d_2	204	75	ואם	ואז	VP
e_2	204	76	שהקנה אותו	שהקנה אותה	VP
f_2	204	76	omits	לפי	VP
g_2	204	76	באיזה	איזה	
h_2	204	76	ואולי	ואולם	V
i_2	204	76	המושכלות	הצורות	
j_2	205	76	וישיבהו משכיל אותה בפועל אחר שהיתה מושכלת בכח	וישיבהו משכיל בפועל אחר שהיה משכיל בכח ובהיות העניין כן הנה אין השכל הפועל משיב הצורה הדמיונית מושכלת בפועל אשר שהיתה מושכלת בכח	
k_2	205	76	אלא אם יפעל זה במקרה	אלא במקרה	
l_2	205	76	יקוים	יקנם	V
m_2	205	76	הטענה	ההקדמה	VP
n_2	205	76	והוא	והיא	VP
o_2	206	77	omits	ממנה	
p_2	207	77	ולא יחוייב במה שיניע באמצעי שיניע בעצמה בזולת אמצעי	ולא יחוייב מפני זה שיניעה בעצמו בזולת אמצעי	
q_2	207	78	אלו המושכלות	אלו המושכלות אשר בכאן	
r_2	207	78	הנה ישיג המושכל אשר הוא בעצמו שכל	הוא המושכל אשר הוא בעצמו שכל	
s_2	207	78	וכי	כי	
t_2	207	78	הצורה הדמיונית מושכל	הצורות הדמיוניות מושכלות	
u_2	207	78	שקרה	שיקרה	VP

Super-script	Page in trans-lation	Page in Leipzig Edition	Faulty Reading	Correct Reading	MS.
v_2	208	78	שאם לא היתה כל תנועתו	שאם לא היתה לתנועתו	VP
w_2	208	79	בלתי מחוייב באחת	בלתי מחוייב מאחת	VP
x_2	209	79	אשר הוא בעינו	אשר שב הוא בעינו	PB
y_2	209	79	סותרת	היא סותרת	
z_2	209	79	בהם	מהם	
a_3	209	80	אבל הוא אולי כמו שהתבאר אחר זה	אבל אולי הוא מחוייב כמו שיתבאר אחר זה	VP
b_3	209	80	omits	אם	VP
c_3	210	80	ובזה	ולזה	
d_3	210	80	בשום צד מפני החדוש שזכרנו	בשום צד מאפני החדוש כמו שקדם וזה מבואר מאד ממה שזכרנו	V
e_3	210	80	שיחממה	שיחממהו	
f_3	210	80	שוב העלה	תשוב העלה	
g_3	210	80–81	אם הנחנו שלא יהיה העלול בשני אלו המציאויות יחד אם הנחנו שיהיה העלול בשני אלו המציאויות יחד לא ימנע כי לא ימנע היות העלול במציאות אשר לעלה אחר המצאו במציאות אשר לעלול	אם הנחנו שיהיה העלול בשני אלו המציאויות יחד אבל שלא ימנע העלול במציאות אשר לעלה אחר המצאו במציאות אשר לעלול	B

Chapter XI

Super-script	Page in trans-lation	Page in Leipzig Edition	Faulty Reading	Correct Reading	MS.
a	212	81	התבאר	יתבאר	
b	213	82	לו	לה	VP
c	213	82	ממנה	ממנו	PB
d	213	82	omits	במקרה	V
e	214	82	תשאש	תשמור	
f	214	83	להשגת הגופיות	להשגות הגופיות	
g	214	83	אשר	כאשר	VP
h	214	83	omits	הסבה	P
i	214	83	omits	הסדור	
j	215	83	יזדכרו	יזדכרו	
k	215	83	omits	אשר תניעם אל זה המושכל ובהיות הענין כן רצוני שיהיה רושם לצורות הדמיוניות	VP
l	215	84	וכבר	ושכבר	
m	215	84	יזדכרו	יזדכרו	

Super-script	Page in trans-lation	Page in Leipzig Edition	Faulty Reading	Correct Reading	MS.
n	215	84	omits	הוא	
o	215	84	בה	בו	P
p	215	84	omits	כמו	
q	215	84	omits	אצלו	
r	216	84	אותו	אותה	VB
s	216	84	שם	בה	
t	216	84	באור	בבאור	
u	216	84	omits	ההוא	

Chapter XII

Super-script	Page in trans-lation	Page in Leipzig Edition	Faulty Reading	Correct Reading	MS.
a	218	85	omits	זה	
b	218	85	ישלים	ישלם	
c	218	85	ועצמיו	ועצביו	
d	219	85	omits	ועוד	
e	219	85	omits	למעוט	
f	219	86	omits	האדם	
g	219	86	האספוג היימיים	האספוג הימי	VB
h	220	86	omits	ועוד	
i	220	86	omits	מהם	
j	220	86	omits	החמר	
k	220	86	omits	האחד זולת הצורות אשר יקבל עד שיגיע אל התכלית	
l	220	87	לקבול	לקבל	
m	220	87	והאחד	והאחר	
n	220	87	omits	כן	
o	220	87	omits	בהכרח	
p	221	87	omits	עד	
q	221	87	תכלית	התכלית	
r	221	87	הליחה המליחה	הליחה המחליאה	
s	221	87	והנה המחליאה היא	והוצאת הליחה המחליאה	
t	221	87	באופן	באופן מה	
u	221	87	הולכת	הולכות	
v	221	87	במספר	כמספר	VB
w	221	87	והוא מה שקרב	והיה מה שקרב	
x	221	88	לדורות	לצורות	
y	222	88	לקודמים	הקודמים	
z	222	88	יכול	יכולה	
a$_1$	222	88	שריה	שרא	V

Super-script	Page in trans-lation	Page in Leipzig Edition	Faulty Reading	Correct Reading	MS.
b_1	222	88	שאין . . . אפשר	שאין . . . אפשרית	
c_1	222	88	omits	תחלה	
d_1	222	88	omits	ההוא	

Chapter XIII

a	223	89	הוא	היא	VP
b	223	89	התכלית האחד	התכלית לאחד	
c	223	89	התשוקה הטבעית	התשוקות הטבעיות	
d	223	89	במה	כמו	
e	224	89	במדרגותו	במדרגת	
f	224	90	צורות האחדות	צורת האחדות	VB
g	224	90	כשקנה	מי שקנה	VB
h	224	90	השכל הנקנה לו מתחלף	השכל הנקנה אשר לו מתחלף	VB
i	224	90	שיקרב	שקרב	
j	224	90	ותענגיו	ותענוגו	
k	224	90	omits	יהיה	
l	224	90	omits	ובכאן הותר הספק השלישי מאלו הספקות וראוי שלא יעלם ממנו שכל אחד מהמצליחים ישמח ויתענג אחר המות במה שהשיג אותו	
m	224	90	זהו	זה	
n	224	90	omits	היא	
o	225	91	omits	שבע תועבות בלבו	

Chapter XIV

a	226	91	מצד מה שיביאהו	מצד מה שיביאוהו	VB
b	226	91	המחלקת	מהמחלקת	

ANALYTICAL TABLE OF CONTENTS OF
THE WARS OF THE LORD

Book 1: *Immortality of the Soul*

I. The Nature of the Human Intellect (chapters 1–2)
   A. The view of Alexander of Aphrodisias (fl. 200 C.E.): the human intellect is not an incorporeal and self-subsistent substance, but merely a corporeal capacity, or disposition, for cognition.
   B. The theory of Themistius (fl. c.375 C.E.): the human intellect is an incorporeal, self-subsistent substance that is everlasting.
   C. The doctrine of Averroes (1126–1198) is a synthesis of Alexander and Themistius, but closer to the latter:
      1. Insofar as the human intellect is a corporeal disposition, it is generated and corruptible.
      2. But insofar as it is a substance, it is identical with the Agent Intellect—the cosmic power responsible for human cognition— and hence is immortal.
   D. The view of certain "modern" (i.e., Christian) scholars: the human intellect is an incorporeal substance created *ex nihilo* and hence not subject to natural corruption.
II. Criticisms of These Theories (chapters 3–5)
   A. Alexander's arguments in behalf of his own doctrine make Themistius' theory improbable (chapter 3).
   B. Averroes' view (chapter 4) is subject to a variety of difficulties, some of which are
      1. If the human intellect is actually identical with the Agent Intellect, and since the Agent Intellect is one, how can we differentiate amongst human intellects and their individual cognitions?
      2. If all human intellects are ultimately identical with the Agent

Intellect, then they are all one and immortality is hence no longer personal and individual.

3. If immortality is impersonal and non-individual, why should one strive to perfect oneself in this life?

C. The doctrine of the "moderns" is subject to many of the defects of the views of both Themistius and Averroes; they all claim that the human intellect is an incorporeal substance. Moreover, it asserts that the soul is created *ex nihilo*, which will be disproved in Book 6, part 1, chapter 17.

D. Gersonides' theory: the human intellect, as Alexander claims, is not an incorporeal substance, but a disposition to receive sensory information and to transform them with the aid of the Agent Intellect into logical concepts. This disposition resides in the imagination, a corporeal faculty of the soul (chapter 5).

III. The Nature of the Agent Intellect (chapter 6)

A. The Agent Intellect comprises all the knowledge that the human intellect is capable of apprehending; in the Agent Intellect this knowledge is unified and ordered, whereas in the human intellect it is usually not.

B. The Agent Intellect is the cause of generation in the sub-lunar world and not solely of man, as Averroes believed.

IV. The Immortality of the Human Intellect (chapters 7–9)

A. The view of Alexander, Themistius and Averroes: human immortality consists in the union or conjunction with the Agent Intellect (chapters 7–8)

B. The doctrine of Avicenna (chapter 9): the human intellect is essentially immortal.

C. The two opinions of Al-Farabi (chapter 9):

1. The doctrine of human immortality is a fiction.

2. Human immortality is attainable through conjunction with the Agent Intellect.

V. Critique of These Theories (chapters 10 and 12)

A. The role of knowledge in attaining immortality and the correct analysis of the nature of human knowledge does not require that we posit the existence of extra-mental, immutable cognitive objects in the physical world called 'universals', the knowledge of which confers immortality. There are no such universals in the physical world (chapter 10).

B. The theory of conjunction in any of its versions is subject to a variety of difficulties (chapter 12):

such communication is sufficiently common to warrant philosophical study (chapter 1).

C. This information exhibits a certain kind of order and plan. But if
it does, how can it concern future contingent events? Insofar as such
knowledge is ordered, or law-governed, the events would have to
be determined; yet, insofar as they are contingent, they could not
be subject to law and order (chapter 2).

   1. This apparent dilemma is a special case of a general apparent
incompatibility between foreknowledge and contingency, which
will be discussed in detail in Book 3.

   2. The problem is solved as follows: knowledge about the future
affairs of men is indeed ordered insofar as there is a general plan
governing the behavior of man that emanates from the heavenly
bodies. However, there is genuine contingency in human affairs
insofar as man has choice, a gift given to man by God.

D. The primary agent, or cause, of this information is the Agent Intellect; the secondary agent, transmitting information through dreams
and divination, is the constellation of heavenly bodies (chapter 3).

E. Although this type of knowledge is chiefly concerned with future
human affairs, occasionally knowledge concerning the theoretical
or practical sciences is communicated in dreams or prophecy as
well. The main purpose of all such knowledge is, in general, the
preservation of man (chapters 4–5).

II. Several Problems Connected with this Type of Cognition (chapters 6–
8)

A. How can the Agent Intellect transmit this information, if knowledge
per se is general but the information concerns particular men and
their particular fortunes or misfortunes? Answer: Although the information inherent in and transmitted by the Agent Intellect is
essentially general, it may be particularized by the *recipient* of the
information.

B. How do we explain the differences in the information received by
various dreamers, diviners and prophets:
Answer: These differences are accounted for by the individual differences in the psychological constitutions of the recipients and their
particular circumstances.

C. What is the difference between dreams and divination on the one
hand and prophecy on the other?
Answer: In dreams and divination, the heavenly bodies play an
important role: they exhibit a certain general plan concerning human
affairs, with which the diviner can resonate and which he can convey

in turn to others. This special capacity of the diviner is primarily attributable to his strong imagination, not to the intellect.

The prophet, however, is endowed not only with a strong imagination but with a highly developed intellect. This intellect enables him to apprehend the Agent Intellect itself and to receive the information that it conveys. Thus, prophecy requires intellectual preparation, whereas divination does not.

D. How is the prophecy of Moses different from the prophecy of the other prophets (chapter 8)?
  1. Answer: In Moses the imagination played no role except in his earliest prophecies;
  2. Moses' intellectual attainments surpassed those of his successors;
  3. Moses was able to isolate or concentrate his attention on intellectual matters to a greater degree than the other prophets (chapter 8).

Book 3: *Divine Knowledge*

I. The Dilemma of Divine Omniscience (chapter 1)
  A. If God knows everything, including particular facts, He would then know particular facts about future human actions; but if He knows such facts, how can they be *free* acts?
  B. The theories of the philosophers:
    1. The extreme thesis: God does not know any particulars, either generally or individually.
    2. The moderate thesis: God does not know particular facts individually, but knows them in a general way, i.e. only insofar as they exemplify a general law or plan.
  C. The view of the theologians of our Torah: God knows *all* facts in all their particularity.
II. The Arguments in Behalf of these Views (chapter 2)
  A. Some of the arguments in behalf of the philosophers' general claim that God does not know particular facts:
    1. Such knowledge is incompatible with God's eternal essence; for this knowledge is temporal, perceptual and diverse, whereas God is a-temporal, pure intellect and absolutely one.
    2. Knowledge of particulars could be infinite, since the number of particulars could be infinite. But the infinite is unknowable.
    3. If God had such knowledge, the dilemma between foreknowledge and freedom would be real.

B. Some of the arguments for the Theological View:
  1. If God were not omniscient in the fullest sense, i.e. if He did not know particulars, He would not be God!
  2. Maimonides' solution: God's mode of cognition is *radically different* from the human mode. Hence, we should not expect to be able to understand how God knows anything, including particular facts.

III. A Critical Analysis of these Various Arguments (chapters 3–4)
  A. Maimonides' solution would entail the complete abandonment of all rational speculation and knowledge about God and His attributes, and not just of His knowledge (chapter 3).
    1. Maimonides' general theory of divine attributes is inadequate.
    2. If we cannot know anything positive about God's knowledge or any one of His attributes, then what prevents us from acquiring false beliefs about God?
  B. The arguments of the philosophers show only that God does not know particulars as particulars, and hence the theological view is false. But they do not prove that God does not know particulars at all or in any way. What has to be shown is whether God does know particulars in some way (chapter 4).

IV. Gersonides' Theory of Divine Cognition (chapter 5)
  A. The empirical facts of dreams, divination, and prophecy indicate that God has *some* kind of knowledge of human affairs.
    1. If the Agent Intellect has such knowledge, surely God has it.
    2. Although God does not know particular things in all their details, He knows the general plan governing them. Moreover, since God knows that man is a free agent, He knows that this plan can be "aborted" by man; hence, He knows that human affairs are contingent, although He does not know the particular outcomes of human choice.
  B. That God does not know particulars as such is not an imperfection in Him, contrary to the doctrine of the theologians.
    1. Divine omniscience is to be defined as: the knowledge of all that can be known.
    2. Since particulars as particulars cannot be known, for the reasons given by the philosophers (II; A), God does not know them. Indeed, to know them is a *logical impossibility*.
    3. As "unknowable" particulars are analogous to "undoables," such as not being able to undo the past or not being able to make the diagonal of a square equal a commensurate ratio.

Just as God is not impotent even though He cannot do these latter things, so is He not ignorant if He cannot know particulars.

C. Genuine contingency exists because of human choice: we have the capacity to choose between alternatives and our choices are not determined by anything, even God's knowledge. Human freedom is therefore unconditioned.

V. The Compatibility of Gersonides' Theory with the Teachings of the Torah (chapter 6)

A. The existence of contingency and the possibility of genuine choice are assumed and explicitly stated by the Torah in many places.

B. The Torah teaches only that God knows *in general* the thoughts and deeds of men.

1. The correct interpretation of Psalms 33:15 shows that God knows the general patterns of human behavior, not the particular acts of individual men.

2. The Torah avers explicitly that God's knowledge and will are immutable.

C. The view of Gersonides was anticipated by Rabbi Abraham ibn Ezra, the great commentator on the Torah.

Book 4 *Divine Providence*

I. The Three Theories of Providence (chapters 1–2)

A. Aristotle: There is no individual providence at all; divine providence extends only generally throughout each natural species.

B. The theologians of the Torah: God is concerned with all individuals in every species.

C. The theory of limited individual providence: only *some* individuals in the human species merit God's concern.

II. Critique of these Theories (chapter 3)

A. Aristotle's denial of individual providence is refuted by the following:

1. the existence of providential dreams, divination and prophecy, all of which concern individuals and are communicated to individuals;

2. the existence of individual providence in the heavenly domain.

B. The theory of the theologians of our Torah is refuted by the following facts:

1. the sufferings of the innocent;

2. the prosperity of the wicked;

3. natural disorders and imperfections;
4. evil is incompatible with God's nature; hence God cannot be the source of evil.

III. A Defense of the Theory of Restricted Individual Providence (chapters 4–6)

   A. Since man alone of all living things has been endowed with intellect and choice, only the *human* species is deserving of special care (chapter 4).

   B. Since individual humans within the species differ considerably in their intellectual and moral levels, divine providence varies accordingly: the higher the degree of intellectual and moral achievement, the greater is the divine providence extended (chapter 5).

   C. The existence of individual providence is compatible with the fact that God has no knowledge of particulars (chapters 5–6).

      1. Just as divine communication is essentially general and becomes particularized by the recipient, so too divine providence is particularized by the individual who warrants it by virtue of his or her personal merit.

      2. Thus, although the nature of divine providence is specific in that it concerns the human species, it is particular insofar as different members of the human species exhibit this providence in varying degrees.

IV. Gersonides' Theodicy (chapter 6)

   A. Gersonides' Principle of Providence: God cannot be the source of evil or suffering.

   B. The causes of suffering in the world are not strictly of divine origin:

      1. Since human beings differ in their intellectual capacities and achievements, they will suffer because of their ignorance, stupidity, or folly.

      2. Many human ills result from man's free-will; precisely because he has choice, man will commit sins, which in turn cause him to suffer.

      3. As will be proved in Book 6, part 1, chapters 17–18, God created the universe from an eternal, formless matter. This material "stuff" is, as Plato said, "recalcitrant to perfection" and is the chief cause of imperfection. Thus, diseases, earthquakes, etc. are the results of the "necessity of matter," not God.

   C. The true good and reward of the righteous is intellectual perfection which can be achieved only in the World-To-Come. Thus, bodily ills are irrelevant to a judgment of true happiness. (Analogously, with respect to the prosperity of the wicked: these material goods are not pertinent to man's true perfection.)

D. Any suffering experienced by the righteous is justified because:
1. that individual has temporarily fallen from his or her high state of perfection;
2. suffering is brought about as the harmful consequences of the evil deeds of one's ancestors. Only those of a very high degree of intellectual and moral perfection can avoid such punishment;
3. a relatively minor ill effect can save the righteous from either a greater evil that they would otherwise suffer by virtue of the providence deriving from the heavenly constellations or the more severe punishment for a minor sin which they have committed.

E. This theory is supported by both the Torah and the teachings of the Rabbis.

F. This theory is in fact taught by Elihu as related in the Book of Job. It is also the view of Maimonides (chapter 7).

Book 5 *Cosmology*

I. Explanations of Various Astonomical Phenomena (Part 2)
A. The study of astronomy is important for a variety of reasons (chapter 1):
1. it is intrinsically valuable since it concerns objects of greater perfection than ourselves, i.e. the heavenly bodies;
2. the heavenly bodies will provide us with information about God and the "separate intellects," or the angels;
3. since the heavenly bodies have effects upon the earth, knowledge of the former increases our knowledge of the latter;
4. the Torah testifies to the importance of this study.

B. Discussions of Specific Celestial Phenomena (chapters 2 and 4–6)
1. Between and surrounding the celestial bodies there is interspersed a formless, liquid matter (chapter 2). In Book 6 it will be shown that this matter is the primordial "stuff" out of which the universe has been created.
2. There is no diurnal sphere beyond and in addition to the sphere of the Zodiac (chapter 4).
3. All the fixed stars are located in one sphere, whereas each planet is uniquely located in its own sphere (chapter 5).
4. Aristotle's explanations of how the sun emits heat are inadequate. The true explanation is that the sun heats the atmosphere through

its rays, not because of reflection or motion as Aristotle thought (chapter 6).

    5. The main effect of the moon is upon the amount of moisture in the earth's atmosphere (chapter 6).

  C. The general structure and movements of the heavenly bodies are directed for the benefit of the Earth. Thus, teleological factors must be considered in cosmology (chapter 3).

  D. There are a number of difficult astronomical problems, the solutions to which become easier once their various teleological influences upon terrestrial phenomena are understood (chapters 7–9).

II. God and the Movers of the Heavenly Spheres (Part 3)

  A. God and the movers of the heavenly bodies, or the separate intellects, are incorporeal substances, the knowledge of which is derived for the most part from information about their effects upon earthly substances, in particular the generation of such phenomena (chapter 1).

  B. There are several different theories attempting to explain how terrestrial substances are generated (chapter 2).

    1. Themistius, Al-Farabi, Avicenna and ibn Bajja assign this role to a separate intellect.

    2. Averroes gives three different explanations, two of which deny that the cause of the generation of terrestial substances is a separate intellect of any kind.

III. Criticisms of these Theories (chapters 3–4):

  A. The view of Themistius and others that the primary cause of terrestrial generation is a Separate Intellect has not been adequately defended by them (chapter 3).

  B. Averroes' counter-thesis that this kind of generation can be explained by purely physical causes without recourse to a separate intellect is wrong, as is clear from his own general theory (chapter 4).

  C. The Themistian view is in general correct, but it has to be reformulated and defended by different and better arguments. (chapter 4)

  D. The true theory of the separate intellects (chapters 5–10)

    1. The previous discussion has shown so far that the cause of terrestrial generation is a Separate Intellect. What role do the separate intellects play in the movement of the heavenly bodies? To answer this question we have to know something about God's role in the terrestrial scheme (chapter 5).

    2. Aristotle's proof (accepted by many medieval philosophers) for

the existence of the separate intellects (including God) from an analysis of motion is invalid. Moving bodies can be explained "naturally" (chapter 6).

3. The various separate intellects and the heavenly spheres that they move are ordered according to a rational system governing the sub-lunar domain (chapters 7–10).

4. The movers of the spheres emanate from God, the "First Separate Intellect" (chapter 8).

E. God (chapters 11–12)

1. The mover of the sphere of the fixed stars is not God, as Averroes claims; God is not the mover of any particular heavenly sphere, but the mover of *all* the spheres via the Separate Intellects that derive from Him (chapter 11).

2. Contrary to the view of Maimonides, God has many positive attributes, knowledge of which we can partially attain by observing His actions as well as by analyzing the logical relationships between one attribute and another (chapter 12).

3. The complete plan of the structure and purpose of all reality is to be found in God, not in the movers of the spheres (chapter 12).

F. The Agent Intellect (chapter 13)

1. The answer to the question posed in chapter 5—What is the primary cause of terrestrial generation?—is: the Agent Intellect.

2. The Agent Intellect, unlike all other separate intellects, is not attached to one heavenly body alone; rather it emanates from *all* the movers of the spheres together.

3. Since the Agent Intellect emanates from all the movers of the spheres, its cognition is more comprehensive than any of theirs, since their knowledge is restricted to the influence resulting from their respective sphere.

G. Concluding thesis: each of the three parts of this Book concerns the highest level of knowledge in each of the three theoretical sciences distinguished by Aristotle:

1. Mathematics: mathematical astronomy is the perfection of the mathematical sciences (part 1).

2. Physics: physical astronomy, or cosmology, is the completion of the study of the natural sciences (part 2).

3. Metaphysics: theology is the highest level of study in metaphysics (part 3).

Book 6: *Creation of the Universe*

I. Thesis: God has voluntarily created the universe out of an eternal, formless matter.

  A. Introduction

    1. Whether a decisive proof can be given for either the creation or the eternity of the world is a deep and serious question (chapter 1). (In fact, Maimonides claimed that there is no such proof for either thesis.)

    2. Another complication is the sheer variety of competing theories. Each of the two contradictory theses has various formulations.

      a. Creation can be interpreted as either: (1) the successive generation of many, perhaps infinite, worlds; or (2) the generation of just *one* universe. Moreover, creation can be either *ex nihilo* or out of some primordial matter.

      b. Eternity can be construed as either: (1) the eternal existence of one universe throughout infinite time, as Aristotle believed; or (2) the continual emanation of the universe from God— or the theory of eternal creation—a view advocated by some of the Muslim Aristotelians, such as Averroes.

    3. Although each of these doctrines has been defended by various arguments, the theories of the eternity of the universe (Aristotle), *ex nihilo* creation (Maimonides) and creation out of matter (Plato) are the more important ones and therefore deserve more careful discussion (chapters 2–3).

    4. The standard arguments in behalf of these three doctrines are not valid (chapter 4).

  B. Proofs for Creation (chapters 5–15)

    1. The direct proofs for creation of the universe are based upon either the teleological order or the presence of non-essential properties in the celestial domain (chapter 6).

    2. The indirect proofs for creation derive from the several paradoxes concerning eternity thesis. If the universe cannot be infinite in duration in the past, then it must have had a temporal beginning (chapters 10–15).

  C. Although the universe had a beginning, it is everlasting and indestructible (chapter 16).

    1. The universe exhibits no inherent, natural cause of decay.

    2. God has no "sufficient reason" to destroy the world.

  D. How the universe was created (chapter 17).

    1. The traditional doctrine of *ex nihilo* creation, which was accepted

by Maimonides, is false, since it leads to many insuperable difficulties.

    2. The Platonic theory of creation out of matter, *properly interpreted*, is the true theory of creation (chapters 17–18).

E. There is only *one* universe (chapter 19).

F. Aristotle's arguments against creation are all invalid (chapters 20–28).

II. Creation in the Torah and the Rabbinic Tradition is identical with the philosophical theory expounded in Part I.

A. The Torah does *not* teach creation *ex nihilo*. Indeed, all the miracles mentioned in the Torah are described as involving some matter (chapter 1).

B. The correct interpretation of *Genesis* 1 shows that the universe was created out of primordial matter (chapters 2–8).

    1. The "six days" do not indicate a temporal sequence, but a causal-natural order in terms of which one element is causally prior to another.

    2. The "light" that was created on "day one" refers to the creation of the separate intellects, or angels, which are prior in the created order.

    3. The "void" mentioned at the outset of creation signifies the primordial matter that was "empty of form."

    4. The "waters" in *Genesis* 1 are never described as being created. These primeval waters, mentioned in verse 2, also refer to the primordial matter (which has been shown to be a liquid in Book 5, part 1, chapter 28).

C. As Maimonides already indicated, the truth of creation makes possible the belief in miracles, whose existence is a fundamental belief of Judaism (chapter 9). However, who is the *agent* of miracles? God, an angel or a prophet? And what is the purpose and domain of miracles?

    1. The principal and proximate agent of miracles is the Agent Intellect; God is only their remote cause and the prophet is only an instrument of their occurrence. (chapter 11)

    2. Miracles are events that occur within nature, more particularly in the sub-human domain, and hence are logically possible, albeit rare or improbable. Moreover, they are concerned with human affairs and usually have beneficial consequences (chapter 12). Often natural phenomena are at least partial causes or instruments of miracles (e.g. the "east wind" at the parting of the sea).

3. The view of some of the Rabbis and perhaps also of Maimonides that the miracles were pre-arranged in the original plan of creation is correct, but only in part. Nevertheless, this "law of miracles" is only conditional: these events will occur *only if* certain antecedent conditions will be satisfied. For example, *if* Pharaoh *decides* to pursue the Israelites, then the sea will be split. In this manner is human freedom preserved (chapter 12).

D. Since miracles often occur in the presence of a prophet, who serves as an instrument of the Agent Intellect, might miracles function as a *test* of a prophet? More generally, how is a prophet confirmed (chapter 13)?

1. Most of the standard tests are insufficient, since all prophecies are conditional: even if the prophet's prediction is not confirmed, he may yet not be a false-prophet. The people's repentance or sudden turn to evil may have reversed the divine decree. In this view, free-will is preserved. The failure or fulfillment of the prophetic prediction is therefore insufficient to confirm prophetic credentials.

2. The only sufficient test of a prophet is whether the miracles announced in the prophecy occur as predicted.